JOURNEYMAN EXAM W(

By Tom Henry and Tim Henry

Based on the 2020 National Electrical Code®

This workbook contains ten closed book (no book) exams, twenty-five open book exams, True or False exam and a Final Exam for a total of over **1850** electrical exam questions with **answers** and references. This workbook is designed to help prepare the electrician for the Journeyman electrical examination.

While every precaution has been taken in the preparation of this book, the author and publisher assumes no responsibility for errors or omissions. Neither is any liability assumed from the use of the information contained herein.

National Electrical Code® and NEC® are Registered Trademarks of the National Fire Protection Association, Inc., Quincy, MA.

First printing January 2020

ISBN 978-1-7334621-0-5

**CODE ELECTRICAL
LEADER IN ELECTRICAL
EDUCATION WORLD WIDE**

*WE DIDN'T INVENT ELECTRICAL TRAINING
.... WE PERFECTED IT.*

ENRY PUBLICATIONS SINCE 1985

Meet the author

READ THE BOOKS THE
ELECTRICIANS READ

Tom Henry

•Certified Chief Electrical Inspector Building Officials of Florida
•Certified Chief Electrical Inspector Southern Building Code Congress
•Former Electrical Inspector Walt Disney World-EPCOT
•Registered Electrical Contractor State of Florida
•Licensed Master Electrician
•Member National Fire Protection Association (NFPA)
•Member International Association of Electrical Inspectors (IAEI)
•Owner of Code Electrical Classes Inc. Winter Park, FL
•Certified Vocational Instructor State of Florida
•Instructor of over 22,000 Electricians
•Author of Electrical Inspection Workbook
•Author of over 70 Electrical books
•Legal consultant involving Electrical fires and deaths
•Over 62 years experience in the Electrical field
•President of Tom Henry's "Learn to be an Electrician" program with over 1900
enrolled from all 50 states and 11 foreign countries

Meet the Vice-President and Co-Author

Tim Henry

•Registered Electrical Contractor State of Florida
•Licensed Master Electrician
•Member National Fire Protection Association (NFPA)
•Vice-President over 30 years of Code Electrical Classes Inc. Winter Park, FL
•Instructor of over 12,000 Electricians
•Co-Author of over ten Electrical books
•Legal consultant involving Electrical fires and deaths
•Over 39 years experience in the Electrical field
•Electrical construction co-editor for the "*Informer*" newsletter
•Director of Tom Henry's "Learn to be an Electrician" program with over 1900 enrolled from all 50 states and several foreign countries

The secret of making something work in your lives is first of all, the deep desire to make it work; then the faith and belief that it can work; then to hold that clear definite vision in your consciousness and see it working out step by step, without one thought of doubt or disbelief.

We act as though comfort and luxury were the chief requirements of life, when all we need to make us really happy is something to be enthusiastic about.

The Electrical License Examination

Understanding the test from 'both sides of the fence' will make the testing session run more smoothly as the administrator will understand test-takers perspective.

Many test takers' livelihoods, professional advancement and professional development depend on the results of the exams they take.

Add to that, the time and money investment that test takers make to prepare themselves for the test experience. Between study materials, coursework, the cost of the exam itself – and the fact that their careers may depend on how they perform, we realize that taking a test can be stressful and anxiety-producing.

We understand that the more you know about what to expect, the more confident and comfortable you'll be on exam day; and the better you'll score!

Many young people entering the field today do not realize it's a skilled trade, it is listed as a profession. Do you know why you are required to be a professional? Because electricity can kill you or someone else working with it. Education and continuing education is required throughout your career. Obtaining your license is just the start of your journey through electrical education. Licensing is a formal and legal way of defining a profession and a means of including in practice those who meet predetermined standards deemed to be necessary for protection of the public. There is a difference when hiring an experienced, qualified and knowledgeable electrician compared to a licensed electrical installer, in court referred to as an electrical worker. **The major purpose of a license is to protect public health and safety by preventing unqualified people from practicing a given profession or occupation**. A license must be treated with respect.

Years ago, a certain state offered to allow a person who did not pass the exam the opportunity to go to a class where an instructor would go over every question not only giving the answer but showing how it was reached. This is education at its finest.

Now I ask what is wrong with this type of education? Well the answer is, they don't want to make the exam too easy or, writing exam questions very difficult and tiring process and we certainly don't want anyone **copying questions** and passing them on to others in which they could possibly locate the question (**but, how would the applicant know it's the correct answer?**) before they take their exam giving them an unfair advantage over the applicant that is limited in time to find the question and then select from multiple choice what they feel is the correct answer?

Your score on the open book exam depends on how familiar you are with the **Code book**. Most exam applicants **run out of time** and are not able to find all the questions and select a choice of answer within the limited time.

Test question writers hope the question is never copied.

Their score is instantaneous but they **never know what questions were wrong** or where their weaknesses are.

The elusive license, is still unattainable at this point. How would the applicant ever find out what the **correct answer** is? They are not permitted to ever knowing the **correct answer**. How are you to be educated if you **never** know the correct answer?

The only time you will ever know the "**correct answer**" is when you read *Tom Henry Books* where from all the years of studying the intent of the NEC from the TCD, TCR giving the substantiation for each of the new safety rules or deletions from the NEC each three years.

At my age 81, I've been through 20 code cycles and written over 70 electrical books which will give you the **correct answer** in full detail.

•The Code is Truly a "National" Code. - The men who freely contribute their time and study to the writing of the Code come from all over the United States and thus the final document represents a nationwide cross-section of opinion.

•The Code is an "American Standard." - The fact that the writers of the Code are organized under the procedure of the American Standards Association makes this possible. This simply means that the Code is officially recognized as representing standard American practice. It is a simple standard; there is no need for necessity for anyone to develop another code; the National Electrical Code is sufficient. Proof of this is the fact that cities and other governmental bodies all over the United States have adopted it as the *safety standard for electrical installations*, in spite of the fact that the Code itself, being written by a technical association, has no legal or mandatory status whatsoever.

The National Electrical Code is based on the fact that **to do less would be a hazard**. Many of the sections of the NEC are a result of known fire; incorporating corrections into the NEC each three years is an attempt to prevent similar occurrences.

Every rule in your safety manual is written in somebody's blood. The freedom and safety that you and I enjoy in our communities in large part is due to the sacrifice of others.

Are receptacles connected in series or parallel?

**How would you answer JOURNEYMAN GENERAL KNOWLEDGE EXAM #2
Question #3?**

3. Receptacles in residential wiring are regularly connected in _____.

(a) parallel   (b) perpendicular   (c) series   (d) diagonal

Your score is instantaneous but you will **never know what questions were wrong** or where their weaknesses are.

How would the applicant ever find out what the **correct answer** is? They are not permitted to ever knowing the **correct answer**. How are you to be educated if you **never** know the correct answer?

Question #3 is a good example, what is the **correct answer**? I assume their choice is (a) parallel, but is that the **correct answer**?

In your time in the electrical trade you have been taught the series circuit and the parallel circuit. The best way for me to show you the **correct answer** is to put it in a drawing.

The branch shown has four duplex or eight single receptacles.

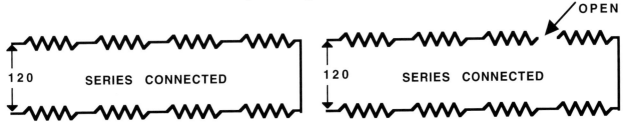

With a series connection and open anywhere in the circuit would drop voltage to ALL the loads. So, series is NOT the answer.

Now, lets check to see if the receptacles are connected in parallel.

PARALLEL CONNECTED

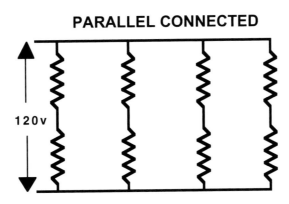

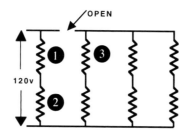

PARALLEL CONNECTED

The sketch above shows an OPEN between the second and third receptacles, but you still have 120 volts at receptacles one and two. So this is **not** a parallel circuit, and it is **not** a series circuit as you would loose power to the entire circuit.

To have a parallel circuit you must "pig tail" the connections as shown below.

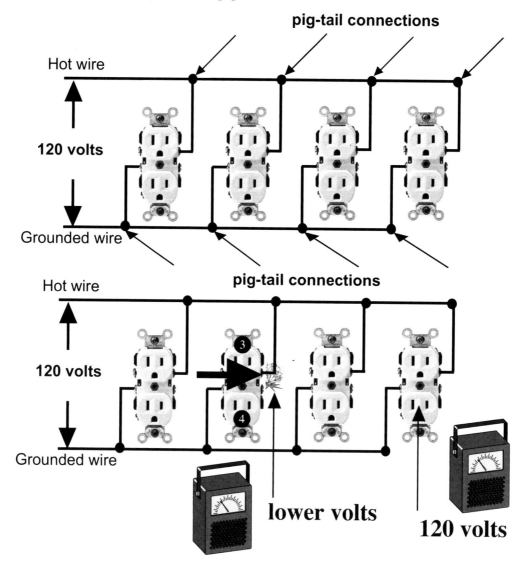

With a **pig-tail** connection to the black and white wires, a loose connection at the terminal would only effect receptacles three and four as all the other receptacles would receive 120 volts by pig-tailing the connections. You would only have one hot wire terminal connection at each receptacle instead of two hot wire terminal connections as on feed- thru connections.

The **feed-thru connection is shown below** as the hot wire and grounded wire are both connected to the screw terminal on the conductive tab.

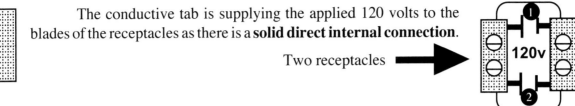

The conductive tab is supplying the applied 120 volts to the blades of the receptacles as there is a **solid direct internal connection**.

Two receptacles ➡️ 120v

The fifth receptacle has a loose screw at the top connection on the conductive tab. The hot wire due to the loose high resistance connection is supplying a voltage drop (**VD**) to the remaining three receptacles (6-7-8) with the **feed-thru** connection.•*You have a total of eight receptacles.*

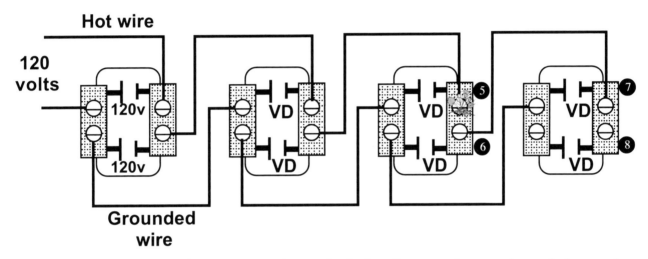

If a loose connection at receptacle two had pig-tail connections as shown below, only receptacles one and two would have a voltage drop. The remaining six receptacles would receive the applied 120 volts.

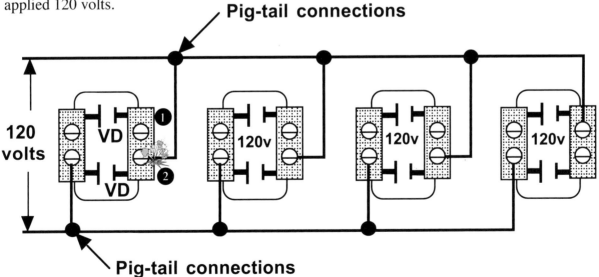

Question 3 should show choice (**a**) as pigtailed to be a parallel circuit: Receptacles in residential wiring are regularly connected in _____.

(**a**) **parallel pigtailed**   (**b**) **perpendicular**   (**c**) **series**   (**d**) **diagonal**

PREPARING FOR GENERAL KNOWLEDGE QUESTIONS

General Knowledge (no book)

This part of the test is where common sense, **apprenticeship and years on the job** are helpful.

When you contact the building department to apply for license exam to receive a blue print of the contents of the exam, remember you are already to be an electrician as they require an apprenticeship and four years on the job to sit for the Journeyman license exam.

But, do they check this to verify your experience? You must first qualify to take the exam. If you falsify your application and lack the experience, this exam will be very difficult.

Safety type questions are asked, questions on practical knowledge as the proper connections to a switch circuit. Ohm's law and basic theory questions are asked closed book. If they want to make the closed book exam more difficult, they ask questions from the Code book. Definitions from Article 100 are a favorite closed book question as they expect the electrician to know the definitions. Prior to the exam, the last thing the applicant should do is scan Article 100 in the Code. Try to retain as many definitions as you can.

The questions can be answered easily in the time limit. It's very simple, either you know the answer or you don't. It doesn't help to sit and scratch your head pondering over the correct answer. It has been proven in test taking that the longer you hesitate in selecting the choice, the more likely you are to talk yourself out of the correct answer.

Read the question and the choice of answers **carefully** and select your choice and move to the next question.

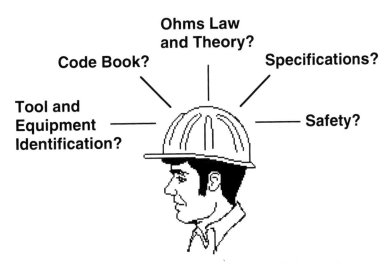

How much do you know, or can remember of the subjects asked?

No book questions (General Knowledge)

•Come up with your own answer, before reading the options. Try to answer the question in your own words if you can, then try to find the answer that most closely matches your idea.

•Don't waste a lot of time on a difficult question and become frustrated, as this may affect your performance on the rest of the test.

•It's better to answer every single question, if you can, and hope that some of your guesses are correct.

•If the answer is only partly true, or applies to only one part of the question, it is probably not the one to choose.

•If the answer is only true under certain conditions, it is probably not the right one. If a question asks about a specific behavior of an elephant, but the answer would only be correct for an elephant in captivity, it doesn't exactly answer the question.

•If an answer is incomplete, or is not correct under every circumstance, eliminate that option. This will leave you with fewer options to choose from, which will increase the odds that you will select the correct answer.

•If you find an answer that looks "almost" complete, see if there is another option that is very similar to that answer, but is complete. This may be the correct choice.

Try choosing the longest answer. Often, the choice that contains the most words is correct, because the teacher needs to include a large number of qualifiers to ensure that the answer can't be contested. The teacher may not take the time to phrase incorrect answers in quite such specific terms.

For example, imagine a driving test with this question: "If you want to turn right, you should be in:" The answers given are: (a) The left lane, (b) The lane that's nearest the direction you want to turn, (c) the right lane,(d) the center lane. The test maker has been most careful in phrasing (correct) option (c), to make sure that this answer can't be disputed.

Qualifying phrases might include over a period of time, in rare cases, or within a small segment of the population.

At the same time, sometimes longer answers can be a trick to try to get you to pick the more elaborate sounding suggestion. Use your best judgment and realize that this strategy isn't a sure thing.

Examine every part of an answer that includes a reason. Answers that are phrased to include a reason are often false. The first part of the answer might be true, but then the teacher will add a modifier that is incorrect or incomplete. This makes the entire statement false.

Look for words like because, if, since, and when.

For example, consider this statement: "Thomas Edison is considered a brilliant visionary because he invented the electric lightbulb." Thomas Edison invented many things, **but he didn't invent the lightbulb**; he invented a longer lasting, incandescent version of the lightbulb.

1878 - Sir Joseph Wilson Swan FRS (Foreign Member of Royal Society) was an English physicist, chemist, and inventor. He is known as an independent **early developer of a successful incandescent light bulb, and is the person responsible for developing and supplying the first incandescent lights used to illuminate homes and public buildings**, including the Savoy Theatre, London, in 1881.

GENERAL KNOWLEDGE EXAM QUESTIONS - Practice

1. When testing a circuit for continuity using the multimeter, the electrician should ___.

(a) insert the test leads and connect the test leads in parallel with the circuit after energizing the circuit
(b) insert the test leads and connect the test leads in series with the circuit after energizing the circuit
(c) insert the test leads and connect the test leads in series with the circuit after de-energizing the circuit
(d) a multimeter cannot be used to test for continuity

2. Which of the following results in loss of electrical energy from the circuit?

(a) Susceptance   (b) Inductive reactance   (c) Capacitive reactance   (d) Resistance

3. The letters MTR on the drawing would indicate ____.

(a) middle of run   (b) manufacture   (c) motor   (d) motor-tie-resistor

4. Ohm's Law cannot be applied for which of the following?

(a) To determine the voltage drop through a resistance.
(b) To determine the impedance of complete motor circuits.
(c) To determine the current produced by a voltage impressed on a resistance.
(d) To determine the voltage required to provide a specific current through a resistance.

5. If the scale is 1/8" = 1' and the conduit run measures 5 3/4" on the drawing, how many lengths of 10' conduit is needed?

(a) 3   (b) 4   (c) 5   (d) 6

6. A newly installed DC motor is running in the wrong direction. What change is necessary to correct this problem?

(a) Shift the brushes toward the direction of rotation.
(b) Interchange the connections of the field winding.
(c) Revolve the pole pieces 180° on their own axis.
(d) Reverse the line leads.

7. On which side of the door should switches be located?

(a) hinged side   (b) opposite of hinged side   (c) back side   (d) door jam vertical

ANSWERS --- GENERAL KNOWLEDGE EXAM QUESTIONS - Practice

1. **(c) insert the test leads and connect the test leads in series with the circuit after de-energizing the circuit.** General knowledge

2. **(d) Resistance** AEH pg. 1.27, sec 50 (AEH is American Electricians Handbook)

3. **(c) motor** Plans review book

4. **(b) To determine the impedance of complete motor circuits.** AEH pg. 1.46 sec 107

5. **(c) 5** Solution: $5.75 \div .125 = 46' \div 10' = 4.6$ or 5 lengths

6. **(b) Interchange the connections of the field winding.** AEH pg. 7.29 sec. 55

7. **(b) opposite of hinged side** General knowledge

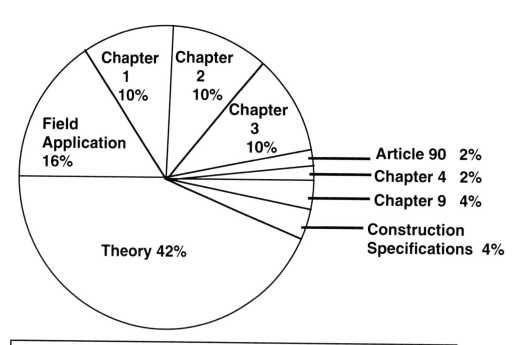

Theory is a big part of an electrical exam. The Ohm's Law book and Theory book by *Tom Henry* are a must!

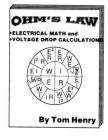
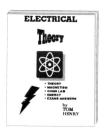

PREPARING FOR AN OPEN BOOK EXAM

Open Book

Most applicants agree this is the most difficult part of an electrical exam. Time becomes such an important factor. 50 open book questions are to be answered in two hours or 100 questions in four hours on the Journeyman exam.

Open book is a test of your knowledge and use of the National Electrical Code. 86% of the open book Journeyman questions are from the Code book.

Your score on the open book exam depends on how familiar you are with the Code book. Most exam applicants run out of time and are not able to find all the answers to the questions within the limited time.

**Journeyman Exam
50 Questions
2 Hour Time Limit**

**That averages to
2.4 minutes
per question**

The key to an open book exam is not to spend too much time on one question. If the question does not contain a key word that you can find in the index, **skip this question**, and continue to the next question. If you spend 3 minutes, 5 minutes, 6 minutes on a question and never find the answer you are eating into the time that should be used for the answers you can find.

In general, there are usually 8 to 10 really difficult questions on an exam. The remaining questions after proper preparation, you will be able to find within the alotted time. Skip these 8 or 10 as you recognize them and move on finding the other answers. If you answer 40 questions correctly out of a total of 50 questions your score would be 80%! That's better than in some cases where the applicant hasn't even answered 20 questions and time has run out. You **can't** spend 5 or 6 minutes on a question. Never leave a question unanswered, unanswered is counted wrong. Always select a multiple choice answer before time runs out.

Proper preparation is so important in passing an open book exam. Don't be guilty of reading a question and feeling, "I know the answer so I won't bother looking in the Code book." The following pages will prove how this can be a big mistake. I teach by being properly prepared with how to find your way around in the Code book. You'll be able to look up all the answers within the time limit.

The difficulty occurs when you say Code book.

THE OPEN BOOK EXAM

       The best reference book for locating words in the Code book is "The Key Word Index". This book contains every word in the Code book with section number and page number. **Now you can find what you're looking for in seconds!** The "Key Word Index" is even pre-drilled with five holes so it can be added to the looseleaf Code book with ease. Now you'll be able to show them out on the job where it says that in the Code book. Try it once and you'll never be without it.

       The "*ULTIMATE*" Code package includes the *2020* NEC looseleaf, *Tom Henry* 68 TABS (installed), KEY WORD INDEX, REMINDER BOOK, 14 pages of FORMULA INSERTS, plus over 3,600 *KEY* Code references **HI-LITED**!

       Will Rogers once said, "You can't come back from someplace you've never been." This book will take you there.

•If you focus first on figuring out what the answer is, **before looking at the options given**, it will force you to think back to the text or the lecture where you first heard this information.
       This process helps to improve your concentration, and will exercise your memory.

•If you are really stuck on a question, make your best guess and put a question mark next to it. If you finish the test with time to spare, go back and reconsider the ones you marked.
       If you do not want to guess, skip the question and put a mark beside it, so you can return to it if you have time at the end of the test.

•Skip answers when you are stuck, but try to get back to them if you can – **it's best to answer every question you can**, within the allotted time frame.

•Forget about always sticking to your first choice. Many people say that your first guess on a test question is usually right, so you should never change your answer. However, recent studies have shown that isn't the case – you're just as likely, or even more likely, to get it right if you change an answer you aren't sure about. So don't stress over whether to change an answer because it wasn't your first choice. **If you change your mind, change your answer**.

•Data collected from takers shows that test-takers who changed some of their answers tended to score higher than those who always stuck with their first choice.
       Test takers in the study most often changed answers from wrong to right, which resulted in a higher score.

To pass the exam is very simple, it takes work! Like with anything in life, you get out of it what you put into it. The more time you spend preparing for the exam, the easier it will become. As you work these exams and grade yourself, hi-lite the answers with a marking pen in your Code book, or better yet purchase the "Ultimate Code Book" which has the complete package for taking an electrical exam.

The key to the exam is that the student must first **understand** the question, which requires **careful reading of each word.**

Read this sentence:

> FINISHED FILES ARE THE RE-
> SULT OF YEARS OF SCIENTIF-
> IC STUDY COMBINED WITH THE
> EXPERIENCE OF YEARS.

Now read it once more, and count the **F's** in the sentence. How many did you find?

(a) 3 (b) 4 (c) 5 (d) 6

If you are a careful reader, you will find all **6** F's.

Most applicants taking an exam are not familiar enough with the Code book and it's easy to understand why only 30 out of 100 pass an electrical exam. Many are *unsuccessful* because they failed to *read* the question correctly.

Your score on the open book exam depends on how familiar you are with the **Code book**. Most exam applicants run out of time and are not able to find all the answers to the questions within the limited time.

Number skills can be tested with math problems or interpreting plans, charts and graphs. You may wonder whether to concentrate on improving your strong areas or on building some background in your fields of *weakness*. Working more practice exams, broader coverage, would be included for those subjects which are more important in your work. Now weigh your strengths and weaknesses against the job requirements and prepare accordingly.

1. Conductors supplying two or more motors shall have an ampacity equal to the sum of the full-load current rating of all the motors plus _____ % of the highest rated motor in the group.

(a) 25   (b) 80   (c) 100   (d) 125

2. In a residence, no point along the floor line in any wall space may be more than __9__ feet from an outlet.

(a) 6   (b) 6 1/2   (c) 12   (d) 10

3. Which of the following statements about a #2 THHN copper conductor is correct?

(a) Its maximum operating temperature is 90° C
(b) It has a nylon insulation
(c) Its area is .067 square inches
(d) It has a DC resistance of .319 ohms per m/ft from Table 8

4. The maximum permissible open circuit voltage of electric-discharge lighting equipment used in a dwelling occupancy is _____ volts.

(a) 1000   (b) 120   (c) 240   (d) 50

5. Voltage shall not exceed 600 volts between conductors on branch circuits supplying only ballasts for electric-discharge lamps in tunnels with a height of not less than _____ feet.

(a) 12   (b) 15   (c) 18   (d) 22

6. Noninsulated busbars will have a minimum space of _____ inches between the bottom of enclosure and busbar.

(a) 6   (b) 8   (c) 10   (d) 12

7. If made up with threadless couplings, a 1" rigid metal conduit shall be supported at least every _____ feet.

(a) 6   (b) 8   (c) 10   (d) 12

1. **(a)** 430.24 Section 430.24 reads: Shall have of an ampacity not less than 125% of the full-load current rating of the highest rated motor plus the sum of the full-load current ratings of all other motors in the group. Question #1 reads: The sum of the full-load current rating of **ALL** the motors plus _____% of the highest rated motor. The highest rated motor was already included at 100% in the question in **ALL** motors, so you need to add 25% more to make it 125%.

2. **(a)** 210.52(A)(1). The key is to read the exact wording in the question. We space outlets 12' apart in a residence, but section 210.52(A)(1) states that **no point along the floor line** in any wall space is more than 6' from an outlet.

3. **(a)** Table 310.4(A). The key is THH**N**, the **N** is a nylon **covering**, not insulation. 0.067 square inches is from Table 8 which is for **bare** conductors. 0.319 ohms per m/ft from Table 8 is for **aluminum** not copper.

4. **(a)** 410.140(B). The key is to check the NEC index for "Electric discharge lighting", check each listing and 1,000 volts or less, 410-XIII will lead you to the answer in section 410.140(B).

5. **(c)** 210.6(D)(1)(b). "Ballasts" and "Electric-discharge lamps" are listed in the index but are no help. "Tunnel" is not even listed in the index. The key, "luminaires voltages" from the index will lead you to section 210.6 and the answer.

6. **(c)** Table 408.5. "Noninsulated" is not listed in the index. "Busbars" is listed, but of no help. The key, think of where you would find a busbar located, in an enclosure, a **panelboard**. Article 408 will lead you to the answer in Table 408.5.

7. **(c)** 344.30. The key word is **"threadless"** couplings. Section 344.30(B)(1) states a conduit shall be supported at least every 10'. 344.30(B)(1) states if made up with **threaded** couplings, you can use Table 344.30(B)(2) for supports.

 When looking at the answer choices and then reading the Code book REMEMBER: 12" is 1 foot, 60 seconds is one minute, twelve is 12, 7 1/2' is 7' 6", 33% is one third, 96" is 8 feet, 18" is 1 1/2', 2 1/2' is 30", 54" is 4 1/2', 2' is 24", and 6' 6" is 6 1/2'.

NEC Code consists of **9 chapters** each dividing into four groupings: General Requirements; Specific Requirements; Communications Systems and Tables

Chapter 1: General
Chapter 2: Wiring and Protection
Chapter 3: Wiring Methods and Materials
Chapter 4: Equipment for General Use
Chapter 5: Special Occupancies
Chapter 6: Special Equipment
Chapter 7: Special Conditions
Chapter 8: Communications Systems
Chapter 9: Tables – Conductor and Raceway Specifications

I agree with questions from theory-Ohm's law, voltage drop, ampacity, tools, plan reading.

But the difficulty for the applicant comes **from asking questions from all nine chapters** of the National Electrical Code.

The preparation for the exam should educate the dangers of the **behavior of electricity**, the overload, short circuit, the explosion, the fire, the injuries, the deaths.

For some electricians, it has been twenty years or more since they have used math formulas, theory, and calculations. For most, the last time was an apprenticeship class. Now, for the exam, we are required to be an expert in the reading of the Code and in applying all of the tables and demand factors to the calculations.

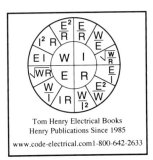

Tom Henry Electrical Books
Henry Publications Since 1985
www.code-electrical.com1-800-642-2633

The most difficult task in preparing for the electrical exam is trying to "memorize" the formulas. You increase the strength of your memory by *overlearning the subject* and that's what our books are about. Our books will show an easier way to study. Study smarter, not harder.

Memorization is the process of committing something to memory. The act of memorization is often a deliberate mental process undertaken in order **to store in memory for later recall.** Memory is the "process of retaining information over time."

Memorization is a frontage road: It runs parallel to the best parts of learning, never intersecting. It's a detour around all the action, *a way of knowing without learning*. Only through sustained effort of **rehearsing information are we able to memorize data for longer than a short period of time.**

We tend to remember things that interest us or are made memorable to us.

Hand-writing is a powerful tool for memorization, and it is even more effective if you do it repeatedly. **Get out a pen and paper and start hand-writing what you need to memorize**.

The **closed book** exam questions your knowledge on "Other than Code questions." Some questions may seem difficult for you, but they represent every conceivable type of question encountered on previous electrical exams.

Instead of marking your choice of answer in the book, write it on a separate paper, that way you can retake the exam over until you feel you understand the question and answer.

The exams are *timed based*, so write down the time you start and finish the practice exam.

25 questions at 2.4 minutes per question = 60 minutes. **Spend an hour a day** working a practice exam and see your scoring increase!

Start now by *reading the question carefully* using your formula sheets and calculator.

To grade your exam:
Count the number of correct answers
and divide by the number of questions 25.
Example: 19 correct answers ÷ 25 questions = 76%

General knowledge categories such as the behavior of electricity, theory, Ohm's Law, ac-dc power, voltage drop, power factor, efficiency, cost, tools, safety, plan reading, specifications, etc.

The **general knowledge** categories test your knowledge of what you have learned from the years spent in the electrical field to **qualify** to take the exam. How much can you remember from your training?

The NEC is updated every 3 years, **general knowledge** categories remain the same over the years in most cases.

There is no NEC section to locate for **general knowledge** questions, you must select the correct answer by **memory**. These are the questions where **formulas** come into play.

Examples of time in the alternating current sine wave exam questions

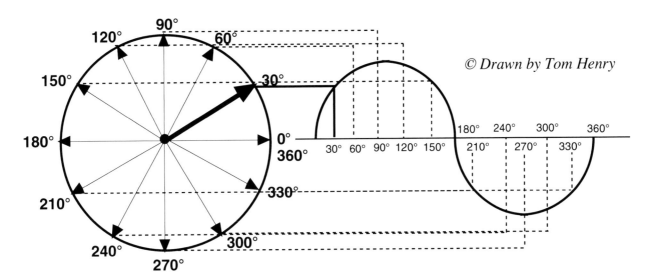

© Drawn by Tom Henry

1. If one complete cycle occurs in 1/60 of a second, the frequency is
_____.
(a) 30 hertz (b) 60 cycle (c) 115 cycle (d) 50 hertz

2. In an AC wave, 30 degrees of phase is _____ of a cycle.
(a) 1/4   (b) 1/3   (c) 1/2   (d) 1/12
Solution: 360° ÷ 30° = 12

3. 60 cycle frequency travels 180 degrees in how many seconds?
(a) 1/60   (b) 1/120   (c) 1/180   (d) 1/30
Solution: 180° ÷ 360° = .5   60 cycles ÷ .5 = 120 or 1/120 second

4. In a 60 cycle system, what length of time does it take to go 90 degrees?
(a) 1/3 second   (b) 1/90 second   (c) 1/60 second   (d) 1/240 second
Solution: 90 ÷ 360° = .25   60 cycles ÷ .25 = 240 or 1/240 second

5. In a 60 cycle system, what length of time does it take to go 270 degrees?
(a) 1/3 second   (b) 1/80 second   (c) 1/60 second   (d) 1/240 second
Solution: 270° ÷ 360° = .75   60 cycles ÷ .75 = 80 or 1/80 second

2020
JOURNEYMAN
GENERAL KNOWLEDGE
EXAM #1

(no-book)

50 QUESTIONS
TIME LIMIT - 1 HOUR

TIME SPENT ☐ **MINUTES**

SCORE ☐ %

JOURNEYMAN GENERAL KNOWLEDGE EXAM #1   TIME LIMIT ONE HOUR

1. What is the most frequently used wire size for interior wiring?

(a) 10 AWG   (b) 12 AWG   (c) 14 AWG   (d) 18 AWG

2. Electric power is almost exclusively generated, transmitted and distributed by three-phase systems because it _____.

(a) costs less than single-phase apparatus   (b) is more efficient
(c) uses less material for a given capacity   (d) all of these

3. An automatic device that operates at preset values is known as a _____.

(a) fuse   (b) relay   (c) contactor   (d) mercury switch

4. Electron is a Greek word for _____.

(a) heat   (b) feather   (c) stone   (d) amber

5. What kind of instrument is an ammeter?

(a) A recording   (b) A DC meter   (c) An indicating   (d) An integrating

6. The purpose of battery cells connected in parallel is to _____.

(a) increase internal resistance   (b) increase in voltage output
(c) increase in current capacity   (d) decrease in current capacity

7. The _____ value is considered as the most important value of a sine wave.

(a) peak   (b) instantaneous   (c) effective   (d) average

8. When two resistances are connected in series, _____.

(a) voltage across them must be the same (b) current in each resistor will be the same
(c) there will be no current in the circuit   (d) they will become inductive

9. A step-down transformer _____.

(a) increases both the voltage and current
(b) lowers the current and increases the voltage
(c) lowers the voltage and increases the current
(d) lowers both the voltage and current

10. Heat is a form of wasted electrical energy dissipated by _____.

(a) inductance (b) capacitance (c) a diode (d) resistance

11. When one resistance in a series circuit is open ____.

(a) the voltage is zero across the open resistance
(b) the current is zero in all the resistances
(c) the current is maximum in the normal resistances
(d) the current increases in the voltage source

12. If the needle of the VOM will no longer align with the zero-ohm mark at the lowest range of resistance but will align on the other resistance ranges, the probable cause is the ____.

(a) meter current is abnormal   (b) needle is bent
(c) terminals were interchanged   (d) supply battery is weak

13. A wire has a resistance of 5 ohms. What will be the resistance of another wire of the same material three times as long and half the cross sectional area?

(a) 7.5Ω (b) 15Ω (c) 30Ω (d) 50Ω

14. A wattmeter measures ____.

(a) AC power only (b) DC reactive power only (c) AC and DC power (d) none of these

15. Which of the following can vary with AC but not with DC?

(a) voltage (b) frequency (c) power (d) magnitude

16. A large series motor should not be started without some mechanical load on it because it will ____.

(a) open the fuse or CB   (b) draw too much current
(c) spark heavily   (d) develop excessive speed and damage itself

17. An inductor works by ____.

(a) introducing resistance into a circuit   (b) charging a piece of wire
(c) storing energy as a magnetic field   (d) choking off high frequency AC

18. A cell that can not be recharged is a _____.

(a) dry cell (b) wet cell (c) secondary cell (d) primary cell

19. A measuring instrument used to measure the diameter of circular mils in a wire is a ____.

(a) wire gauge (b) micrometer (c) millimeter (d) milliammeter

20. The start winding of a split-phase induction motor is switched out of the circuit by a device called ____.

(a) proximity switch (b) zero speed switch (c) magnetic contactor (d) centrifugal switch

21. An ideal step-up transformer with 100 turns in the primary and 2500 turns in the secondary carries a load of 2 amps in the secondary windings. The current of the primary winding is ____ .

(a) 25 amps (b) 50 amps (c) 250 amps (d) 500 amps

22. A device used to remove sharp burrs or rough edges is a ____.

(a) hickey (b) bender (c) reamer (d) rotometer

23. The presence of current is only made known by the effect it produces. Three important effects are ____.

(a) heating, magnetic and chemical   (b) generation, chemical and electric shock
(c) heating, magnetic and electric shock (d) heating, electric shock and generation

24. ____ is a wiring method using knobs, tubes, and flexible non-metallic tubing for the protection and support of single insulated conductors concealed in hollow spaces of walls and ceilings of buildings.

(a) Knob and tube wiring   (b) Open wiring on insulators
(c) Open wiring with knobs, tubes, etc. (d) Concealed knob and tube wiring

25. On a drawing, a circle with the letter B stands for ____.

(a) buzzer outlet (b) pushbutton outlet (c) bell outlet (d) outlet with blank cover

26. A ____ is not a standard size fuse.

(a) 45 amp (b) 75 amp (c) 80 amp (d) 125 amp

27. ____ currents are wasteful currents which flow in the core of a transformer and produce heat.

(a) Sneak (b) Magnetizing (c) Eddy (d) Residual

28. In electricity, the positive electric charge refers to ____.

(a) atoms (b) electrons (c) neutrons (d) protons

29. The rate of doing work is ____.

(a) power   (b) current   (c) energy   (d) force

30. A transformer consists of ____.

(a) a parallel resonant circuit   (b) two coils wound on a common core
(c) a capacitor and an inductor   (d) an inductance and resistance

31. The effect of a discharge of electricity due to ionization of surrounding air by high voltage is ____.

(a) corona effect   (b) Hall effect   (c) Compton effect   (d) Miller effect

32. An ammeter must always be connected in the circuit under test ____.

(a) positive to negative and negative to negative
(b) positive to positive and negative to positive
(c) positive to negative and negative to positive
(d) positive to positive and negative to negative

33. ____ is the poorest conductor of electricity.

(a) Steel   (b) Aluminum   (c) Silver   (d) Carbon

34. A meter used to test the armatures and stators of electric motors, generators, and other equipment for a short circuit is called a ____.

(a) multimeter   (b) megohmeter   (c) bolometer   (d) growler

35. In a transformer, the primary circuit sees the impedance of the ____ winding.

(a) secondary   (b) primary   (c) both primary and secondary   (d) isolation

36. When the temperature of a conductor is decreased, the resistance will be ____.

(a) increased   (b) steady   (c) decreased   (d) zero

37. ____ is the process by which one conductor produces or induces a voltage in another conductor even though there is no mechanical coupling between the two conductors.

(a) Cutting of fluxes   (b) Short circuit   (c) Induction   (d) Eddy current

38. A/an ____ motor has no commutator.

(a) shunt   (b) induction   (c) universal   (d) repulsion

39. The inert gas present in an incandescent bulb is primarily intended to ____.

(a) increase lumen output
(b) decrease filament evaporation
(c) activate the surface of the filament
(d) reduce hazards when the glass bulb is shattered

40. A short circuit can be detected by using ____ .

(a) a megger   (b) an ammeter   (c) an oscilloscope   (d) an ohmmeter

41. Which of the following has the least number of valence electrons?

(a) insulator   (b) semi-insulator   (c) conductor   (d) semiconductor

42. To increase voltage output, battery cells are connected in ____.

(a) series   (b) parallel   (c) series-parallel   (d) parallel-series

43. If a low resistance is connected in parallel with a higher resistance, the combined resistance is ____.

(a) always less than the low resistance
(b) always more than the high resistance
(c) always between the values of high and low resistance
(d) higher or lower than the low resistance depending on the value of the higher resistance

44. The purpose of a ballast in a fluorescent lamp assembly is ____.

(a) to regulate the lumens output   (b) to limit the current through the lamp
(c) to improve the overall power factor   (d) to regulate the voltage across the lamp

45. Branch circuits are classified according to the maximum ____.

(a) power consumed   (b) voltage across it
(c) load being served   (d) setting of the overcurrent device

46. A capacitor opposes change in ____.

(a) current   (b) voltage   (c) voltage and current   (d) neither voltage nor current

47. On a simple ohmmeter, the 0Ω mark is located ____.

(a) in the middle   (b) at the far left   (c) at the far right   (d) anywhere

48. Which of the following is the main function of a DC motor?

(a) To change mechanical energy to electrical energy
(b) To change electrical energy to mechanical energy
(c) To change chemical energy to mechanical energy
(d) To generate power

49. A short length of conductor used to make a connection between terminals or around a break in the circuit is a _____.

(a) jumper   (b) bonding wire   (c) tie wire   (d) guy wire

50. A fuse link should be made from a material with a ____ melting point.

(a) high   (b) low   (c) moderate   (d) strong

2020
JOURNEYMAN
GENERAL KNOWLEDGE
EXAM #2

(no-book)

50 QUESTIONS
TIME LIMIT - 1 HOUR

TIME SPENT [ ] **MINUTES**

SCORE [ ] %

JOURNEYMAN GENERAL KNOWLEDGE EXAM #2   TIME LIMIT ONE HOUR

1. Your foreman asked you to measure the insulation resistance of some conductors. To do this you would use a _____.

(a) hydrometer   (b) megger   (c) bell tester   (d) wattmeter

2. The main difference between a pipe thread and a machine thread is that the pipe thread is _____.

(a) finer   (b) longer   (c) uneven   (d) tapered

3. Receptacles in residential wiring are regularly connected in _____.

(a) parallel   (b) perpendicular   (c) series   (d) diagonal

4. A foreman in charge of a crew of men preparing to work on a low voltage tension circuit should caution them to _____.

(a) work only when the load is zero
(b) consider the circuit hot at all times
(c) never work on any circuit alone
(d) wait until the circuit has been killed

5. The term pneumatic refers to _____.

(a) electricity   (b) steam   (c) air   (d) oil

6. What type of fastner would you use to mount a box to a hollow tile wall?

(a) expansion bolts   (b) toggle bolts
(c) rawl plugs   (d) bolts with backing plates

7. Which of the following locations would most likely require installation of a ground fault circuit interrupter?

(a) living room   (b) closet   (c) bedroom   (d) bathroom

8. The lubricant used to make pulling wires through a conduit easier is _____.

(a) grease   (b) powdered pumice   (c) vaseline   (d) powdered soapstone

9. The instrument by which electric power is measured is a ____.

(a) ammeter   (b) rectifier   (c) voltmeter   (d) wattmeter

10. The connection between the grounded circuit conductor and the equipment grounding conductor at the service is called the ____ bonding jumper.

(a) circuit   (b) equipment   (c) main   (d) appliance

11. The larger the conductor, the ____.

(a) higher the resistance   (b) lower the ampacity
(c) higher the voltage   (d) lower the resistance

12. A hook on the end of a fish tape is **not** to ____.

(a) keep it from catching on joints and bends
(b) tie a swab to
(c) tie the wires, to be pulled
(d) protect the end of the wire

13. Which of the following is an LL conduit body?

(a)   (b)   (c)   (d)

14. When soldering two copper conductors together, they are kept clean while heating by ____.

(a) the use of flux
(b) applying the solder quickly
(c) rubbing often with emery cloth
(d) not permitting the open flame to touch them

15. Metal cabinets used for lighting circuits are grounded to ____.

(a) reduce shock hazard
(b) eliminate electrolysis
(c) assure that the fuse will blow in a defective circuit
(d) simplify the wiring

16. In sockets, extension cord is protected by means of the _____ knot.

(a) underwriters' (b) clove hitch (c) sheepshank (d) western union

17. A branch circuit that supplies a number of outlets for lighting and appliances is a/an _____ branch circuit.

(a) individual (b) multi-purpose (c) general purpose (d) utility

18. When three equal resistors are connected in parallel, the total resistance is _____.

(a) equal to the resistance of each   (b) less than any one resistor
(c) greater than any one resistance   (d) none of these

19. The efficiency of a motor is a measure of _____.

(a) the natural speed of the motor
(b) the torque the motor produces
(c) how well it converts electrical energy into mechanical energy
(d) the power output of the motor in horsepower

20. When stripping insulation from an aluminum conductor _____.

I.   remove insulation as you would sharpen a pencil
II. ring the conductor and slip the insulation off the conductor
III. peel the insulation back and then cut outwards

(a) I, II and III (b) I and II only (c) I and III only (d) II and III only

21. The _____ angle is the angle between the real power and the apparent power.

(a) lag (b) power factor (c) voltage-current (d) watt

22. The most heat is created when current flows through which of the following?

(a) a 10 ohm condenser   (b) a 10 ohm inductance coil
(c) a 10 ohm resistor   (d) heat would be equal

23. 60 cycle frequency travels 180 degrees in how many seconds?

(a) 1/60 (b) 1/120 (c) 1/180 (d) 1/30

24. The current-carrying capacity of conductors expressed in amperes is _____.

(a) demand (b) pressure (c) ampacity (d) duty-cycle

25. The electrician's tapered reamer is used for ____.

(a) reaming the threads on couplings
(b) reaming the holes in bushings
(c) reaming the ends of rigid conduit after it is cut
(d) making holes in boxes

26. Electricity is sold by the kilowatt which is ____ watts.

(a) 10,000   (b) 1000   (c) 100   (d) 100,000

27. Three-way switching does **not** use the following conductor:

(a) ungrounded   (b) traveler   (c) grounded   (d) switch leg

28. The greater the number of free electrons, the better the ____ of a metal.

(a) insulation value   (b) resistance   (c) voltage drop   (d) conductivity

29. To cut Wiremold you would ____.

(a) use a chisel
(b) use an approved cutter like an M.M. cutter
(c) use a pair of tin snips
(d) use a hacksaw and remove the burr with a file

30. Electrical contacts are opened or closed when the electrical current energizes the coils of a device called a ____.

(a) thermostat   (b) reactor   (c) condenser   (d) relay

31. A clamp-on ammeter will measure ____.

(a) voltage when clamped on a single conductor
(b) current when clamped on a multi-conductor cable
(c) accurately only when parallel to cable
(d) accurately only when clamped perpendicular to a conductor

32. When a current leaves its intended path and returns to the source bypassing the load the circuit is ____.

(a) open   (b) shorted   (c) incomplete   (d) broken

33. The electric pressure or electromotive force is measured by the ____.

(a) volt (b) electric meter (c) watt (d) kilowatt

34. Conduit installed in a concrete slab is considered a ____.

(a) damp location (b) moist location (c) wet location (d) dry location

35. It is best as a safety measure, not to use water to extinguish electrical equipment fires. The main reason is that water ____.

(a) may transmit shock to the user
(b) will turn to steam
(c) will not put the fire out
(d) may damage the wiring

36. The total opposition to current flow in an AC circuit is expressed in ohms and is called ____.

(a) impedance (b) conductance (c) reluctance (d) resistance

37. Which of the items below is a rotometer?

(a)   (b)   (c)   (d)

38. When a person is burned the basic care steps are ____.

(a) cover and cool the burned area   (b) prevent infection
(c) care for shock   (d) all of these

39. A multimeter is a combination of ____.

(a) ammeter, ohmmeter and wattmeter   (b) voltmeter, ohmmeter and ammeter
(c) voltmeter, ammeter and megger   (d) voltmeter, wattmeter and ammeter

40. A good magnetic material is ____.

(a) brass (b) copper (c) iron (d) aluminum

41. Since fuses are rated by an amperage and voltage a fuse will work on ____.

(a) AC only   (b) AC or DC   (c) DC only   (d) any voltage

42. A fuse puller is used in replacing ____.

(a) cartridge fuses   (b) plug fuses   (c) link fuses   (d) ribbon fuses

43. A pendant fixture is a ____.

(a) hanging fixture   (b) recessed fixture   (c) bracket fixture   (d) none of these

44. To fasten an outlet box between the studs in a wall constructed of metal lath and plaster, you would use ____.

(a) cement or mortar   (b) iron wire
(c) nylon lath twine   (d) an approved box hanger

45. The unit of measurement for electrical resistance to current is the ____.

(a) watt   (b) ohm   (c) volt   (d) amp

46. A low energy power circuit ____.

(a) is a remote-control circuit
(b) is a signal circuit
(c) has its power supplied by transformers and batteries
(d) none of these

47. To convert AC or DC you will use a ____.

(a) generator   (b) rectifier   (c) vibrator   (d) auto-transformer

48. S_3 is a symbol used on a drawing to indicate a ____ switch.

(a) flush   (b) single-pole   (c) four-way   (d) three-way

49. Action requiring personal intervention for its control:

(a) controller   (b) automatic   (c) periodic duty   (d) non-automatic

50. A voltmeter is connected in ____ with the load.

(a) series   (b) parallel   (c) series-parallel   (d) series-shunt

2020
JOURNEYMAN
GENERAL KNOWLEDGE
EXAM #3

(no-book)

50 QUESTIONS
TIME LIMIT - 1 HOUR

TIME SPENT ☐ **MINUTES**

SCORE ☐ %

JOURNEYMAN GENERAL KNOWLEDGE EXAM #3   TIME LIMIT ONE HOUR

1. To control a ceiling light from five different locations it requires which of the following?

(a) four 3-way switches and one 4-way switch
(b) three 4-way switches and two 3-way switches
(c) three 3-way switches and two 4-way switches
(d) four 4-way switches and one 3-way switch

2. The advantage of AC over DC includes which of the following?

(a) better speed control   (b) lower resistance at higher current
(c) ease of voltage variation   (d) impedance is greater

3. Which of the following is considered the best electrical conductor?

(a) iron wire   (b) copper wire   (c) aluminum wire   (d) tin wire

4. The liquid in a battery is called the _____.

(a) askarel   (b) festoon   (c) hermetic   (d) electrolyte

5. A color code is used in multiple-conductor cables. For a 3-conductor cable the colors would be ___.

(a) one black, one red and one white
(b) two black and one red
(c) one white, one black and one blue
(d) two red and one black

6. Explanatory material in the Code is characterized by _____.

(a) the word "shall"   (b) FPN   (c) the word "may"   (d) the word "could"

7. The identified grounded conductor of a lighting circuit is always connected to the screw of a light socket to _____.

(a) reduce the possibility of accidental shock
(b) ground the light fixture
(c) improve the efficiency of the lamp
(d) provide the easiest place to connect the wire

.

8. A _____ box may be weatherproof.

(a) watertight   (b) rainproof   (c) raintight   (d) all of these

9. The Code requires that all AC phase conductors where used, the neutral and all equipment grounding conductors be grouped together when using metal enclosures or raceways. The principal reason for this is _____.

(a) currents would circulate through individual raceways
(b) less expensive to install a single raceway
(c) less labor hours for pulling wires in a single raceway
(d) conductors are easier to pull in a single raceway

10. Installing more than three current carrying conductors in the same conduit requires _____.

(a) a larger conduit   (b) high heat rated conductors
(c) derating of ampacity   (d) continuous loading

11. A _____ helps prevent arcing in movable contacts.

(a) spring   (b) condenser   (c) resistor   (d) hydrometer

12. The _____ circuit is that portion of a wiring system prior to the final overcurrent protective device protecting the circuit.

(a) service   (b) feeder   (c) power   (d) branch

13. When tightening a screw on a terminal, the end of the conductor should wrap around the screw in the same direction that you are turning the screw so that _____.

(a) when you pull on the conductor it will tighten
(b) the screw will not become loose
(c) the conductor will act as a locking nut
(d) the conductor will not turn off

14. Determining a positive wire on a single-phase circuit is _____.

(a) possible with a wattmeter   (b) possible with a voltmeter
(c) possible with an ammeter   (d) an impossibility

15. A _____ is used for testing specific gravity.

(a) thermocouple   (b) megger   (c) hydrometer   (d) galvanometer

16. An autotransformer differs from other types of transformers in that ____.

(a) its primary winding is always larger than its secondary winding
(b) it can be used only in automobiles
(c) its primary and secondary windings are common to each other
(d) it must be wound with heavier wire

17. In residential buildings, small appliance loads should have two or more _____.

(a) 15 ampere branch circuits   **(b) 20 ampere branch circuits**
(c) 40 ampere branch circuits   **(d) 50 ampere branch circuit**s

18. If the end of a cartridge fuse becomes warmer than normal, you should ____.

(a) tighten the fuse clips
(b) lower the voltage on the circuit
(c) notify the utility company
(d) change the fuse

19. Which of the following is the poorest conductor of electricity?

(a) mercury   (b) aluminum   (c) carbon   (d) silver

20. The primary winding of a loaded step-down transformer has ____ compared to the secondary winding.

(a) lower voltage and current   **(b) higher voltage and current**
(c) higher voltage and lower current **(d) lower voltage and higher current**

21. Copper is used for the tip of a soldering iron because ____.

(a) copper will not melt   **(b) copper is a very good conductor of heat**
(c) solder will not stick to other alloys **(d) copper is less expensive**

22. The sum of the voltage drop around a circuit is equal to the source voltage is ____.

(a) Kirchhoff's law   (b) Ohm's law   (c) Nevin's theory   (d) Faraday's law

23. Piezoelectric is caused by crystals or binding ____.

(a) chemical   (b) battery   (c) pressure   (d) heat

24. Heavy-duty lampholders include ____.

(a) admedium lampholders rated at 660 watts
(b) lampholders used on circuits larger than 20 amperes
(c) lampholders rated at not less than 750 watts
(d) all of the above

25. The reason for installing electrical conductors in a conduit is ____.

(a) to provide a ground
(b) to increase the ampacity of the conductors
(c) to protect the conductors from damage
(d) to avoid derating for continuous loading of conductors

26. Discoloring of one end of a fuse normally indicates ____.

(a) increased current   (b) excessive voltage   (c) low resistance   (d) poor contact

27. Wing nuts are useful on equipment where ____.

(a) cotter pins are used   (b) the nuts must be removed frequently
(c) a wrench cannot be used   (d) screws cannot be used

28. When resistors are connected in series, the total resistance is ____.

(a) the sum of the individual resistance values
(b) the equivalent of the smallest resistance value
(c) the equivalent of the largest resistance value
(d) less than the value of the smallest resistance

29. If a 120 volt incandescent light bulb is operating at a voltage of 125 volts, the result will be ____.

(a) it may be enough to blow a fuse
(b) the bulb won't be as bright
(c) shorter life of the bulb
(d) the wattage will be less than rated

30. Laminations are used in transformers to prevent ____.

(a) copper loss   (b) weight   (c) eddy current loss   (d) counter EMF

31. The Code requires which of the following colors for the equipment grounding conductor?

(a) white or gray   (b) green or green with yellow stripes
(c) yellow   (d) blue with a yellow stripe

32. Sometimes mercury toggle switches are used in place of a regular toggle switch because they ____.

(a) are easier to connect   (b) do not wear out as quickly
(c) are less expensive   (d) they glow in the dark

33. The assigned color for the high-leg conductor of a three-phase, 4-wire delta secondary is ____.

(a) red   (b) black   (c) blue   (d) orange

34. The Code rule for maximum 90 degree bends in a conduit between two boxes is four, the most likely reason for the total 360 degree limitation is ____.

(a) it is unsafe
(b) it makes pulling the conductors through the conduit too difficult
(c) you can damage the galvanized coating on the conduit
(d) too many bends require extra wire to be pulled

35. The correct word to define wiring which is not concealed is ____.

(a) open   (b) uncovered   (c) exposed   (d) bare

36. A solenoid is a ____.

(a) relay   (b) permanent magnet   (c) dynamo   (d) electromagnet

37. An electrician should always consider the circuit to be "hot" unless he definitely knows otherwise. The main reason is to avoid ____.

(a) personal injury   (b) having to find the panel
(c) saving time   (d) shutting off the wrong circuit

38. The best thing to cut PVC conduit within a tight area is ____.

(a) a short hacksaw   (b) a nylon string   (c) a knife   (d) a pipe cutter

39. If a live conductor is contacted accidentally, the severity of the electrical shock is determined primarily by ____.

(a) the size of the conductor   (b) whether the current is DC or AC
(c) the current in the conductor   (d) the contact resistance

40. Ohm's law is ____.

(a) an equation for determining power
(b) the relationship between voltage, current and power
(c) the relationship between voltage, current and resistance
(d) a measurement of wattage losses

41. What is the normal taper on a standard conduit thread-cutting die?

(a) 1/2" per foot   (b) 1/4" per foot   (c) 3/8" per foot   (d) 3/4" per foot

42. In an AC circuit the ratio of the power in watts to the total volt-amps is called the ____.

(a) demand factor   (b) power factor   (c) turns-ratio   (d) diversity factor

43. A continuous load is where the maximum current is expected to continue for ____ hours or more.

(a) five   (b) two   (c) three   (d) four

44. Which phase is probably open when you test Phase A and Phase B and get a low voltage reading, test Phase B and C and get a normal reading and test Phase A and C and get a low voltage reading?

(a) Phase A   (b) Phase B   (c) Phase C   (d) None of these

45. A ladder which is painted is a safety hazard mainly because the paint ____.

(a) may conceal weak spots in the rails or rungs
(b) is slippery after drying
(c) causes the wood to crack more quickly
(d) peels and the sharp edges of the paint may cut the hands

46. The chemical used as the agent in fire extinguishers to fight electrical fires is ____.

(a) CO_2 (b) K_OH (c) H_2O (d) L_O6

47. A location classified as _____ may be temporarily subject to dampness and wetness.

(a) dry (b) damp (c) moist (d) wet

48. The average dry cell battery gives an approximate voltage of _____.

(a) 1.5 (b) 1.2 (c) 1.7 (d) 2.0

49. The _____ circuit is that portion of a wiring system beyond the final overcurrent protection.

(a) lighting (b) feeder (c) signal (d) branch

50. Which of the following will **not** affect the resistance of a circuit?

(a) Length of the Conductor   (b) Diameter of the Conductor
(c) Insulation of the Conductor   (d) Temperature

2020
JOURNEYMAN
GENERAL KNOWLEDGE
EXAM #4

(no-book)

50 QUESTIONS
TIME LIMIT - 1 HOUR

TIME SPENT [   ] **MINUTES**

SCORE [   ] %

JOURNEYMAN GENERAL KNOWLEDGE EXAM #4   TIME LIMIT ONE HOUR

1. The electromotive force required to cause a current to flow may be obtained ____.

I. thermally   II. mechanically   III. chemically

(a) I only   (b) I and III only   (c) II and III only   (d) I, II and III

2. Which of the following is **not** true?

(a) A fluorescent fixture is more efficient than an incandescent fixture.
(b) Room temperature has an affect on the operation of a fluorescent lamp.
(c) Fluorescent fixtures have a good power factor with the current leading the voltage.
(d) The life of a fluorescent bulb is affected by starting and stopping.

3. Resistance opposes the flow of current in a circuit and is measured in ____.

(a) farads   (b) joules   (c) ohms   (d) henrys

4. Which of the following is true?

(a) Wooden plugs may be used for mounting electrical equipment in concrete.
(b) The high-leg conductor of a 4-wire delta is identified blue in color.
(c) The minimum size service permitted by the Code for a residence is 100 amps.
(d) The ungrounded conductor is connected to the screw shell of a lampholder.

5. Multiple start buttons in a motor control circuit are connected in ____.

(a) series   (b) parallel   (c) series-parallel   (d) none of these

6. Which of the following is **not** true?

(a) Feeder demand factors are applicable to household electric ranges.
(b) A green colored conductor can be used as an ungrounded circuit conductor.
(c) Insulated conductors #6 or smaller shall be white or gray, no marking tape permitted.
(d) All joints or splices must be electrically and mechanically secure before soldering.

7. Special permission is ____.

(a) granted by the electrical foreman on the job
(b) verbal permission by the inspector
(c) given only once on one blueprint change request
(d) the written consent of the authority having jurisdiction

8. One million volts can also be expressed as ____.

(a) 1 millivolt   (b) 1 kilovolt   (c) 1 megavolt   (d) 1 microvolt

9. Resistance in a circuit may be ____.

I. resistance of the conductors   II. resistance due to imperfect contact

(a) I only   (b) II only   (c) both I and II   (d) neither I nor II

10. Which of the following is **not** true?

(a) All receptacles on 15 and 20 amp branch circuits must be of the grounding type.
(b) Splices and joints shall be covered with an insulation equivalent to the conductor insulation.
(c) The size of the conductor determines the rating of the circuit.
(d) All 15 and 20 amp receptacles installed in a dwelling bathroom shall have GFCI protection.

11. A magnetic field is created around a conductor ____.

(a) whenever current flows in the wire, provided the wire is made of magnetic material
(b) only when the wire carries a large current
(c) whenever current flows in the conductor
(d) only if the conductor is formed into a loop

12. A universal motor has brushes that ride on the ____.

(a) commutator   (b) stator   (c) inter-pole   (d) field

13. How many kw hours are consumed by 25 - 60 watt light bulbs burning 5 hours in a 120v circuit?

(a) 1.5   (b) 180   (c) 7.5   (d) 75

14. A dynamo is ____.

(a) a pole line insulator
(b) a tool used to test dielectric strength
(c) a meter used for checking the R.P.M. of a motor
(d) a machine for converting mechanical energy into electrical energy

15. Which of the following is/are generally used for field magnets?

I. copper   II. steel   III. wrought iron

(a) I and II only   (b) I and III only   (c) II and III only   (d) I, II and III

16. The difference between a neutral and a grounded circuit conductor is ___.

(a) only a neutral will have equal potential to the ungrounded conductor
(b) only a neutral's outer covering is white or natural gray
(c) only a neutral carries unbalanced current
(d) there is no difference

17. The normal rotation of an induction motor is ____ facing the front of the motor. (The front of a motor is the end opposite the shaft).

(a) clockwise (b) counterclockwise

18. A function of a relay is to ____.

(a) turn on another circuit   **(b) produce thermal electricity**
(c) limit the flow of electrons   **(d) create a resistance in the field winding**

19. Which of the following is **not** true?

(a) It is an electrical impossibility to have a circuit with only inductive reactance because the metallic wire has a resistance.
(b) The voltage of a circuit is the greatest effective difference of potential that exists between any two conductors of a circuit.
(c) The current is said to lag the voltage in a circuit that has only capacitive reactance.
(d) Power factor is the phase displacement of current and voltage in an AC circuit.

20. Unity power factor, which means that the current is in phase with the voltage, would be ____.

(a) .50 (b) .80 (c) 0.10 (d) 1.0

21. Rheostats and potentiometers are types of ____ resistors.

(a) film (b) variable (c) fixed (d) wirewound

22. A laminated pole is ____.

(a) one built up of layers or iron sheets, stamped from sheet metal and insulated
(b) used in transmission lines over 100kv
(c) a pole soaked in creosote
(d) found in the western part of the U.S.A.

23. Which of the following is true?

(a) Conductors of different systems may not occupy the same enclosure.
(b) Knife switches should be mounted in a horizontal position.
(c) 75 amps is a standard size fuse.
(d) Circuits are grounded to limit excess voltage to ground, which might occur from lightning or exposure to other higher voltage sources.

24. Electrical power is a measure of _____.

(a) work wasted   (b) voltage   (c) rate at which work is performed   (d) total work performed

25. What percentage of the maximum (peak) voltage is the effective (R.M.S.) voltage?

(a) 100%   (b) 70.7%   (c) 63.7%   (d) 57.7%

26. A low factor is commonly caused by _____.

I. induction motors   II. synchronous motors   III. fluorescent lights

(a) III only   (b) II and III only   (c) I and III only   (d) I, II and III

27. Which of the following is **not** true?

(a) Conduit painted with enamel cannot be used outdoors.
(b) All AC phase wires, neutral and equipment grounding conductors if used, must be installed in the same raceway.
(c)   PVC shall have a minimum burial depth of 24".
(d) EMT raceway can be installed in an air conditioning-space heating duct.

28. Which of the following is **not** true?

(a) Equal currents flow in the branches of parallel circuits.
(b) The total resistance of a parallel circuit is less than the smallest resistor in the circuit.
(c) The total current in a parallel circuit is the sum of the branch currents.
(d) In a parallel circuit, there is more than one path for the current flow.

29. Hysteresis is _____.

(a) the tool used to read the specific gravity of a battery
(b) the lagging of magnetism, in a magnetic metal, behind the magnetizing flux which produces it
(c) the opposite of impedance
(d) none of these

30. The electric pressure of a circuit would be the ____.

(a) voltage   (b) amperage   (c) resistance   (d) wattage

31. Permeability is ____.

(a) the opposite of conductance
(b) a measure of the ease with which magnetism passes through any substance
(c) the total resistance to current flow
(d) the liquid substance in a battery

32. The Wheatstone bridge method is used for accurate measurements of ____.

(a) voltage   (b) amperage   (c) resistance   (d) wattage

33. When a circuit breaker is in the OPEN position ____.

I.   you have a short in the ungrounded conductor
II. you have a short in the grounded conductror

(a) I only   (b) II only   (c) either I or II   (d) both I and II

34. In solving series-parallel circuits, generally you would ____.

(a) treat it as a series circuit   (b) reduce it to its simplest form
(c) assume that all loads are equal   (d) treat it as a parallel circuit

35. A commutator is ____.

(a) a ditching machine
(b) the inter-poles of a generator
(c) a device for causing the alternating currents generated in the armature to flow in the same
     direction in the external circuit
(d) a transformer with a common conductor

36. Which of the following is true?

(a) EMT may be threaded
(b) The "white" colored conductor connected to the silver colored post on a duplex receptacle
     on a 120v two-wire branch circuit is called the "neutral" conductor.
(c) Plastic water pipe is approved to be used for electrical conduit.
(d) The screw shell of a lampholder may support a fixture weighing 6 pounds.

37. To fasten a box to a terra cotta wall you should use which of the following?

(a) wooden plug   (b) lag bolt   (c) expansion bolt   (d) toggle bolt

38. If a 240 volt heater is used on 120 volts, the amount of heat produced will be ____.

(a) twice as great   (b) four times as great   (c) 1/4 as much   (d) the same

39. Which of the following about a strap wrench is/are true?

I. you can turn pipe using one hand   II. use in a tight corner   III. use on different sizes of pipe

(a) I only   (b) II only   (c) III only   (d) I, II and III

40. When soldering a joint, the flux is used to ____.

(a) keep the wire cool   (b) keep the surface clean
(c) lubricate the joint   (d) maintain a tight connection

41. The transferring of electrons from one material to another would be ____.

(a) electrochemistry   (b) static electricity   (c) solar electricity   (d) piezoelectricity

42. A minimum thickness of ____ inch/inches of concrete over conduits and raceways should be used to prevent cracking.

(a) 1   (b) 2   (c) 3   (d) 4

43. Wire connectors are generally classified as ____ type(s).

I. thermal   II. pressure

(a) I only   (b) II only   (c) both I and II   (d) neither I nor II

44. One of the disadvantages of indenter or crimp connectors is ____.

(a) they must be re-crimped at each annual maintenance inspection
(b) that special tools are required to make the joint
(c) eventually they will loosen
(d) they can only be used for copper conductors

45. The usual service conditions under which a transformer should be able to carry its rated load are ____.

I. at rated secondary voltage or not in excess of 105% of the rated value
II. at rated frequency
III. temperature of the surrounding cooling air at no time exceeding 40°C (104°F) and average temperature of the surrounding cooling air during any 24-hour period not exceeding 30°C (86°F)

(a) I only (b) II only (c) III only (d) I, II, and III

46. Which of the following is **not** true?

(a) An autotransformer may be used as part of the ballast for lighting circuits.
(b) A branch circuit can never be supplied through an autotransformer.
(c) The losses of the autotransformer are less than those of a two-coil transformer.
(d) Autotransformers may be used as starting compensators for AC motors.

47. Conductors supplying two or more motors shall have an ampacity equal to the sum of the full-load current rating of all the motors plus ____ % of the highest rated motor in the group.

(a) 25 (b) 80 (c) 100 (d) 125

48. The symbol for a wye connection is ____.

(a) Σ (b) Δ (c) ø (d) Y

49. Which of the following meters is a wattmeter?

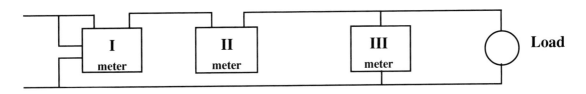

(a) I only (b) II only (c) III only (d) I, II or III

50. The voltage of a circuit is best defined as ____.

(a) the potential between two conductors
(b) the greatest difference of potential between two conductors
(c) the effective difference of potential between two conductors
(d) the average RMS difference of potential between any two conductors

2020
JOURNEYMAN
GENERAL KNOWLEDGE
EXAM #5

(no-book)

50 QUESTIONS
TIME LIMIT - 1 HOUR

TIME SPENT [ ] **MINUTES**

SCORE [ ] %

JOURNEYMAN GENERAL KNOWLEDGE EXAM #5   TIME LIMIT ONE HOUR

1. Something that would effect the ampacity of a conductor would be ____.

I. voltage   II. amperage   III. length   IV. temperature

(a) I only   (b) II only   (c) III only   (d) IV only

2. Alternating currents may be increased or decreased by means of a ____.

(a) motor   (b) transformer   (c) dynamo   (d) megger

3. Fixtures supported by the framing members of suspended ceiling systems shall be securely fastened to the ceiling framing member by mechanical means such as ____.

I. bolts or screws   II. rivets   III. clips identified for this use

(a) I only   (b) II only   (c) III only   (d) I, II or III

4. Which has the highest electrical resistance?

(a) brass   (b) iron   (c) water   (d) paper

5. Conductor sizes are expressed ____.

(a) only in circular mils   (b) in AWG or in circular mils
(c) in diameter or area   (d) in AWG or millimeters

6. Of the following, which one is **not** a type of file?

(a) half round   (b) bastard   (c) tubular   (d) mill

7. Oil is used in many large transformers to ____.

(a) prevent breakdown due to friction   (b) lubricate the core
(c) cool and insulate the transformer   (d) lubricate the coils

8. Fractional horsepower universal motors have brushes usually made of ____.

(a) copper strands   (b) mica   (c) carbon   (d) thin wire rings

9. When administering first aid to a worker suffering from fright as a result of falling from a ladder, the most important thing to do is ____.

(a) position the person to a sitting position
(b) cover the person and keep the person warm
(c) apply artificial respiration immediately
(d) check the rungs of the ladder

10. Which of the following would be used as a stop button?

(a)   **(b)**   **(c)**   **(d)**

11. If a co-worker is burned by acid from a storage battery, the proper first aid treatment is to wash with ____.

(a) iodine and leave it open to the air
(b) vinegar and apply a wet dressing
(c) water and apply vaseline
(d) lye and apply a dry bandage

12. A type of motor that will **not** operate on DC is the ____.

(a) series   (b) short shunt   (c) long shunt compound   (d) squirrel cage

13. Receptacles installed on ____ ampere branch circuits shall be of the grounding type.

(a) 15 and 20   (b) 25   (c) 30   (d) 40

14. Where conductors carrying alternating current are installed in metal enclosures or metal raceways, they shall be so arranged as to avoid heating the surrounding metal by induction, to accomplish this ____ shall be grouped together.

I.   all phase conductors
II. where used, the neutral
III. all equipment grounding conductors

(a) I only   (b) I and II only   (c) I and III only   (d) I, II and III

15. A(an) ____ changes AC to DC.

(a) battery   (b) capacitor   (c) alternator   (d) rectifier

16. A steel measuring tape is undesirable for use around electrical equipment. The **least** important reason is the ____.

(a) danger of entanglement in rotating machines
(b) shock hazard
(c) short circuit hazard
(d) magnetic effect

17. ____ is the ability of a material to permit the flow of electrons.

(a) Voltage   (b) Current   (c) Resistance   (d) Conductance

18. Which of the following two wires are grounded wires in a three-wire cable?

(a) red and white   (b) white and black   (c) bare and red   (d) white and bare

19. A fitting is ____.

(a) part of a wiring system that is intended primarily to perform an electrical function
(b) pulling cable into a confined area
(c) to be suitable or proper for
(d) part of a wiring system that is intended primarily to perform a mechanical function

20. The neutral conductor ____.

(a) is always the "white" grounded conductor
(b) has 70% applied for a household clothes dryer for a branch circuit
(c) never apply ampacity corrections
(d) carries the unbalanced current

21. An appliance that is easily moved from one place to another in normal use is a/an ____ appliance.

(a) on wheels   (b) dwelling-unit   (c) moveable   (d) portable

22. All wiring must be installed so that when completed ____.

(a) it meets the current-carrying requirements of the load
(b) it is free of shorts and unintentional grounds
(c) it is acceptable to Code compliance authorities
(d) it will withstand a hy-pot test

23. Rosin is preferable to acid as a flux for soldering wire because rosin is ____.

(a) a dry powder   (b) a better conductor   (c) a nonconductor   (d) noncorrosive

24. Utilization equipment is equipment which utilizes ____ energy for mechanical, chemical, heating, lighting or similar purposes.

I. chemical   II. electric   III. heat

(a) I only   (b) II only   (c) III only   (d) I, II and III

25. The **main** purpose of using a cutting fluid when threading conduit is to ____.

(a) prevent the formation of rust
(b) wash away the metal chips
(c) improve the finish of the thread
(d) prevent the formation of electrolytic pockets

26. Of the following, the best indication of the condition of the charge of a lead acid battery is the ____.

(a) temperature of the electrolyte   (b) level of the electrolyte
(c) open circuit cell voltage   (d) specific gravity

27. In general, the most important point to watch in the operation of transformers is the ____.

(a) core loss   (b) exciting current   (c) temperature   (d) primary voltage

28. When mounting electrical equipment, wooden plugs driven into holes in ____ shall **not** be used.

I. masonry   II. concrete   III. plaster

(a) I only   (b) II only   (c) III only   (d) I, II or III

29. Mica is commonly used in electrical construction for ____.

(a) commutator bar separators   (b) heater cord insulation
(c) strain insulators   (d) switchboard panels

30. If a fuse becomes hot under normal load, a probable cause is ____.

(a) excessive tension in the fuse clips   (b) rating of the fuse is too low
(c) insufficient pressure at the fuse clips   (d) rating of the fuse is too high

31. For maximum safety the magnetic contactors used for reversing the direction of rotation of a motor should be ____.

(a) operated from independent sources
(b) electrically interlocked
(c) mechanically interlocked
(d) electrically and mechanically interlocked

32. Large squirrel cage induction motors are usually started at a voltage considerably lower than the line voltage to ____.

(a) allow the rotor current to build up gradually
(b) permit starting under full load
(c) avoid excessive starting current
(d) obtain a low starting speed

33. Which of the following is a motor starter?

(a)   (b)   (c)   (d)

34. If the voltage on a light bulb is increased 10%, the bulb will ____.

(a) fail by insulation breakdown
(b) have a longer life
(c) burn more brightly
(d) consume less power

35. All edges that are invisible should be represented in a drawing by lines that are ____.

(a) dotted   (b) curved   (c) solid   (d) broken

36. A light bulb usually contains ____.

(a) air   (b) neon   (c) H2O   (d) either a vacuum or gas

37. The service disconnecting means shall be installed ____.

I. outside a building   II. inside a building   III. at the nearest point of entrance

(a) I only   (b) II only   (c) III only   (d) either I or II

38. Critical burns are potentially ____.

(a) life-threatening   (b) disfiguring   (c) disabling   (d) all of these

39. A set of lights switched from three different places can be controlled by ____ switch(es).

(a) two 3-way and one 4-way   **(b) two 3-way and one 2-way**
(c) 2 single-pole   **(d) four pole**

40. A fellow electrician is not breathing after receiving an electrical shock, but is no longer in contact with the electricity, the most important thing for you to do is _____.

(a) start artificial respiration immediately   **(b) cover the person and keep warm**
(c) move the person to a window   **(d) remove the persons shoes**

41. A wrench you would **not** use to connect rigid metal conduit is a ____ wrench.

(a) box end   (b) chain   (c) strap   (d) stillson

42. The instrument that would prove **least** useful in testing for opens, grounds, and shorts after the wiring has been completed is the ____.

(a) voltmeter   (b) ammeter   (c) ohmmeter   (d) megger

43. A stranded wire is given the same size designation as a solid wire if it has the same ____.

(a) weight per foot   **(b) overall diameter**
(c) strength   **(d) cross-sectional area**

44. A lighting fixture is to be controlled independently from two different locations. The type of switch required in each of the two locations is a ____.

(a) double-pole, double-throw
(b) double-pole, single-throw
(c) single-pole, double throw
(d) single-pole, single-throw

45. The rating "1000 ohms, 10 watts" would generally apply to a ____.

(a) transformer   (b) relay   (c) resistor   (d) heater

46. The open circuit test on a transformer is a test for measuring its ____.

(a) insulation resistance
(b) copper losses
(c) iron losses
(d) equivalent resistance of the transformer

47. The proper way to open a knife switch carrying a heavy load is to ____.

(a) open it with care, to avoid damage to the auxiliary blade by the arc
(b) open it slowly so that there will not be a flashover at the contacts
(c) tie a 5 foot rope on the switch handle and stand clear of the switch
(d) open it with a jerk so as to quickly break any arc

48. When thermal overload relays are used for the protection of polyphase induction motors, their primary purpose is to protect the motors in case of ____.

(a) short circuit between phases
(b) low line voltage
(c) reversal of phases in the supply
(d) sustained overload

49. The National Electrical Code is sponsored by the ____.

(a) Underwriters Lab
(b) National Safety Council
(c) National Electrical Manufacturers Association
(d) National Fire Protection Association

50. Which of the following is an LB conduit body?

 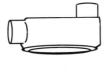  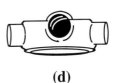

(a)   **(b)**   **(c)**   **(d)**

2020
JOURNEYMAN
GENERAL KNOWLEDGE
EXAM #6

(no-book)

50 QUESTIONS
TIME LIMIT - 1 HOUR

TIME SPENT [ ] **MINUTES**

SCORE [ ] %

JOURNEYMAN GENERAL KNOWLEDGE EXAM #6   TIME LIMIT ONE HOUR

1. An advantage of an electromagnet over a permanent magnet is that ____.

(a) an electromagnet can be switched on and off
(b) permanent magnets must always be cylindrical
(c) an electromagnet requires no power source
(d) an electromagnet does not have specific polarity

2. An excellent diffuser surface is one that ____.

(a) diffuses all the incident light   **(b) scatters light uniformly in all directions**
(c) absorbs all the incident light   **(d) transmits all the incident light**

3. Light is converted into electricity ____.

(a) in a wet cell   (b) in a dry cell   (c) in a photovoltaic cell   (d) none of these

4. The rotating part of a DC motor is known as ____.

(a) armature   (b) pole   (c) stator   (d) winding

5. A device used to pull wires through a conduit is called ____.

(a) wire tong   (b) puller   (c) fish tape   (d) reel

6. In making a resistance test, remember that the resistance of a short circuit is ____.

(a) approximately zero   **(b) midway between high and low**
(c) infinite   **(d) slightly above the midrange**

7. To increase current capacity, battery cells are connected in ____.

(a) series   (b) parallel   (c) series-parallel   (d) parallel-series

8. The hot resistance of an incandescent lamp is approximately ____ times its cold resistance.

(a) 4   (b) 6   (c) 8   (d) 10

9. The proper way of measuring an unknown voltage with a multi-tester is to ____.

(a) de-energize the circuit first
(b) start measuring at the lowest range of the meter
(c) start measuring at the highest range
(d) start measuring at the mid range of the meter

10. A capacitor stores ____.

(a) a charge   (b) voltage   (c) current   (d) power

11. ____ has the lowest dielectric strength.

(a) Paper   (b) Glass   (c) Mica   (d) Teflon

12. A form of air switch in which the moving element is a hinged blade wedge between stationary contact blades when closed is a ____ switch.

(a) safety   (b) knife   (c) snap   (d) toggle

13. If a bare live conductor is touched accidentally, the severity of the electric shock is determined primarily by ____.

(a) the size of the wire
(b) the amperage flowing in the wire
(c) the type of electricity, whether AC or DC
(d) the contact resistance between the bare wire and the person at the point of contact

14. The voltage per turn of the primary of a transformer is ____ the voltage per turn of the secondary.

(a) more than   (b) less than   (c) twice   (d) the same as

15. An open resistor when checked with an ohmmeter reads ____.

(a) infinite   (b) zero   (c) low but not zero   (d) high but within the tolerance

16. The larger the diameter of a wire, the ____ is its resistance.

(a) higher   (b) stable   (c) unstable   (d) lesser

17. Service heads and goosenecks in service entrance cable shall be ____ point of attachment of the service drops to the building.

(a) above the   (b) below the   (c) at the back of   (d) at the center of

18. Type TW conductor is a ____ type.

(a) heat resistant and thermoplastic   (b) moisture and heat resistant thermoplastic
(c) moisture and heat resistant   (d) moisture resistant and thermoplastic

19. Steel is hard to magnetize because of its ____.

(a) high density   (b) high permeability   (c) high retentivity   (d) low permeability

20. A repulsion motor is equipped with a ____.

(a) rectifier   (b) commutator   (c) repeller   (d) emitter

21. When the temperature of a copper wire is raised, the resistance ____.

(a) will decrease   (b) will increase   (c) will be steady   (d) is zero

22. The capacitor in a capacitor-start induction-run AC motor is connected in series with the ____ winding.

(a) running   (b) starting   (c) compensating   (d) field

23. The ____ is defined as the shortest distance measured between a point on the top surface of any direct buried conductor, cable, conduit and the top surface of finish grade.

(a) duct   (b) grade   (c) cover   (d) depth

24. An ohmmeter consists of a meter movement in series with ____.

(a) a battery   (b) a capacitor   (c) a spring   (d) an inductor

25. Grease is a lubricant that is basically a combination of ____.

(a) oil and water   (b) oil and soap   (c) oil and dirt   (d) oil, water and soap

26. The continuity of a coil of winding may be determined by measuring the resistance of the coil. If the resistance measured is infinite, the coil winding is ____.

(a) partially shorted   (b) totally shorted   (c) open   (d) in good condition

27. A three-way switch is equivalent to a ____ switch.

(a) DPST   (b) DPDT   (c) SPST   (d) SPDT

28. The main reason that electrical appliances are connected in parallel rather than series is ____.

(a) appliances connected in series are too noisy
(b) parallel connection is simpler than a series connection
(c) each appliance will draw more current if connected in series
(d) it makes the operation of each appliance independent with each other

29. A step-up transformer increases ____.

(a) power   (b) current   (c) frequency   (d) voltage

30. A circuit with a lagging current means the circuit is ____.

(a) capacitive   (b) reactive   (c) inductive   (d) at resonance

31. If a conductor has a resistance of 0.2Ω and the length is doubled, the resistance becomes ____.

(a) 0.20Ω (b) 0.02Ω (c) 0.4Ω (d) 0.04Ω

32. Insulating materials have the function of ____.

(a) storing very high currents
(b) conducting very large currents
(c) preventing a short circuit between conducting wires
(d) preventing an open circuit between the voltage source and the load

33. For current to flow, the very basic circuit requirements are ____.

(a) voltage source, a switch and a conductor   (b) voltage source and a switch
(c) voltage source, a dielectric and a conductor   (d) voltage source and a conductor

34. A device or equipment which is suspended from overhead either by means of a flexible cord carrying current, or otherwise is a ____.

(a) rosette   (b) fixture   (c) air terminal   (d) pendant

35. In a series circuit with unequal resistances ____.

(a) the highest resistance has the highest voltage
(b) the lowest resistance has the most current
(c) the lowest resistance has the highest voltage
(d) the highest resistance has the most current

36. The kilowatt-hour meter can be classified as a/an ____ instrument.

(a) indicating   (b) digital   (c) recording   (d) deflecting

37. Transformer cores are built up from laminations rather than from solid metal so that ____.

(a) cooling process is better   (b) eddy current loss is reduced
(c) air circulation is improved   (d) oil penetrates the core better

38. An instrument used to check the motor shaft alignment is called a ____.

(a) dynamometer   (b) potentiometer   (c) dial indicator   (d) micrometer

39. In AC circuits, the ratio of kw/kva represents the ____ factor.

(a) quality   (b) corona   (c) power   (d) wave

40. Capacitance increases with ____.

(a) higher values of applied voltage
(b) smaller plate area and less distance between plates
(c) larger plate area and smaller distance between plates
(d) larger plate area and greater distance between plates

41. A tool used by a lineman to remove insulation from large cables is called a/an ____.

(a) wire gauge   (b) lineman's pliers   (c) wire stripper   (d) electrician's knife

42. The condition of a liquid electrolyte in a battery is measured in terms of its ____.

(a) acidity   (b) specific gravity   (c) viscosity   (d) water content

43. In a parallel circuit, the total resistance is ____.

(a) the sum of all resistances
(b) the reciprocal of all the resistances
(c) larger than the largest resistance in the combination
(d) smaller than the smallest resistance in the combination

44. A ____ is a machine used to transform mechanical energy into electrical energy.

(a) transformer   (b) electric motor   (c) generator   (d) rectifier

45. A/an ____ is a material with atoms in which the electrons tend to stay in their orbits.

(a) conductor   (b) insulator   (c) inductor   (d) resistor

46. Hysteresis losses ____.

(a) is caused by the cooling of magnets
(b) generally increase with direct current in a coil
(c) can not be produced in an iron core, because it is a conductor
(d) are caused by high frequency alternating current in a coil with an iron core

47. In magnetic and electric circuit analogy, magnetic flux is the analog of _____.

(a) conductance   (b) resistance   (c) voltage   (d) current

48. A device that reverses the magnetic field polarity to keep a DC motor rotating is a/an _____.

(a) commutator   (b) field coil   (c) armature coil   (d) solenoid

49. The resistance of a wire is directly proportional to the _____ and inversely proportional to the cross-sectional area.

(a) resistivity   (b) volume   (c) length   (d) permeability

50. The energy in a battery cell depends mainly on _____.

(a) its physical size   (b) its voltage   (c) the density   (d) the current drawn from it

2020
JOURNEYMAN
GENERAL KNOWLEDGE
EXAM #7

(no-book)

50 QUESTIONS
TIME LIMIT - 1 HOUR

TIME SPENT ⬜ **MINUTES**

SCORE ⬜ %

46ᵀᴴ

JOURNEYMAN GENERAL KNOWLEDGE EXAM #7   TIME LIMIT ONE HOUR

1. Electrical current is measured in terms of _____.

(a) electron pressure   (b) electrons passing a point per second
(c) watts   (d) resistance

2. A stop switch is wired _____ in a motor circuit.

(a) series   (b) series-shunt   (c) series-parallel   (d) parallel

3. An autotransformer has _____.

(a) one coil   (b) two coils   (c) three coils   (d) four coils

4. What type of meter is shown below?

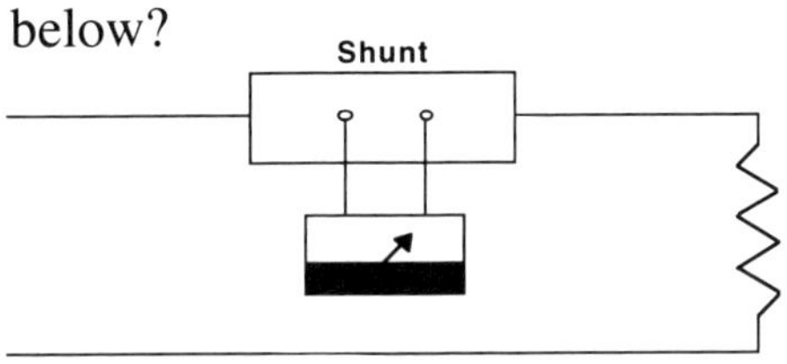

(a) wattmeter   (b) ammeter   (c) ohmmeter   (d) voltmeter

5. Concrete, brick or tile walls are considered as being _____.

(a) isolated   (b) insulators   (c) grounded   (d) dry locations

6.  ⬛   is the symbol for a _____ panel.

(a) power   (b) wall-mounted   (c) lighting   (d) surface-mounted

7. A corroded electrical connection _____.

(a) decreases the voltage drop   (b) decreases the resistance of the connection
(c) increases the resistance at the connection   (d) increases the ampacity at the connection

8. An AC ammeter or voltmeter is calibrated to read RMS values; this means the meter is reading the _____ value.

(a) maximum   (b) peak   (c) average   (d) effective

9. The correct connection for the two 120 volt lights to the single-pole switch would be ____.

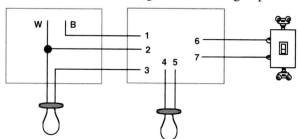

(a) 1-4 2-6 3-5-7 (b) 1-6 2-5 3-4-7 (c) 1-7 2-5-6 3-4 (d) 1-5 2-6-7 3-4

10. The location of a wall receptacle outlet in the bathroom of a dwelling shall be installed ____.

(a) the Code does not specify the location　　**(b) adjacent to the toilet**
(c) within 36" of outside edge of basin　　**(d) across from the shower**

11. On a delta three-phase four-wire secondary, how many hot wires may use the common neutral?

(a) 1 (b) 2 (c) 3 (d) 4

12. It shall be permissible to apply a demand factor of ____ to the nameplate-rating load of four or more appliances fastened in place served by the same feeder in a dwelling.

(a) 70% (b) 75% (c) 60% (d) 80%

13. Insulated nonmetallic boxes are made of ____.

I. polyvinyl chloride II. bakelite III. Bower-Barff lacquer

(a) I only (b) II only (c) I and II only (d) I, II and III

14. Tungsten-filament lamps can be used on ____ circuits.

(a) AC (b) DC (c) AC and DC (d) none of these

15. An overcurrent protective device with a circuit opening fusible part that is heated and severed by the passage of overcurrent through it is called a ____.

(a) current-limiter (b) fuse (c) circuit breaker (d) thermal overload

16. The service conductors between the terminals of the service equipment and a point usually outside the building, clear of building walls, where joined by tap or splice to the service drop is called the ____.

(a) service drop (b) service-entrance conductors (c) service equipment (d) none of these

17. If you needed to know the provisions for the installation of stationary storage batteries, you would refer to Article ____ of the Code.

(a) 225   (b) 445   (c) 460   (d) 480

18. A chain wrench can be used ____.

I. with one hand after the chain is around the conduit
II. in confined places and close to walls
III. for all sizes of conduit

(a) I and II only   (b) I and III only   (c) II and III only   (d) I, II and III

19. To cut rigid conduit you should ___.

(a) use 3-wheel pipe cutter   **(b) use a cold chisel and ream the ends**
(c) use hack saw and ream the ends   **(d) order it cut to size**

20. A fixture that exceeds ____ in any dimension shall not be supported by the screw shell of a lampholder.

(a) 8"   (b) 12"   (c) 16"   (d) 20"

21. Is it permissible to install direct current and alternating current conductors in the same outlet box?

(a) yes, if insulated for the maximum voltage of any conductor   **(b) no, never**
(c) yes, if the ampacity is the same for both conductors   **(d) yes, in dry places**

22. Electrical equipment shall be installed ____.

(a) better than the minimum Code allows
(b) according to the local Code when more stringent than the N.E.C.
(c) according to the N.E.C. regardless of local Code
(d) according to the local Code when less stringent than the N.E.C.

23. Voltage drop in a wire is ___.

(a) the wire resistance times the voltage   **(b) a percentage of the applied voltage**
(c) a function of insulation   **(d) part of the load voltage**

24. What type of capacitor is used as a start capacitor with a compressor motor?

(a) paper   (b) electrolytic   (c) ceramic   (d) mica

25. Galvanized conduit has a finish exterior and interior of ____.

(a) lead   (b) copper   (c) nickel   (d) zinc

26. Which of the following is the best type of saw to use to cut a 3" diameter hole through 1/2" plywood?

(a) circular saw   (b) saber saw   (c) hack saw   (d) cross-cut saw

27. Which of the following machine screws has the smallest diameter?

(a) 6-32 x 1"   (b) 10-32 x 3/4"   (c) 8-32 x 1/2"   (d) 10-24 x 3/8"

28. Which of the following is the most important factor contributing to an electricians safety on the job?

(a) work at a slow pace   (b) always wear leather gloves
(c) be alert at all times   (d) never be late for break

29. A one-quarter bend in a raceway is equivalent to an angle of ____ degrees.

(a) 90   (b) 45   (c) 25   (d) 180

30. A 3Ω, a 6Ω, a 9Ω and a 12Ω resistor are connected in parallel. Which resistor will consume the most power?

(a) 3Ω   (b) 6Ω   (c) 9Ω   (d) 12Ω

31. Listed ceiling (paddle) fans that do not exceed ____ pounds in weight, with or without accessories, shall be permitted to be supported by outlet boxes identified for such use.

(a) 35   (b) 45   (c) 50   (d) 60

32. The best way to lay out a 40 foot long straight line on a floor is to ____.

(a) use a steel measuring tape with dark crayon   (b) use a plumb bob with long string
(c) use a long 2 x 4 and a lead pencil   (d) use a chalk line

33. Silver is used on electrical contacts to ____.

(a) avoid corrosion   (b) improve efficiency   (c) improve continuity   (d) improve appearance

34. Electricians should be familiar with the rules and regulations of their job mainly to ____.

(a) eliminate overtime   (b) increase wages   (c) perform their duties properly   (d) save time

35. To determine if the raceway is truly vertical, an electrician would use a ____.

(a) plumb bob   (b) transit level   (c) square   (d) level

36. In order to prevent a safety hazard, an electrician should never ____.

(a) strike a hardened steel surface with a hardened steel hammer
(b) use a soft brass hammer to strike a soft brass surface
(c) strike a soft iron surface with a hardened steel hammer
(d) use a soft iron hammer to strike a hardened steel surface

37. Service drop conductors not in excess of 600 volts shall have a minimum clearance of ____ feet over residential property and driveways, and those commercial areas not subject to truck traffic.

(a) 10   (b) 12   (c) 15   (d) 18

38. When conduit or tubing nipples having a maximum length not to exceed 24" are installed between boxes, they shall be permitted to be filled ____ percent of its total cross-sectional area.

(a) 31   (b) 40   (c) 53   (d) 60

39. Before using rubber gloves when working on high voltage equipment, the gloves should be ____.

(a) cleaned inside and out   (b) tested to withstand the high voltage
(c) oiled inside and out   (d) brand new

40. Stranded wire should be ____ before being placed under a screw head.

(a) tinned   (b) twisted together tightly   (c) coated with an inhibitor   (d) sanded

41. A 3Ω, 6Ω, 9Ω and a 12Ω resistor are connected in series. The resistor that will consume the most power is the ____ .

(a) 3Ω   (b) 6Ω   (c) 9Ω   (d) 12Ω

42. What Article of the NEC refers to grounding?

(a) 230   (b) 240   (c) 250   (d) 300

43. The total of the following numbers 8 5/8", 6 1/4", 7 3/16" and 5 1/4" is ____.

(a) 27 5/16"   (b) 26 1/8"   (c) 28 7/8"   (d) none of these

44. A fusestat is different than the ordinary plug fuse because a fusestat ____.

(a) doesn't have threads
(b) has left-hand threads
(c) has different size threads
(d) has an aluminum screwshell

45. The symbol ─⊖─ usually indicates a (an) ____.

(a) switch   (b) receptacle   (c) ceiling outlet   (d) exhaust fan

46. A fuse on a 20 amp branch circuit has blown. The fuse is replaced with a 20 amp fuse and the fuse blows when the switch is turned on. The electrician should _____.

(a) check the ground rod connection first
(b) change to a circuit breaker
(c) install a 30 amp fuse
(d) check the circuit for a problem

47. To sharpen an electrician's knife, you would use a ____ stone.

(a) rubber   (b) carborundum   (c) rosin   (d) bakelite

48. The decimal equivalent of 3/16" is ____.

(a) 0.125   (b) 0.1875   (c) 5.33   (d) none of these

49. When drilling into a steel I-beam, the most likely cause for breaking a drill bit would be ____.

(a) the drill bit is too dull
(b) too slow a drill speed
(c) too much pressure on the bit
(d) too much cutting oil on bit

50. Which of the fuses is blown?

(a) L1 fuse is blown   (b) L2 fuse is blown   (c) both fuses are blown   (d) neither fuse is blown

2020
JOURNEYMAN
GENERAL KNOWLEDGE
EXAM #8

(no-book)

50 QUESTIONS
TIME LIMIT - 1 HOUR

TIME SPENT ☐ **MINUTES**

SCORE ☐ %

JOURNEYMAN GENERAL KNOWLEDGE EXAM #8   TIME LIMIT ONE HOUR

1. A/an _____ is a protective device for limiting surge voltages by discharging or bypassing surge current, and it also prevents continued flow of follow current while remaining capable of repeating these functions.

(a) surge arrester   (b) automatic fuse   (c) fuse   (d) circuit breaker

2. A/an _____ conductor is one having one or more layers of non-conducting materials that are not recognized as insulation.

(a) bare   (b) covered   (c) insulated   (d) wrapped

3. In a D.C. circuit, the ratio of watts to voltamperes is _____.

(a) unity   (b) greater than one   (c) less than one   (d) cannot tell what it might be

4. A current limiting overcurrent protective device is a device which will _____ the current flowing in the faulted circuit.

(a) reduce   (b) increase   (c) maintain   (d) none of these

5. The horsepower rating of a motor _____.

(a) is a measure of motor efficiency   (b) is the input to the motor
(c) cannot be changed to watts   (d) is the output of the motor

6. A common fuse and circuit breaker works on the principal that _____.

(a) voltage develops heat   (b) voltage breaks down insulation
(c) current develops heat   (d) current expands a wire

7. The voltage will lead the current when the _____ in the circuit.

(a) inductive reactance exceeds the capacitive reactance
(b) reactance exceeds the resistance in the circuit
(c) resistance exceeds reactance
(d) capacitive reactance exceeds the inductive reactance

8. Which of the following is an Allen head bolt?

(a)   (b)   (c)   (d)

9. ____ is performing a function without the necessity of human intervention.

(a) **Remote-control** (b) **Automatic** (c) **Semi-automatic** (d) **Controller**

10. A 1000 watt, 120 volt lamp uses electrical energy at the same rate as a 14.4 ohm resistor on ____.

(a) **120 volts** (b) **115 volts** (c) **208 volts** (d) **240 volts**

11. When using compressed air to clean electrical equipment, the air pressure should not exceed 50 pounds. The main reason is higher pressures ____.

(a) **may loosen insulating tape**   (b) **may blow dust to surrounding equipment**
(c) **introduces a personal hazard to the user**   (d) **may rupture the air hose**

12. Which of the following is **not** used to fasten equipment to concrete?

(a) **expansion bolt** (b) **lead shield** (c) **rawl plug** (d) **steel bushing**

13. 3-way and 4-way switches to operate a light shall have the wiring connected in the ____ conductor.

(a) **grounded** (b) **identified** (c) **ungrounded** (d) **neutral**

14. The decimal equivalent of 9/16 is ____.

(a) **0.5625** (b) **0.675** (c) **0.875** (d) **none of these**

15. The information most useful in preventing the recurrence of a similar type accident when making out an accident report would be ____.

(a) **the nature of the injury**   (b) **the cause of the accident**
(c) **the weather conditions at the time** (d) **the age of the person involved**

16. What is the total wattage of this circuit?

120v   60 ohm   80 ohm

(a) **3.5** (b) **420** (c) **16,800** (d) **140**

17. Artificial respiration after a severe electrical shock is necessary when the shock results in ____.

(a) **broken limbs** (b) **bleeding** (c) **stoppage of breathing** (d) **unconsciousness**

18. If the circuit voltage is increased, all else remains the same, only the _____ will change.

(a) resistance   (b) current   (c) ampacity   (d) conductivity

19. The two methods of making joints or connections for insulated cables are soldered connections and by means of solderless connection devices (wirenuts). The advantage(s) of a solderless connection (wirenut) is/are _____.

I.   will not fail under short circuit due to melting of solder
II. mechanical strength as great as solder
III. reduces the time required to make a splice

(a) I only   (b) I and II only   (c) II and III only   (d) I, II and III

20. Which of the following plugs is a polarized plug?

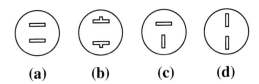

(a)   (b)   (c)   (d)

21. When accidentally splashing a chemical into the eyes, the best immediate first aid solution is to _____.

(a) look directly into the sun   (b) rub eyes with dry cloth
(c) flush eyes with clean water   (d) close eyes quickly

22. It is generally not good practice to supply lamps and motors from the same circuit because _____.

I.   it is more economical to operate motors on a higher voltage than that of a lighting circuit
II. overloads and short circuits are more common on motor circuits and would put the lights out
III. when a motor is started it would cause the lights to dim or blink

(a) I only   (b) II only   (c) III only   (d) I, II and III

23. Which of the following is the correct wiring to a light controlled by two 3-way switches?

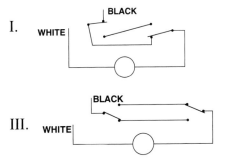

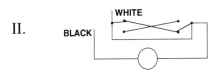

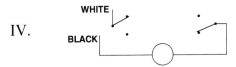

(a) I only   (b) II only   (c) III only   (d) IV only

24. The Code considers low voltage to be _____.

(a) 480 volts or less   (b) 1000 volts or less   (c) 24 volts   (d) 12 volts

25. The cross-sectional area of the busbar is ____ square inch.

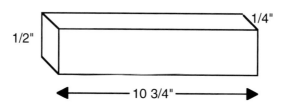

(a) 0.125   (b) 1.34375   (c) 11.5   (d) none of these

26. A high spot temperature in a corroded electrical connection is caused by a (an) ____.

(a) increase in the flow of current through the connection
(b) decrease in the voltage drop across the connection
(c) increase in the voltage drop across the connection
(d) decrease in the effective resistance of the connection

27. ____ is the symbol used for the delta connection.

(a) Ω (b) Σ (c) ø   (d) Δ

28. Because aluminum is not a magnetic metal, there will be ____ present when aluminum conductors are grouped in a raceway.

(a) no heat due to voltage   (b) no heating due to hysteresis
(c) no induced currents   (d) none of these

29. A switch is a device for ____.

I.   making or braking connections
II. changing connections
III. interruption of circuit under short-circuit conditions

(a) I only   (b) I and II only   (c) II and III only   (d) I, II and III

30. At least two persons are required to be present during a high-voltage test because ____.

(a) one person can cover while the one is on break   (b) high voltage is too heavy for one
(c) if one person is hurt the other person can help   (d) it eliminates overtime

31. One of the essential functions of any switch is to maintain a ____.

(a) good high-resistance contact in the closed position
(b) good low-resistance contact in the closed position
(c) good low-resistance contact in the open position
(d) good high-resistance contact in the open position

32. Which of the following is a 30 amp receptacle?

  (a)   **(b)**   **(c)**   **(d)**

33. When the ground resistance exceeds the allowable value of 25 ohms, the resistance can be reduced by ____.

I.   paralleling ground rods   II. using a longer ground rod
III. using a larger diameter ground rod   IV. chemical teatment of the soil

(a) II and III only   (b) I, II and III only   (c) II, III and IV only   (d) I, II, III and IV

34. Silver and gold are better conductors of electricity than copper; however, the main reason copper is used is its ____.

(a) weight   (b) strength   (c) melting point   (d) cost is less

35. Standard lengths of conduit are in 10 foot lengths. A required feeder raceway is 18 yards in length, how many lengths of 10 foot conduit would you need?

(a) 4   (b) 5   (c) 6   (d) none of these

36. The term "open circuit" means ____.

(a) the wiring is in an open area   **(b) the wiring is exposed on a building**
(c) all parts of the circuit are not in contact   **(d) the circuit has one end exposed**

37. Which of the items below is used to test specific gravity?

 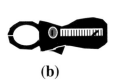  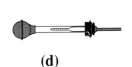

  (a)   **(b)**   **(c)**   **(d)**

38. Conduit should be installed as to prevent the collection of water in it between outlets. The conduit should not have a _____.

(a) low point at an outlet   (b) high point at an outlet
(c) high point between successive outlets   (d) low point between successive outlets

39. Brass is an alloy of _____.

(a) zinc and copper   (b) lead and copper   (c) tin and lead   (d) lead and tin

40. Which type of the following portable fire extinguishers should be used on a live electrical fire?

(a) carbon dioxide   (b) water   (c) foam   (d) soda-acid

41. Enclosed knife switches that require the switch to be open before the housing door can be opened, are called _____ switches.

(a) release   (b) air-break   (c) safety   (d) service

42. Which of the following is a solenoid?

(a)	(b)	(c)	(d)

43. What Article of the Code addresses high-voltage (over 1000 volts)?

(a) 450   (b) 230   (c) 680   (d) 490

44. A close nipple _____.

(a) is always 1/2" or less in length   (b) has no threads
(c) has only internal threads   (d) has threads over its entire length

45. When applying rubber tape to an electrical splice, it would be necessary to _____.

(a) stretch the tape properly during the application
(b) apply an adhesive to the splice before applying the tape
(c) apply the rubber tape after any other tape
(d) apply heat to the tape when installing

46. A stranded wire with the same AWG as a solid wire _____.

(a) is used for higher voltages
(c) is larger in total diameter
(b) has a higher ampacity
(d) has the same resistance

47. A limit switch is used on a piece of machinery to open the circuit when the _____.

(a) current exceeds a preset limit
(c) pressure exceeds a preset limit
(b) travel reaches a preset limit
(d) temperature reaches a preset limit

48. With switches 1 and 2 closed, the combined resistance of the circuit is _____ ohms.

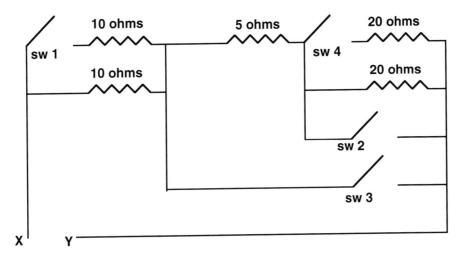

(a) 30 (b) 25 (c) 10 (d) 3

49. When rigid metal conduits are buried, the minimum cover required by the Code is _____.

(a) 6"   (b) 12"   (c) 18"   (d) 24"

50. Which of the following is **not** considered part of a luminaire?

(a) ballast
(b) a lampholder
(c) lamp or lamps
(d) parts designed to position the light source

2020
JOURNEYMAN
GENERAL KNOWLEDGE
EXAM #9

(no-book)

50 QUESTIONS
TIME LIMIT - 1 HOUR

TIME SPENT [ ] **MINUTES**

SCORE [ ] %

JOURNEYMAN GENERAL KNOWLEDGE EXAM #9   TIME LIMIT ONE HOUR

1. Locknuts are sometimes used in making electrical connections on studs. In these cases, the purpose of the locknuts is to ____.

(a) be able to connect several wires to one stud
(b) make it difficult to tamper with the connection
(c) make a tighter connection
(d) prevent the connection from loosening under vibration

2. To cut rigid conduit, you should ____.

(a) use a 3-wheel pipe cutter
(b) use a cold chisel and ream the ends
(c) use a hacksaw and ream the ends
(d) order it cut to size

3. In the course of normal operation the instrument which will be **least** effective in indicating that a generator may overheat because it is overloaded, is ____.

(a) a wattmeter   (b) a voltmeter   (c) an ammeter   (d) a stator thermocouple

4. Two switches in one box under one face-plate is called a ____.

(a) double-pole switch   (b) two-gang switch   (c) 2-way switch   (d) mistake

5. A conduit body is ____.

(a) a cast fitting such as an FD or FS box
(b) a standard 10 foot length of conduit
(c) a sealtight enclosure
(d) an "LB" or "T", or similar fitting

6. A dwelling unit is ____.

(a) one unit of an apartment
(b) one or more rooms used by one or more persons
(c) one or more rooms with space for eating, living, and sleeping
(d) a single unit, providing complete and independent living facilities for one or more persons, including permanent provisions for living, sleeping, cooking, and sanitation.

7. Enclosed means, surrounded by a _____ which will prevent persons from accidentally contacting energized parts.

I. wall   II. fence   III. housing or case

(a) I only   (b) II only   (c) III only   (d) I, II or III

8. Where the conductor material is not specified in the Code, the conductors are assumed to be _____.

(a) busbars   (b) aluminum   (c) copper-clad aluminum   (d) copper

9. The voltage lost across a portion of a circuit is called the _____.

(a) power loss   (b) power factor   (c) voltage drop   (d) apparent va

10. In a series circuit _____ is common.

(a) resistance   (b) current   (c) voltage   (d) wattage

11. Batteries supply _____ current.

(a) positive   (b) negative   (c) direct   (d) alternating

12. Electron flow produced by means of applying pressure to a material is called _____.

(a) photo conduction   (b) electrochemistry   (c) piezoelectricity   (d) thermoelectricity

13. Raceways shall be provided with _____ to compensate for thermal expansion and contraction.

(a) accordion joints   (b) thermal fittings   (c) expansion joints   (d) contro-spansion

14. An alternation is _____.

(a) one-half cycle   (b) one hertz   (c) one alternator   (d) two cycles

15. What is the function of a neon glow tester?

I.   Determines if circuit is alive
II. Determines polarity of DC circuits
III. Determines if circuit is AC or DC

(a) I only   (b) II only   (c) III only   (d) I, II and III

16. What chapter in the Code is Mobile Homes referred to?

(a) Chapter 3   (b) Chapter 5   (c) Chapter 6   (d) Chapter 8

17. Never approach a victim of an electrical injury until you ____.

(a) find a witness   (b) are sure the power is turned off
(c) have a first-aid kit   (d) contact the supervisor

18. A wattmeter indicates ____.

I. real power   II. apparent power if PF is not in unity   III. power factor

(a) I only   (b) II only   (c) III only   (d) I, II and III

19. The connection of a ground clamp to a grounding electrode shall be ____.

(a) accessible   (b) visible   (c) readily accessible   (d) in sight

20. The current will lead the voltage when ____.

(a) inductive reactance exceeds the capacitive reactance in the circuit
(b) reactance exceeds the resistance in the circuit
(c) resistance exceeds the reactance in the circuit
(d) capacitive reactance exceeds the inductive reactance in the circuit

21. Mandatory rules of the Code are identified by the use of the word ____.

(a) should   (b) shall   (c) must   (d) could

22. Which of the following is **not** one of the considerations that must be evaluated in judging equipment?

(a) wire-bending and connection space   (b) arcing effects
(c) longevity   (d) electrical insulation

23. To increase the range of an AC ammeter which one of the following is most commonly used?

(a) a current transformer
(b) a condenser
(c) an inductance
(d) a straight shunt (not U-shaped)

24. If a test lamp lights when placed in series with a condenser and a suitable source of DC, it is a good indication that the condenser is ____.

(a) fully charged   (b) short-circuited   (c) open-circuited   (d) fully discharged

25. To transmit power economically over considerable distances, it is necessary that the voltages be high. High voltages are readily obtainable with ____ currents.

(a) rectified   (b) AC   (c) DC   (d) carrier

26. Two 500 watt lamps connected in series across a 110 volt line draws 2 amperes. The total power consumed is ____ watts.

(a) 50   (b) 150   (c) 220   (d) 1000

27. The resistance of a copper wire to the flow of electricity ____.

(a) decreases as the length of the wire increases
(b) decreases as the diameter of the wire decreases
(c) increases as the diameter of the wire increases
(d) increases as the length of the wire increases

28. Enclosed knife switches that require the switch to be open before the housing door can be opened, are called ____ switches.

(a) release   (b) air-break   (c) safety   (d) service

29. A type of cable protected by a spiral metal cover is called ____ in the field.

(a) BX   (b) greenfield   (c) sealtight   (d) Romex

30. The resistance of a circuit may vary due to ____.

(a) a loose connection   (b) change in voltage   (c) change in current   (d) induction

31. Grounding conductors running with circuit conductors may be ____.

I. uninsulated
II. a continuous green, if covered
III. continuous green with yellow stripe, if covered

(a) I only   (b) II only   (c) III only   (d) I, II and III

32. For voltage and current to be in phase, ____.

I. the circuit impedance has only resistance
II. the voltage and current appear at their zero and peak values at the same time

(a) I only   (b) II only   (c) both I and II   (d) neither I nor II

33. The definition of ampacity is ____.

(a) the current-carrying capacity of conductors expressed in volt-amps
(b) the current-carrying capacity expressed in amperes
(c) the current-carrying capacity of conductors expressed in wattage
(d) the current in amperes a conductor can carry continuously under the conditions of use without exceeding its temperature rating

34. Continuous duty is ____.

(a) a load where the maximum current is expected to continue for three hours or more
(b) a load where the maximum current is expected to continue for one hour or more
(c) intermittent operation in which the load conditions are regularly recurrent
(d) operation at a substantially constant load for an indefinitely long time

35. A location classified as dry may be temporarily subject to ____.

I. wetness   II. dampness

(a) I only   (b) II only   (c) both I and II   (d) neither I nor II

36. A ____ is an enclosure designed either for surface or flush mounting and provided with a frame, mat, or trim in which a swinging door or doors are or may be hung.

(a) cabinet   (b) panelboard   (c) cutout box   (d) switchboard

37. A 15 ohm resistance carrying 20 amperes of current uses ____ watts of power.

(a) 300   (b) 3000   (c) 6000   (d) none of these

38. When using a #14-2 with ground Romex, the ground ____ carry current under normal operation.

(a) will   (b) will not   (c) will sometimes   (d) none of these

39. As compared with solid wire, stranded wire of the same gauge size is ____.

(a) **better for higher voltages**　(b) **given a higher ampacity**
(c) **easier to skin**　(d) **larger in total diameter**

40. The type of AC system commonly used to supply both commercial light and power is the ____.

(a) **3-phase, 3-wire**　(b) **3-phase, 4-wire**　(c) **2-phase, 3-wire**　(d) **single-phase, 2-wire**

41. To make a good soldered connection between two stranded wires, it is **least** important to ____.

(a) **use enough heat to make the solder flow freely**
(b) **clean the wires carefully**
(c) **twist the wires together before soldering**
(d) **apply solder to each strand before twisting the two wires together**

42. The most important reason for using a condulet-type fitting in preference to making a bend in a one inch conduit is to ____.

(a) **avoid the possible flattening of the conduit when making the bend**
(b) **cut down the amount of conduit needed**
(c) **make a neater job**
(d) **make wire pulling easier**

43. When skinning a small wire, the insulation should be "penciled down" rather than cut square to ____.

(a) **allow more room for the splice**
(b) **save time in making the splice**
(c) **decrease the danger of nicking the wire**
(d) **prevent the braid from fraying**

44. Rubber insulation on an electrical conductor would quickly be damaged by continuous contact with ____.

(a) **water**　(b) **acid**　(c) **oil**　(d) **alkali**

45. A tester using an ordinary light bulb is commonly used to test ____.

(a) **whether a circuit is AC or DC**　(b) **for polarity of a DC circuit**
(c) **an overloaded circuit**　(d) **for grounds on 120 volt circuits**

46. Pigtails are used on brushes to ____.

(a) compensate for wear
(b) supply the proper brush tension
(c) make a good electrical connection
(d) hold the brush in the holder

47. With respect to fluorescent lamps, it is correct to state ____.

(a) the filaments seldom burn out
(b) the starters and tubes must be replaced at the same time
(c) they are easier to install than incandescent light bulbs
(d) their efficiency is less than the efficiency of incandescent light bulbs

48. A ____ stores energy in much the same manner as a spring stores mechanical energy.

(a) resistor   (b) coil   (c) condenser   (d) none of these

49. An overcurrent trip unit of a circuit shall be connected in series with each ____.

(a) transformer
(b) grounded conductor
(c) overcurrent device
(d) ungrounded conductor

50. ____ lighting is a string of outdoor lights suspended between two points.

(a) Pole   (b) Festoon   (c) Equipment   (d) Outline

2020
JOURNEYMAN
GENERAL KNOWLEDGE
EXAM #10

(no-book)

50 QUESTIONS
TIME LIMIT - 1 HOUR

TIME SPENT [ ] **MINUTES**

SCORE [ ] %

JOURNEYMAN GENERAL KNOWLEDGE EXAM #10   **TIME LIMIT ONE HOUR**

1. Using 1.5 volt dry cells, the voltage between A and B would be _____.

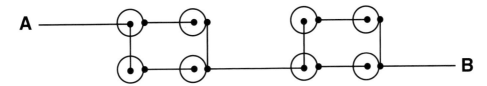

(a) **1.5**   (b) **4**   (c) **6**   (d) **12**

2. A rigid conduit connecting to an outlet box should have a _____.

(a) **bushing and locknut on the outside**
(b) **bushing on the outside and a locknut on the inside**
(c) **locknut and bushing on the inside**
(d) **locknut on the outside and a bushing on the inside**

3. Identified, as used in the Code in reference to a conductor or its terminals, means that such a conductor or terminal is to be recognized as _____.

(a) **grounded**   (b) **bonded**   (c) **colored**   (d) **marked**

4. A toaster will produce less heat on low voltage because _____.

(a) **its total watt output decreases**   (b) **the current will decrease**
(c) **the resistance has not changed**   (d) **all of these**

5. If the current flow through a conductor is increased, the magnetic field around the conductor _____.

(a) **is unchanged**   (b) **becomes stronger**   (c) **collapses**   (d) **becomes weaker**

6. Comparing a #6 conductor to a #10 conductor of equal lengths, the #6 will have lower _____.

(a) **cost**   (b) **weight**   (c) **resistance**   (d) **strength**

7. The definition of ambient temperature is _____.

(a) **the temperature of the conductor**
(b) **the insulation rating of the conductor**
(c) **the temperature of the area surrounding the conductor**
(d) **the differential temperature**

8. The primary reason for using a hacksaw blade with fine teeth rather than coarse teeth when cutting large stranded conductors is ____.

(a) a coarse blade would overheat the conductor
(b) a coarse blade breaks too easily
(c) to avoid snagging or pulling strands
(d) a fine blade will bend easier

9. The standard residential service is a 3-wire, 240 volt single-phase system. The maximum voltage to ground in this system would be ____ volts.

(a) 115   (b) 120   (c) 199   (d) 208

10. When working on a motor, the electrician should ____ to prevent accidental starting of the motor.

(a) remove the fuses   (b) ground the motor
(c) shut off the switch   (d) remove the belts

11. It is the responsibility of the electrician to make sure his tools are in good condition because ____.

(a) defective tools can cause accidents
(b) the boss may want to use them
(c) the company will pay for only one set of tools
(d) a good job requires perfect tools

12. Continually overloading a conductor is a poor practice because it causes ____.

(a) the conductor to melt   (b) the insulation to deteriorate
(c) the conductor to shrink   (d) damage to the raceway

13. For better illumination you would ____.

(a) random spacing of lights
(b) even spacing, numerous lights
(c) evenly spaced, higher ceilings
(d) cluster lights

14. A junction box above a lay-in ceiling is considered ____.

(a) concealed   (b) accessible   (c) readily accessible   (d) recessed

15. Which of the following metals is most commonly used in the filament of a bulb?

(a) aluminum   (b) mercury   (c) tungsten   (d) platinum

16. Electrical equipment can be defined as _____.

I. fittings   II. appliances   III. devices   IV. fixtures

(a) I only   (b) I and IV only   (c) I, III and IV   (d) all of these

17. If two equal resistance conductors are connected in parallel, the resistance of the two conductors is equal to _____.

(a) the resistance of one conductor
(b) twice the resistance of one conductor
(c) one-half the resistance of one conductor
(d) the resistance of both conductors

18. Wire connection should encircle binding posts in the _____ manner the nut turns to tighten.

(a) opposite   (b) same   (c) reverse   (d) different

19. Which of the following is a limit switch?

(a)   (b)   (c)   (d)

20. The primary and secondary windings of a transformer always have _____.

(a) a common magnetic circuit
(b) the same size wire
(c) separate magnetic circuits
(d) the same number of turns

21. Which of the following is **not** the force which moves electrons?

(a) EMF   (b) voltage   (c) potential   (d) current

22. A motor with a wide speed range is a _____.

(a) DC motor   (b) AC motor   (c) synchronous motor   (d) induction motor

23. The "stator" of an AC generator is another name for the ____.

(a) rotating portion (b) slip rings (c) stationary portion (d) housing

24. Where galvanized conduit is used, the main purpose of the galvanizing is to ____.

(a) slow down rust   (b) provide better continuity
(c) provide better strength   (d) provide a better surface for painting

25. To lubricate a motor sleeve bearing, you would use ____.

(a) grease (b) vaseline (c) oil (d) graphite

26. When soldering conductors, flux is used ____.

(a) to heat the conductors quicker
(b) to keep the surfaces clean
(c) to prevent loss of heat
(d) to bond the conductors

27. ____ means so constructed or protected that exposure to the weather will not interfere with successful operation.

(a) Rainproof (b) Weather tight (c) Weather resistant (d) All weather

28. The current used for charging storage batteries is ____.

(a) square-wave (b) direct (c) alternating (d) variable

29. You should close a knife switch firmly and rapidly as there will be less ____.

(a) likelihood of arcing   (b) wear on the contacts
(c) danger of shock   (d) energy used

30. If one complete cycle occurs in 1/30 of a second, the frequency is ____.

(a) 30 hertz (b) 60 cycle (c) 115 cycle (d) 60 hertz

31. An instrument that measures electrical energy is called the ____.

(a) galvanometer (b) wattmeter (c) dynamometer (d) watthour meter

32. In electrical wiring, "wire nuts" are used to _____.

(a) connect wires to terminals　**(b) join wires and insulate the joint**
(c) connect the electrode　**(d) tighten the panel studs**

33. Which of the following would be the best metal for a magnet?

(a) steel　**(b) aluminum**　**(c) lead**　**(d) tin**

34. An electrician may use a megger _____.

(a) to determine the RPM of a motor
(b) to determine the output of a motor
(c) to check wattage
(d) to test a lighting circuit for a ground

35. The **least** important thing in soldering two conductors together is to _____.

(a) use plenty of solder　**(b) use sufficient heat**
(c) clean the conductors　**(d) use the proper flux**

36. The property of a circuit tending to prevent the flow of current and at the same time causing energy to be converted into heat is referred to as _____.

(a) the inductance　**(b) the resistance**　**(c) the capacitance**　**(d) the reluctance**

37. Rigid conduit is generally secured to outlet boxes by _____.

(a) beam clamps　**(b) locknuts and bushings**　**(c) set screws**　**(d) offsets**

38. Which one of the following is **not** a safe practice when lifting heavy items?

(a) use the arm and leg muscles
(b) keep your back as upright as possible
(c) keep lifting a heavy object until you get help
(d) keep your feet spread apart

39. A thermocouple will transform _____ into electricity.

(a) current　**(b) heat**　**(c) work**　**(d) watts**

40. In a residence, the wall switch controlling the ceiling light is usually ____.

(a) connected across both lines
(b) a double pole switch
(c) connected in one line only
(d) a 4-way switch

41. A switch which opens automatically when the current exceeds a predetermined limit would be called a ____.

(a) limit switch   (b) circuit breaker   (c) DT disconnect   (d) contactor

42. A wattmeter is a combination of which two of the following meters?

I. ammeter   II. ohmeter   III. phase meter   IV. volt meter   V. power factor meter

(a) II and III   (b) I and V   (c) I and IV   (d) II and V

43. What would the ohmmeter read ?

(a) 100 Ω   (b) 200 Ω   (c) 125Ω   (d) 50 Ω

44. Acid is not considered a good flux when soldering conductors because it ____.

(a) smells bad   (b) is corrosive   (c) is non-conductive   (d) costs too much

45. If the spring tension on a cartridge fuse clip is weak, the result most likely would be ____.

(a) the fuse would blow immediately
(b) the fuse clips would become warm
(c) the voltage to the load would increase
(d) the supply voltage would increase

46. The branch-circuit loads specified by the Code for lighting and receptacles are considered ____.

(a) minimum loads   (b) maximum loads   (c) loads to be served   (d) peak loads

47.The conductor with the highest insulation temperature rating is ____.

(a) UF   (b) TW   (c) THWN   (d) THHN

48. After cutting a conduit, to remove the rough edges on both ends, the conduit ends should be
____.

(a) reamed   (b) filed   (c) sanded   (d) ground

49. To fasten a raceway to a solid concrete ceiling, you would use ____.

(a) toggle bolts   (b) expansion bolts   (c) wooden plugs   (d) rawl plugs

50. A commutator of a generator should be cleaned with which of the following?

(a) emery cloth   (b) graphite   (c) a smooth file   (d) fine sandpaper

2020

TRUE or FALSE EXAM

(no-book)

50 QUESTIONS
TIME LIMIT - 30 Minutes

TIME SPENT ⬜ **MINUTES**

SCORE ⬜ %

50 EXAM QUESTIONS - TRUE or FALSE   **Time Limit 30 Minutes**

1. A Code rule may be waived or alternative methods of installation approved that may be contrary to the Code, if the authority having jurisdiction gives verbal or written consent.

☐ **True**   ☐ **False**

2. Where no statutory requirement exists, the authority having jurisdiction could be a property owner or his/her agent, such as an architect or engineer.

☐ **True**   ☐ **False**

3. The term "luminaire" is a complete lighting unit consisting of a light source such as a lamp or lamps, together with the parts designed to position the light source and connect it to the power source. It may also include parts to protect the light source or the ballast or to distribute the light. A lampholder itself is not a luminaire.

☐ **True**   ☐ **False**

4. The circuit of a control apparatus or system that carries the electric signals directing the performance of the controller but does not carry the main power current is a motor control circuit.

☐ **True**   ☐ **False**

5. A raintight enclosure is constructed or protected so that exposure to a beating rain will not result in the entrance of water under specified test conditions.

☐ **True**   ☐ **False**

6. Type FCC systems are permitted both for general-purpose and appliance branch circuits; they are not permitted for individual branch circuits.

☐ **True**   ☐ **False**

7. Type AC cable installed through, or parallel to, framing members must be protected against physical damage from penetration by screws or nails.

☐ **True**   ☐ **False**

8. Surface extensions from a flush-mounted box must be made by mounting and mechanically securing an extension ring over the flush box.

☐ **True**   ☐ **False**

9. Type NM cable can be installed as open runs in dropped or suspended ceilings in other than one and two-family and multifamily dwellings.

☐ **True**   ☐ **False**

10. In Class I, Division 1 and 2 locations, locknut-bushing and double-locknut types of fittings are depended on for bonding purposes.

☐ **True**   ☐ **False**

11. Lighting systems operating at 30 volts or less need not be listed for the purpose.

☐ **True**   ☐ **False**

12. Listed spa and hot tub packaged units installed indoors, rated 20 amps or less, are permitted to be cord-and-plug connected.

☐ **True**   ☐ **False**

13. Masts and metal structures supporting antennas must be grounded in accordance with the requirements of Article 250.

☐ **True**   ☐ **False**

14. An equipment grounding conductor is not required in rigid nonmetallic conduit if the grounded conductor is used to ground equipment as permitted in section 250.142.

☐ **True**   ☐ **False**

15. There is never a case where HDPE can be installed in a hazardous location.

☐ **True**   ☐ **False**

16. ENT is not permitted in hazardous (classified) locations, except for intrinsically safe applications.

☐ **True**   ☐ **False**

17. Metal wireways can be installed either exposed or concealed under all conditions.

☐ **True**   ☐ **False**

18. Extensions from wireways by raceway or cable wiring methods are not permitted.

☐ **True** ☐ **False**

19. Each section of cablebus must be marked with the manufacturer's name or trade designation and the minimum diameter, number, votage rating, and ampacity of the conductors to be installed. Markings must be so located as to be visible after installation.

☐ **True** ☐ **False**

20. The derating factors in 310.15(B)(3)(a) apply to a nonmetallic wireway.

☐ **True** ☐ **False**

21. FMC can be installed exposed or concealed where not subject to physical damage.

☐ **True** ☐ **False**

22. Strut-type channel raceway enclosures must have a means for connecting an equipment grounding conductor. The raceway is permitted as an equipment grounding conductor in accordance with 250.118(14).

☐ **True** ☐ **False**

23. Metal surfaces that are within 5' of the inside walls of an indoor spa or hot tub, and not separated from the indoor spa or hot tub area by a permanent barrier, are not required to be bonded.

☐ **True** ☐ **False**

24. Only wiring, raceways, and cables used directly in connection with the elevator must be inside the hoistway and the machine room.

☐ **True** ☐ **False**

25. Optional standby system wiring is permitted to occupy the same raceways, cables, boxes, and cabinets with other general wiring.

☐ **True** ☐ **False**

26. Overhead service conductors can be supported to hardwood trees.

☐ **True**   ☐ **False**

27. Power-limited fire alarm (PLFA) cables can be supported by strapping, taping, or attaching to the exterior of a conduit or raceway.

☐ **True**   ☐ **False**

28. Nonmetallic cable trays are permitted in corrosive areas and in areas requiring voltage isolation.

☐ **True**   ☐ **False**

29. The conductors supported by messenger is permitted to come into contact with the messenger supports or any structural members, walls, or pipes.

☐ **True**   ☐ **False**

30. Fixture wires cannot be used for branch-circuit wiring.

☐ **True**   ☐ **False**

31. Single-throw knife switches must be installed so that gravity will tend to close the switch.

☐ **True**   ☐ **False**

32.Incandescent luminaires that have open lamps, and pendant-type luminaires, can be installed in clothes closets where proper clearance is maintained from combustible products.

☐ **True**   ☐ **False**

33. The intent of Article 392 is to limit the use of cable trays to industrial establishments only.

☐ **True**   ☐ **False**

34. A receptacle must not be installed within, or directly over, a bathtub or shower space.

☐ **True**   ☐ **False**

35. Switches must not be installed within wet locations in tub or shower spaces unless installed as part of a listed tub or shower assembly.

□ **True**   □ **False**

36. Trees can be used to support outdoor luminaires.

□ **True**   □ **False**

37. Receptacles installed behind a bed in the guest rooms in hotels and motels must be located so as to prevent the bed from contacting an attachment plug, or the receptacle must be provided with a suitable guard.

□ **True**   □ **False**

38. Running threads of IMC must not be used on conduit for connection at couplings.

□ **True**   □ **False**

39. Supplementary overcurrent devices used in luminaires or appliances are not required to be readily accessible.

□ **True**   □ **False**

40. The antenna mast and antenna discharge unit grounding conductor must be guarded from physical damage.

□ **True**   □ **False**

41. The Code covers underground installations in mines and self-propelled mobile surface mining machinery and its attendant electrical trailing cable.

□ **True**   □ **False**

42. Each motor must be provided with an individual controller.

□ **True**   □ **False**

43. A branch-circuit overcurrent protection device such as a plug fuse may serve as the disconnecting means for a stationary motor of 1/8 hp or less.

☐ True   ☐ False

44. The controller is required to open all conductors to the motor.

☐ True   ☐ False

45. The continuity of the grounding conductor system used to reduce electrical shock hazards at carnivals, fairs, and similar locations must be verified each time the portable electrical equipment is connected.

☐ True   ☐ False

46. The dedicated space above a panelboard extends to a dropped or suspended ceiling, which is considered a structural ceiling.

☐ True   ☐ False

47. A box or conduit body is not required for splices and taps in direct-buried conductors and cables as long as the splice is made with a splicing device that is identified for the purpose.

☐ True   ☐ False

48. An individual 20 amp circuit is permitted to supply power to a single bathroom in a dwelling for receptacle outlet(s) and other equipment within the same room.

☐ True   ☐ False

49. AC circuits of less than 50 volts must be grounded if supplied by a transformer whose supply system exceeds 150 volts to ground.

☐ True   ☐ False

50. An exothermic or irreversible compression connection to fireproofed structural metal is required to be accessible.

☐ True   ☐ False

2020

JOURNEYMAN
OPEN
BOOK
EXAM #1

50 QUESTIONS
TIME LIMIT - 2 HOURS

TIME SPENT [ ] **MINUTES**

SCORE [ ] %

JOURNEYMAN OPEN BOOK EXAM #1   **Two Hour Time Limit**

1. A seal between electrical systems and flammable or combustible process fluids where a failure could allow the migration of process fluids into the premises' wiring system is the definition of ___.

(a) plenum seal   (b) process seal   (c) innerduct seal   (d) apparatus seal

2. An attachment fitting is different as ____.

(a) no cord is associated with the fitting   (b) it can only be used on low voltage circuits
(c) it must have double locknuts   (d) it provides no locking support

3. Motors rated less than ____ and connected to a lighting circuit shall be considered general lighting load.

(a) 1/8 HP   (b) 1/4 HP   (c) 250 watts   (d) 300 watts

4. Fixed industrial process heating equipment requiring supply conductors with over ____ insulation shall be cleary and permanently marked.

(a) 60°   (b) 70°   (c) 76°   (d) 90°

5. GFCI protection shall be provided for lighting outlets not exceeding ____ volts installed in crawl spaces.

(a) 30   (b) 50   (c) 90   (d) 120

6. An energy-reducing active arc flash mitigation system helps in reducing ____ duration in the electrical distribution center.

(a) flash   (b) arcing   (c) short-circuit   (d) amperage

7. Type MV cable terminated in equipment or installed in pull boxes or vaults shall be secured and supported by metallic or nonmetallic supports suitable to withstand the weight by cable ties listed and identified for securement and support, or other approved means, at intervals not exceeding 5' from terminations at a maximum of ____ between supports.

(a) 5'   (b) 6'   (c) 8'   (d) 10'

8. Connections to an aluminum or copper busbar not less than ____ ____ and of sufficient length to accommodate at least three terminations for communication systems in addition to other connections.

(a) 1/4" thick - 2" wide (b) 1/2" thick - 2" wide   (c) 1/4" thick - 4" wide   (d) 1/2" thick - 4" wide

9. The power monitoring equipment total area of all conductors, splices, taps, and equipment at any cross section of the wiring space does not exceed ___ of the csa of that space.

(a) 75%   (b) 60%   (c) 40%   (d) 20%

10. At least one 120 volt, 20 ampere branch circuit shall be installed to supply receptacle outlets in ____ with electric power.

I. readily accessible outdoor receptacles   II. detached garages   III. attached garages

(a) III only   (b) II only   (c) I and II   (d) I, II and III

11. Each meeting room of not more than ____ sq.ft. in other than dwelling units shall have outlets for nonlocking-type, 125 volt, 15 or 20 ampere receptacles.

(a) 250   (b) 500   (c) 750   (d) 1000

12. The appliance GFCI shall be readily accessible, listed, and located in one or more of the following locations:
I.   An integral part of an attachment plug
II. A device or outlet within the supply circuit
III. Within the branch circuit overcurrent device

(a) I only   (b) II only   (c) I and III   (d) I, II and III

13. EMT shall be permitted to be installed in cinder concrete or cinder fill where subject to permanent moisture when protected on all sides by a layer of noncinder concrete at least 2" thick or when the tubing is installed at least ____ under the fill.

(a) 6"   (b) 12"   (c) 18"   (d) 24"

14. Exposed runs of MC cable shall closely follow the surface of the building finish or of ____.

(a) the roof   (b) concrete wall   (c) running boards   (d) the floor

15. HVAC multimotor and combination-load equipment where installed outdoors on a roof, an equipment grounding conductor of the wire type shall be installed in outdoor portions of metallic raceway systems that use ____.

(a) compression-type fittings   (b) threaded fittings   (c) insulated fittings   (d) bushings

16. All appliances operating at ____ volts or more shall be listed.

(a) 50   (b) 75   (c) 120   (d) 240

17. All cut ends of LFMC shall be ____ inside and outside to remove rough edges.

(a) filed   (b) sanded   (c) trimmed   (d) de-burred

18. Low voltage heating power unit shall be an isolating type with a rated output not exceeding ____ volts peak ac.

(a) 30   (b) 42.4   (c) 60   (d) 25

19. In airports where maintenance and supervision conditions ensure that only qualified persons can access, install, or service the cable, airfield lighting cable used in series circuits that are rated up to ____ volts and are powered by constant current regulators shall be permitted to be installed in cable trays.

(a) 1000   (b) 2500   (c) 3000   (d) 5000

20. Tapped conductors shall not be permitted for portable generators rated ____ or less where field wiring connection terminals are not accessible.

(a) 15 kW   (b) 17.5 kW   (c) 22 kW   (d) 25 kW

21. All luminaires, lampholders, and ____ shall be listed.

(a) fixture wires   (b) retrofit kits   (c) lamps   (d) ballasts

22. Vending machines not utilizing a cord and plug connection shall be ____.

(a) guarded   (b) fixed in place   (c) stationary   (d) GFCI protected circuit

23. The maximum length of the branch-circuit wiring from the overcurrent device to the first outlet shall not exceed ____ feet for a #14 AWG conductor for a listed supplement arc protection circuit breaker installed at the orgin of the branch circuit in combination with a listed outlet type branch-circuit type AFCI installed at the first outlet box on the branch circuit with all conditions met.

(a) 50   (b) 75   (c) 85   (d) 100

24. Nameplates for all stationary generators and portable generators rated more than ____ watts shall also give the power rating, the subtransient and transient reactances, the insulation system class, etc.

(a) 5kW   (b) 7.5 kW   (c) 15,000   (d) all of these

25. Single-conductor power to an MDC shall be permitted to be used only in sizes _____ AWG or larger.

(a) #2   (b) #4   (c) #6   (d) #8

26. Rooftop decks that are accessible from inside the RV shall have at least one receptacle installed within the perimeter of the rooftop deck. The receptacle shall not be located more than _____ above the balcony, deck, or porch surface. The receptacle shall comply with the requirements of 406.9(B) for wet locations.

(a) 48"   (b) 6'   (b) 8'   (d) 10'

27. Where _____ or tinsel cord is approved for and used with a specific listed appliance or luminaire, it shall be considered to be protected when applied within the appliance or luminaire listing requirements.

(a) fixture wire   (b) festoon wire   (c) flexible cord   (d) multiconductor cable

28. Article 640 does not cover _____.

(a) electronic organs   (b) speech input systems
(c) electronic musical instruments   (d) fire and burglary alarm signaling devices

29. NM cables shall be concealed within walls, floors, or ceilings that provide a thermal barrier of material that has at least a _____ finish rating as identified in listings of fire-rated assemblies.

(a) 15-minute   (b) 1 hour   (c) 2 hour   (d) 3 hour

30. Use of the system employed by the Listing organization allows the _____ to identify a Listed product.

(a) qualified person   (b) electrician   (c) owner   (d) AHJ

31. Where subject to exposure to _____ vapors, splashing, or immersion, materials or coatings shall either be inherently resistant to chemicals based on their listing or be identified for the specific chemical reagent.

(a) gasoline   (b) oil   (c) chemical solvents   (d) corrosive environments

32. Where a listed metal or nonmetallic conduit or tubing or Type MC cable is encased in not less than _____ inches of concrete for the portion of the branch circuit between the branch-circuit overcurrent device and the first outlet, it shall be permitted to install a listed outlet branch-circuit type AFCI at the first outlet to provide protection for the remaining portion of the branch circuit.

(a) 1 1/2   (b) 2   (c) 3   (d) 4

33. Where a feeder is supplied from a dc system operating at more than 60 volts, each ungrounded conductor of ____ AWG or larger shall be identified by polarity at all termination, connection, and splice joints by marking tape, tagging, or other approved means.

(a) #14 (b) #10 (c) #8 (d) #4

34. GFCI protection is required where receptacles are installed within ____of the outside edge of the bathtub or shower stall.

(a) 6' (b) 8' (c) 10' (d) 12'

35. In seating areas or similar surfaces, receptacles shall not be installed in a face-up position unless the receptacle is ____.

(a) part of an assembly listed either as household furnishings or as commercial furnishings
(b) part of an assembly listed as a furniture power distribution unit, if cord and plugged connected
(c) installed in a listed floor box
(d) any of these

36. Examples of increased or additional hazards include, but are not limited to, ____.

(a) motors associated with adjustable speed drives   (b) submersible motors
(c) motors rated in excess of 100 hp   (d) all of these

37. Tire inflation machines and automotive vacuum machines provided for ____ use shall be protected by a GFCI.

(a) commercial   (b) personnel   (c) compact vehicle   (d) bicycle

38. Type MC cable shall be permitted to be unsupported where the cable is of the interlocked armor type in lengths not exceeding ____ from the last point where it is securely fastened and is necessary to minimize the transmission of vibration from equipment or to provide flexibility for equipment that requires movement after installation.

(a) 24" (b) 30" (c) 36" (d) 48"

39. All nonlocking type 125v, 15 and 20 amp receptacles that are controlled by an automatic control device shall be marked with the symbol shown below ____.

(a) (b) (c) (d)

40. Documentation of engineered design by a licensed professional engineer engaged primarily in the design of such systems for the spacing between conductors shall be available upon request of the AHJ and this is stated in Article ____.

(a) 517   (b) 501   (c) 300   (d) 399

41. Illumination shall be provided for working spaces containing battery systems. The lighting outlets shall not be controlled by ____ means only.

(a) timers   (b) photo cell   (c) automatic   (d) low voltage

42. Arc-fault circuit-interrupter type and ground-fault circuit-interrupter type receptacles shall be installed in a/an ____ location.

(a) exposed   (b) accessible   (c) readily accessible   (d) concealed

43. Approved drainage openings not larger than ____ inch shall be permitted to be installed in the field in boxes or conduit bodies rated for use in damp or wet locations.

(a) 0.125   (b) 1/8”   (c) 0.250   (d) 3/16”

44. Where metal fences are located within 16' of the exposed electrical conductors or equipment, the fence shall be bonded to the grounding electrode system with wire-type bonding jumpers by ____.

(a) any gate or other opening in the fence shall be bonded across the opening by a buried bonding jumper
(b) the barbed wire strands above the fence shall be bonded to the grounding electrode system
(c) where bare overhead conductors cross the fence, bonding jumpers shall be installed on each side of the crossing
(d) all of these

45. Luminaires installed in exposed or concealed locations under metal-corrugated sheet roof decking shall be installed and supported so there is not less than ____ measured from the lowest surface of the roof decking to the top of the luminaire.

(a) 1 1/2”   (b) 1”   (c) 3/4”   (d) 5/8”

46. Threads cut into conduit anywhere other than the factory are called ____ threads.

(a) hand-cut   (b) field-cut   (c) course   (d) tampered

47. Any combustible wall or ceiling finish exposed between the edge of a luminaire canopy or pan and an outlet box having a surface area of ____ inch square or more shall be covered with noncombustible material.

(a) 80   (b) 100   (c) 125   (d) 180

48. ____ shall be constructed and installed so that electrical and mechanical continuity of the complete system are assured.

(a) Wireways   (b) Surface metal raceways   (c) Auxiliary gutters   (d) Multioutlet assemblies

49. ____ RMC shall be permitted to be installed for direct burial and swimming pool applications.

(a) Stainless steel   (b) Galvanized steel   (c) Aluminum   (d) Red brass

50. Where the distance above the roof to the bottom of the raceway is less than ____, a temperature adder of 60°F shall be added to the outdoor temperature to determine the applicable ambient temperature.

(a) 7/8"   (b) 1"   (c) 1 1/4"   (d) 2"

2020

JOURNEYMAN
OPEN
BOOK
EXAM #2

50 QUESTIONS
TIME LIMIT - 2 HOURS

TIME SPENT [   ] MINUTES

SCORE [   ] %

JOURNEYMAN OPEN BOOK EXAM #2   **Two Hour Time Limit**

1. Type AC cable must provide _____ for equipment grounding.

(a) an adequate path
(b) a green terminal on all fittings
(c) a solid green copper conductor in all cables
(d) all of these

2. The ampacity of capacitor circuit conductors must not be less than _____ of capacitor current.

(a) 80%   (b) 100%   (c) 125%   (d) 135%

3. Type MV cable is defined as a single or multiconductor solid dielectric insulated cable rated _____ volts or higher.

(a) 300   (b) 601   (c) 1,000   (d) 2,001

4. A waste disposal can be cord-and-plug connected, but the cord must not be less than 18" or more than _____ in length and must be protected from physical damage.

(a) 24"   (b) 30"   (c) 36"   (d) 48"

5. Cables with entirely nonmetallic sheaths are permitted to enter the top of a surface-mounted enclosure through one or more nonflexible raceways not less than 18" or more than _____ in length if all the requirements are met.

(a) 6'   (b) 10'   (c) 12'   (d) 20'

6. Type USE or SE cable must have a minimum of _____ conductors (including the uninsulated one) in order for one of the conductors to be uninsulated.

(a) one   (b) two   (c) three   (d) four

7. Bends made in interlocked or corrugated sheath metal clad cable must maintain a bending radius of at least _____ the external diameter of the metallic sheath.

(a) 5 times   (b) 6 times   (c) 7 times   (d) 8 times

8. Luminaires containing a metal halide lamp, other than a thick-glass parabolic reflector lamp (PAR), must be provided with a containment barrier that encloses the lamp, or the luminaire must be provided with a physical means that only allows the use of a(n) _____.

(a) Type PAR lamp   (b) incandescent lamp   (c) Type "O" lamp   (d) none of these

9. Threadless couplings and connectors used with RMC and installed in wet locations must be
____.

(a) approved for damp locations   (b) listed for damp locations
(c) approved for wet locations   (d) listed for wet locations

10. Loop wiring ____ in a cellular metal raceway.

(a) is considered a splice or tap when used   (b) is not considered a splice or tap
(c) is not permitted   (d) none of these

11. The derating factors for sheet metal auxiliary gutters shall be applied only where the number of
current-carrying conductors exceeds ____.

(a) 15 conductors (b) 25 conductors (c) 30 conductors (d) no limit on number of conductors

12. The number of conductors allowed in LFNC must not exceed that permitted in ____.

(a) Table 7 (b) Appendix D (c) Table 1 (d) Table 4

13. It is permissible to extend busways vertically through dry floors if totally enclosed (unventilated)
where passing through, and for a minimum distance of ____ above the floor to provide adequate
protection from physical damage.

(a) 6' (b) 8' (c) 10' (d) 12'

14. The maximum number of conductors permitted in any surface raceway must be ____.

(a) no more than 40% of the inside diameter
(b) no more than 75% of the csa
(c) that which is permitted in Table 4
(d) no greater than the number it was designed for

15. When applying the demand factors of Table 220.56, in no case can the feeder or service demand
load be less than the sum of the ____.

(a) largest two kitchen equipment loads   (b) heat and air conditioning loads
(c) rating of the appliance loads   (d) total receptacle load

16. A single piece of equipment consisting of a multiple receptacle comprised of ____ or more
receptacles must be computed at not less than 90 va per receptacle.

(a) one (b) two (c) three (d) four

17. There must be no reduction in the size of the grounded conductor on _____ type loads.

(a) resistive   (b) nonlinear   (c) linear   (d) symmetrical

18. _____ provided with permanent provisions for cooking must have branch circuits and outlets installed to meet the rules for dwelling units.

(a) Commercial kitchens   (b) Guest rooms   (c) Guest suites   (d) b and c

19. A _____ is an accommodation with two or more contiguous rooms comprising a compartment, with or without doors between such rooms, that provides living, sleeping, sanitary, and storage facilities.

(a) single-family dwelling   (b) guest room   (c) dwelling unit   (d) guest suite

20. Per the Code, the volume of a 3" x 2" x 2" device box is _____ cubic inches.

(a) 10   (b) 12   (c) 14   (d) 15

21. In cellular concrete floor raceways, a grounding conductor must connect the insert receptacle to a _____.

(a) grounded terminal located within the insert
(b) negative ground connection provided in the raceway
(c) negative ground connection provided on the header
(d) positive ground connection provided on the header

22. The AC ohms-to-neutral impedance per 1,000 feet of #4/0 aluminum in a steel raceway is _____.

(a) 0.05Ω   (b) 0.010Ω   (c) 0.101Ω   (d) 0.10Ω

23. A GFCI must be installed in the branch circuit supplying swimming pool lights that operate at voltages greater than _____

(a) 6 volts   (b) 10 volts   (c) 12 volts   (d) the low volage contact limit

24. Conductors located above a heated ceiling are considered as operating in an ambient temperature of _____.

(a) 20°C   (b) 30°C   (c) 50°C   (d) 75°C

25. For cellular concrete floor raceways, junction boxes must be _____ the floor grade and sealed against the free entrance of water or concrete.

(a) leveled to   (b) adjacent to   (c) perpendicular to   (d) above

26. The minimum spacing of busbars of opposite polarity held in free air inside a panelboard is ____ when operating at not over 125 volts, nominal.

(a) 1/2"   (b) 3/4"   (c) 1"   (d) 3"

27. Where knob-and-tube conductors pass through wood cross members in plastered partitions, conductors must be protected by non-combustible, nonabsorbent, insulating tubes extending not less than ____ beyond the wood member.

(a) 3"   (b) 4"   (c) 6"   (d) 8"

28. Type IGS cable is a factory assembly of one or more conductors, each individually insulated and enclosed in a loose-fit, non-metallic flexible conduit as an integrated gas spacer cable rated ____ volts.

(a) 0 through 300   (b) 0 through 600   (c) 0 through 1,000   (d) 0 through 22,000

29. Which of the following is true about MI cable?

(a) It may be used in any hazardous location.
(b) It must be securely supported at intervals not exceeding 10'
(c) A single run of cable must not contain more than the equivalent of four quarter bends.
(d) none of these

30. Nonmetallic cable trays must be made of ____ material.

(a) plastic   (b) fire-resistant   (c) flame-retardant   (d) corrosive

31. Neon tubing, other than Listed ____ accessible to pedestrians, must be protected from physical damage.

(a) fixed equipment   (b) wet location portable signs
(c) Class II locations   (d) dry location portable signs

32. When equipment or devices are installed in ducts or plenum chambers used to transport environmental air, and illumination is necessary to facilitate maintenance and repair, enclosed ____ - type luminaires are permitted.

(a) cord-and-plug   (b) gasketed   (c) screw   (d) pendant

33. Transformers with ventilating openings must be installed so that the ventilating openings ____.

(a) are not blocked by walls or obstructions   (b) are aesthetically located
(c) are vented to the exterior of the building   (d) are 18" minimum above the floor

34. The Type 3 SPD connection shall be a minimum ____ of conductor distance from the service.

(a) 10'   (b) 20'   (c) 30'   (d) 50'

35. The disconnecting means is not required at the building or structure where documented safe switching procedures are established and maintained, and where the installation is monitored by ____.

(a) the AHJ   (b) the management   (c) the supervisor   (d) qualified individuals

36. For installations of resistors and reactors, a thermal barrier is required if the space between them and any combustible material is less than ____.

(a) 2"   (b) 4"   (c) 6"   (d) 12"

37. Vertical runs of metal wireways must be securely supported at intervals not exceeding ____ and must not have more than one joint between supports.

(a) 8'   (b) 10'   (c) 12'   (d) 15'

38. Electric-discharge luminaires having an open-circuit voltage exceeding ____ must not be installed in or on dwelling occupancies.

(a) 240 volts   (b) 300 volts   (c) 120 volts   (d) 1,000 volts

39. A value assigned to a circuit or system for the purpose of conveniently designating its voltage class such as 120/240 volt is called ____ voltage.

(a) average   (b) source   (c) nominal   (d) effective

40. A 240 volt single-phase room air conditioner shall be considered as a single-phase motor unit if its rating is not more than ____.

(a) 20 amps   (b) 25 amps   (c) 30 amps   (d) 40 amps

41. The maximum permitted weight of a ceiling fan mounted directly to an outlet box is ____.

(a) 35 pounds   (b) 50 pounds   (c) 70 pounds   (d) 75 pounds

42. Structures of _____ shall be provided for support of overhead conductors over 1000 volts.

(a) concrete (b) metal (c) wood (d) any of these

43. AFCIs shall be installed on branch circuits supplying _____.

(a) closets (b) bedrooms (c) kitchens (d) all of these

44. In a building without a fire sprinkler system, ENT is permitted to be installed above a suspended ceiling if the suspended ceiling provides a thermal barrier having at least a _____ minute finish rating.

(a) 12 (b) 15 (c) 20 (d) 30

45. NUCC must be capable of being supplied on reels without damage or _____, and must be of sufficient strength to withstand abuse without damage to conduit or conductors.

(a) bending (b) distortion (c) crushing (d) wetness

46. Motor overload protection is not required where _____.

(a) short-circuit protection is provided
(b) ground-fault protection is pre-set
(c) conductors are oversized for the motor
(d) it might introduce additional or increased hazards

47. When grounding AC systems, the grounding electrode conductor must be connected to the grounded service conductor at _____.

(a) the meter equipment   (b) the service disconnect
(c) the load end of the service drop   (d) any of these

48. The grounding electrode conductor shall be installed in one continuous length without a splice or joint, unless _____.

(a) spliced by connecting to a busbar
(b) spliced by the exothermic welding process
(c) spliced by irreversible compression-type connectors listed as grounding and bonding
(d) any of these

49. When the resistance-to-ground of a single ground rod exceeds 25Ω, _____.

(a) the ground rod must be removed
(b) no additional electrodes are required
(c) at least one additional electrode must be installed
(d) it must be connected to a PVC pipe at least 50' in length

50. Individual open conductors entering a building must enter through roof bushings or through the wall in an upward slant through individual, noncombustible, nonabsorbent insulating _____.

(a) bushings   (b) tubes   (c) raceways   (d) chases

2020

JOURNEYMAN
OPEN
BOOK
EXAM #3

50 QUESTIONS
TIME LIMIT - 2 HOURS

TIME SPENT ☐ MINUTES

SCORE ☐ %

JOURNEYMAN OPEN BOOK EXAM #3   **Two Hour Time Limit**

1. The minimum size service lateral to a branch circuit limited load is ___ copper.

(a) #8   (b) #10   (c) #12   (d) none of these

2. A household-type appliance with surface heating elements having a maximum demand of more than ___ amperes computed in accordance with Table 220.19 shall have its power supply subdivided into two or more circuits, each of which is provided with overcurrent protection rated at not over ___ amperes.

(a) 40-40   (b) 50-40   (c) 50-60   (d) 60-50

3. A 2400 volt lead cable can be bent up to ___ times its diameter.

(a) 6   (b) 8   (c) 10   (d) 12

4. A steel cable tray of .79 square inches is used as an equipment ground conductor. The maximum rating of the circuit breaker permitted for this application is ___ amps.

(a) 1000   (b) 600   (c) 200   (d) 400

5. Medium voltage cable insulation is rated for voltages ___ volts and higher.

(a) 150   (b) 600   (c) 1000   (d) 2001

6. A fixture rated at 7 amps requires a size ___ minimum fixture wire.

(a) #16   (b) #18   (c) #14   (d) #12

7. Battery stands shall be permitted to contact adjacent walls or structures, provided that the battery shelf has a free air space for not less than ____ of its length.

(a) 45%   (b) 70%   (c) 80%   (d) 90%

8. A bathroom in a dwelling has a counter space of seven feet including the sink. How many receptacles are required to serve this area?

(a) 1   (b) 3   (c) 4   (d) none are required

9. To ensure effective continuity between enclosures, ___ shall be removed from the conduit threads.

(a) ends   (b) enamel   (c) galvanize finish   (d) aluminum

10. An installation requires a device box with a capacity of 10.25 cubic inches. What is the minimum size box allowed?

(a) 2" x 2" x 3"   (b) 3" x 2" x 2 1/4"   (c) 3" x 2" x 2"   (d) 2" x 3" x 3"

11. The maximum percent of overcurrent protection allowed is ___ of the input current to an autotransformer when less than 9 amps.

(a) 167%   (b) 150%   (c) 300%   (d) 125%

12. A show window is calculated at ___ va per linear foot.

(a) 180   (b) 1500   (c) 1800   (d) 200

13. Aluminum fittings and enclosures shall be permitted to be used with ___.

(a) both ferrous and nonferrous conduits   (b) PVC schedule 80 conduit
(c) electrical nonmetallic tubing   (d) steel electrical metallic tubing

14. Type UF cable is manufactured in sizes #14 through # ___ copper.

(a) 4/0   (b) 4   (c) 6   (d) 10

15. Synchronous motors of the low torque, low speed type, such as are used to drive reciprocating compressors, pumps, etc., that start unloaded, do not require a fuse rating or circuit breaker setting in excess of ___ percent of full load current.

(a) 150   (b) 200   (c) 250   (d) 400

16. All 125 volt single phase receptacles within ___ feet of the inside walls of a hydromassage tub shall be protected by a ground fault circuit interrupter(s).

(a) 6   (b) 10   (c) 12   (d) none of these

17. Of the two to six service disconnecting means in a panel, only a disconnect used for ___ is permitted to be remote from the other disconnects.

(a) control wiring   (b) a water pump intended for fire protection
(c) elevator panels   (d) supply to across the line starting

18. A lighting fixture under a canopy is considered to be in a ___ location.

(a) damp   (b) wet   (c) dry   (d) hazardous

19. Resistors and reactors for use over 600 volts, shall not be installed in close enough proximity to combustible materials to constitute a fire hazard and shall have a clearance of not less than ___ from combustible materials.

(a) 6"   (b) 1'   (c) 18"   (d) 2'

20. To reach a lighting fixture junction box, you had to stand on a ladder. This junction box is considered to be ___.

(a) concealed   (b) readily accessible   (c) accessible   (d) hidden

21. To settle a disagreement between an inspector and a contractor foreman, the ___ would have the final say.

(a) local authority having jurisdiction   (b) local electrical board
(c) the IBEW   (d) the engineer

22. The maximum number of 15 amp receptacles permitted on a free standing office partition is ___.

(a) 10   (b) 13   (c) 2   (d) 6

23. Transformer vaults shall have adequate structural strength and a minimum fire resistance of at least ___ hours. Unless protected by automatic sprinklers.

(a) 6   (b) 1 1/2   (c) 3   (d) not required

24. Flexible cords ___ and larger are used to supply approved appliances and are considered protected from overcurrent by overcurrent devices.

(a) #18   (b) #16   (c) #14   (d) #12

25. Panelboards, switches, gutters, wireways or transformers are permitted to be mounted above or below one another if ___.

(a) rated 300v or less
(b) flush along the back edge
(c) they extend not more than 6 inches beyond the front of the equipment
(d) flush along the front edge

26. In other than dwellings, ___ must have GFCI protection in a commercial building.

(a) sinks   (b) outdoor receptacle   (c) bathroom receptacle   (d) all of these

27. Size #18 or #16 fixture wires and flexible cords shall be permitted for the control and operating circuits of X-ray and auxiliary equipment where protected by not larger than ___ ampere overcurrent device.

(a) 15   (b) 20   (c) 25   (d) 30

28. Which of the following does not require a switched outlet according to the NEC?

(a) walk through garage door
(b) walk through porch door
(c) attic entrance
(d) drive through garage door

29. The highest current at rated voltage that a device is intended to interrupt under standard test conditions is know as ___.

(a) overload   (b) inverse time rated   (c) thermal protector   (d) interrupting rating

30. Where fluorescent lighting fixtures are supported independently of the outlet box, they shall be connected by metal raceways, nonmetallic raceways or ___ may be used.

I. nonmetallic sheathed cable (romex)   II. MI cable   III. AC cable   IV. MC cable

(a) I and II only   (b) II and III only   (c) III only   (d) I, II, III, and IV

31. ___ is/are considered as service equipment by the NEC.

I. Meter socket enclosure   II. Service disconnecting means   III. Panelboard

(a) I only   (b) I and II only   (c) II and III only   (d) I, II, and III

32. The sum of the diameters of all single conductors shall not exceed ___ when installed in a ventilated channel cable tray 4 inches inside width.

(a) 2 inches   (b) 3 inches   (c) 4 inches   (d) none of these

33. Each autotransformer of 1000 volts or less shall be protected by an individual overcurrent device installed in series with each ungrounded conductor and ___.

I. the overcurrent device shall be rated or set at not more than 125% of the rated full load input current of the autotransformer
II. an overcurrent device shall be installed in series with the shunt winding common to both the input and output circuits of the autotransformer

(a) I only   (b) II only   (c) I or II   (d) neither I nor II

34. In no case shall the distance between supports of nonmetallic wireway exceed ____ feet.

(a) 3 (b) 5 (c) 8 (d) 10

35. A dry type transformer not rated over 112 1/2 kva installed indoors, shall have a separation of at least ___ inches from combustible material.

(a) 24 (b) 18 (c) 12 (d) 6

36. The residual voltage of a capacitor shall be reduced to ___ volts, nominal, or less with 1 minute after the capacitor is disconnected from the source of supply.

(a) 0 (b) 15 (c) 30 (d) 50

37. Where more than one building or other structure is on the same property and under single management, each building or other structure served shall be provided with means for disconnecting all ___ conductors located nearest the point of entrance of the supply conductors.

I. grounded   II. ungrounded   III. ungrounded and grounded

(a) I only (b) II only (c) III only (d) I, II and III

38. Where single phase loads are connected on the load side of a phase converter, they shall not be connected to the ___.

(a) high leg (b) grounded phase (c) manufactured phase (d) neutral

39. For an installation consisting of not more than two 2-wire branch circuits, the service disconnecting means shall have a rating of not less than ___ amperes.

(a) 20 (b) 30 (c) 60 (d) 100

40. The term pool includes swimming, wading and therapeutic pools and the term fountain includes ___.

I. ornamental pools   II. drinking fountains   III. display pools   IV. reflection pools

(a) I & II only (b) II & III only (c) III & IV only (d) I, III, & IV only

41. Where the overcurrent device is rated over ___ amperes, the ampacity of the conductors it protects shall be equal to or greater than the rating of the overcurrent device.

(a) 100 (b) 200 (c) 500 (d) 800

42. When derating the ampacity of multiconductor cables to be installed in cable tray, the ampacity deration shall be based on ___.

I. the total number of current carrying conductors in the cable tray
II. the total number of current carrying conductors in the cable

(a) I only   (b) II only   (c) either I or II   (d) both I and II

43. Where necessary to prevent ___, an automatic overcurrent device protecting service conductors supplying only a specific load, such as a water heater, shall be permitted to be locked or sealed where located so as to be accessible.

(a) tripping   (b) corrosion   (c) heat build up   (d) tampering

44. A complete lighting unit consisting of a lamp or lamps together with the parts designed to distribute the light, to position and protect the lamps and ballast, and to connect the lamps to the power supply is a ____.

(a) luminaire   **(b) class I, division I light fixture**
(c) class I, division II light fixture   **(d) intrinsically safe light fixture**

45. A bonding jumper shall be used to connect the equipment grounding conductors of the derived system to the grounded conductor. This connection shall be made ___.

I.   at any point on the separately derived system from the source to the first system disconnect
II. at any point on the separately derived system from the source to the first overcurrent device
III. at the source if the system has no disconnecting means or overcurrent device

(a) I only   (b) II only   (c) III only   (d) I, II or III

46. A/an ___ shall be used to connect the grounding terminal of a grounding type receptacle to a grounded box.

(a) neutral conductor   **(b) branch circuit**
(c) equipment bonding jumper   **(d) bonding jumper main**

47. Thermoplastic-insulated fixture wire shall be durably marked with the AWG size, voltage rating and other required markings on the surface at intervals not exceeding ___ inches.

(a) 6   (b) 12   (c) 18   (d) 24

48. Fuses shall be plainly marked with ___.

I. ampere rating II. voltage rating III. interrupting rating where other than 10,000 amperes

(a) I only (b) I & II only (c) I & III only (d) I, II & III

49. Strut-type channel raceway shall be secured at intervals not exceeding ___ feet and within 3 feet of each outlet box.

(a) 3 (b) 4 1/2 (c) 10 (d) 12

50. Several motors, each not exceeding 1 horsepower in rating, shall be permitted on a nominal 120 volt branch circuit protected at not over __ amperes.

(a) 15 (b) 20 (c) 30 (d) 40

2020

JOURNEYMAN OPEN BOOK EXAM #4

50 QUESTIONS
TIME LIMIT - 2 HOURS

TIME SPENT [   ] MINUTES

SCORE [   ] %

JOURNEYMAN OPEN BOOK EXAM #4   **Two Hour Time Limit**

1. Direct buried coaxial cable shall be separated at least _____ from conductors of any light or power.

(a) 12"   (b) 18"   (c) 24"   (d) 30"

2. Where low-voltage fire alarm system cables penetrate a fire-resistance-rated wall, _____.

(a) openings shall be firestopped
(b) no special considerations are required
(c) cables cannot penetrate through a firewall
(d) a junction box on each side of the wall shall be connected by a rigid steel nipple

3. The purpose of the National Electrical Code is to provide _____.

(a) a design specification for electrical installations
(b) installations which are adequate for good service
(c) efficient electrical installations
(d) safe electrical installations

4. Which is the requirement for a dry-type transformer rated 112 1/2 kVA or less installed indoors?

(a) It shall be installed in a vault.
(b) Dry-type transformers shall not be installed indoors.
(c) It shall be installed in a room of fire-resistant construction.
(d) It shall have a separation of at least 12" from combustible materials.

5. The working clearance in front of a switchboard or switchgear shall be not less than _____.

(a) 24"   (b) 30"   (c) 36"   (d) 48"

6. With the exception of cord and plug-connected appliances, the disconnecting means for air conditioning and refrigerating equipment shall be _____.

(a) readily accessible
(b) located within sight
(c) permitted to be installed on or within the equipment
(d) All of the above

7. Panelboards equipped with snap switches rated at 30 amperes or less shall have overcurrent protection not in excess of _____ amperes.

(a) 60   (b) 100   (c) 150   (d) 200

8. To provide short-circuit and ground-fault protection for a branch circuit supplying a motor or motors, a feeder conductor supplying that branch shall be provided with a ____.

(a) thermal relay   **(b) protective device**
(c) motor control device   **(d) control transformer**

9. The minimum clearance required between a high pressure sodium lighting fixture and combustible ceiling framing is ____.

(a) 1/4"   (b) 1/2"   (c) 5/8"   (d) 11/16"

10. Conductors for small motors shall not be smaller than ____ AWG unless otherwise permitted in Article 430.

(a) #12   (b) #14   (c) #20   (d) #22

11. Where conductors supply several motors or groups of motors, and where the circuitry is so interlocked as to prevent the starting and running of a second motor or group of motors, the conductor size shall be determined from ____.

(a) 75% of the sum of the full-load current ratings only
(b) 80% of the sum of the full-load current ratings only
(c) the summation of the currents of motors and other loads operated at the same time
(d) the sum of the full-load current ratings plus 25% of the highest rated motor

12. An electrically operated waste disposer, installed in the kitchen of a dwelling unit, shall have a cord not less than ____ and not more than ____ in length.

(a) 18"; 36"
(b) 18"; 24"
(c) 16"; 36"
(d) 12"; 24"

13. Where a surface-mounted fixture containing a ballast is to be installed on combustible low-density cellulose fiberboard, it shall be spaced not less than ____ from the surface.

(a) 1/2"   (b) 1'   (c) 1 1/2"   (d) 3"

14. Unless the use of a motor is specified, it shall be considered as ____ duty.

(a) periodic
(b) continuous
(c) intermittent
(d) medium

15. In a 10-unit apartment building, the disconnecting means for fixed appliances shall be located
____.

(a) within sight of the appliance or 50' in distance
(b) inside the individual dwelling unit only
(c) anywhere within the building, and accessible
(d) within the individual unit, or on the same floor in the building

16. Disregarding any exceptions, the identification of terminals to which a grounded conductor is to
be connected shall be ____.

(a) a green colored not readily removable, terminal screw with a hexagonal head
(b) substantially white in color
(c) either (a) or (b)
(d) none of the above

17. The width of working space in front of electric equipment shall be the width of the equipment
or ____, whichever is greater.

(a) 18" (b) 24" (c) 30" (d) 36"

18. The number of ungrounded conductors which may be utilized with a single common neutral
conductor on an outside lighting circuit is ____.

(a) 2 (b) 6 (c) 8 (d) no limit specified

19. An individual outlet with taps not over 18" long is connected to a 50 ampere circuit. The tap
conductor ampacity shall not be less than ____ amperes.

(a) 15 (b) 20 (c) 30 (d) 40

20. At least one receptacle outlet per unit, accessible at grade level, shall be installed at the front and
back on ____.

(a) commercial buildings
(b) office buildings only
(c) motels
(d) one and two family dwellings

21. Which of the following receptacles may be connected to the small appliance branch circuit?

(a) Outside receptacles
(b) Electric clock in a dining room
(c) Hallway receptacle which is within 20 feet of kitchen
(d) Garage ceiling receptacle for automatic garage door opener

22. Sealed cans of gasoline may be stored in a _____ area.

(a) Class I, Division 1
(b) Class I, Division 2
(c) Class II, Division 1
(d) Class II, Division 2

23. A portable light to be placed on the floor underneath automobiles in a commercial garage shall be ____.

(a) any identified portable light
(b) identified for Class I, Division 1 locations
(c) identified for Class I, Division 2 locations
(d) identified for Class II, Division 1 locations

24. According to the National Electrical Code, a hospital's essential electrical system shall be comprised of ____ separate branches.

I. life safety system   II. critical system   III. equipment system

(a) I only   (b) II only   (c) III only   (d) all of these

25. The grounded conductor at a service entrance shall not be smaller than the required size of the ____ conductor.

(a) phase   (b) service   (c) equipment   (d) as specified in Table 250.102(C1)

26. A 1" liquidtight flexible metal conduit 5 foot in length contains no equipment grounding conductor and is terminated in fittings listed for grounding. The maximum size overcurrent device to protect the conductors is ____ amperes.

(a) 20   (b) 30   (c) 40   (d) 60

27. Where the ampacity of a conductor does not correspond with the standard ampere rating of a fuse or circuit breaker, the next higher standard size is permitted only if the rating does not exceed ____ amperes.

(a) 600   (b) 800   (c) 1,000   (d) 1,200

28. A ground ring shall be in direct contact with the earth at a depth below the earth surface not less than ____ .

(a) 1 1/2'   (b) 2'   (c) 2 1/2'   (d) 3'

29. Where wet contact is likely to occur in a permanent amusement attraction, ungrounded 2-wire DC control circuits shall be limited to _____ maximum for continuous DC or 12.4 volts peak for DC that is interrupted at a rate of 10 to 200 Hz.

(a) 12 volts   (b) .031 va   (c) 24 watts   (d) 30 volts

30. Luminaires with GFCI protection located over a spa shall be permitted provided the mounting height is not less than _____.

(a) 6'   (b) 7'6"   (c) 8'   (d) 12'

31. A Class 1 Power-Limited circuit shall be supplied by a source having a rated output not more than _____ volts.

(a) 6   (b) 12   (c) 24   (d) 30

32. A 240v service cable passing over an outside spa shall have a vertical clearance from the water level of at least _____.

(a) 14.5'   (b) 18"   (c) 22.5'   (d) 25'

33. If one piece of equipment shall be within sight of another piece of equipment, the equipment shall be visible to each other and within _____ feet of each other.

(a) 20   (b) 30   (c) 40   (d) 50

34. Type AC cables shall be permitted for use _____.

(a) in wet or damp locations
(b) as portable power cables
(c) in exposed work
(d) in direct burial in earth, if conductors lead-covered

35. Disregarding exceptions, where ungrounded conductors of _____ or larger enter a raceway in a cabinet, pull box, junction box or auxiliary gutter, the conductor shall be protected by an insulated bushing.

(a) #6   (b) #4   (c) #2   (d) #1/0

36. A 3/8" flexible fixture "whip" with external connectors may contain one bare #12 grounding conductor plus _____ #12 THHN circuit conductors.

(a) 2   (b) 3   (c) 4   (d) 6

37. Disregarding any exceptions, surface metal raceways shall be permitted ____.

(a) in dry locations
(b) in any hazardous location
(c) where subject to corrosive vapors
(d) where the voltage is 300 volts or more between conductors

38. Nonmetallic sheathed (NM) cable shall be secured in place at intervals not exceeding ____.

(a) 36" (b) 42" (c) 54" (d) 4' 3"

39. Disregarding any exceptions, the smallest size liquidtight flexible metal conduit that shall be used is ____.

(a) 3/8" (b) 1/2" (c) 5/8" (d) 3/4"

40. Rigid metal conduit shall be fastened in place within ____ feet of each box, outlet, cabinet or fitting and may be increased to ____ feet where structural members interfere.

(a) 1;2 (b) 2;4 (c) 3;5 (d) 4;6

41. When driving a rod electrode into the soil and rock bottom is encountered, what other method may be used?

(a) Bury the conductor in earth at least 18".
(b) Connect to the primary water main.
(c) Connect to the nearest building steel.
(d) Bury the rod in a trench at least 2 1/2' deep.

42. Flexible metal conduit and tubing shall be permitted for equipment grounding if ____.

(a) the circuit conductors contained therein are protected
(b) the length in any ground return path does not exceed 6 feet
(c) the conduit or tubing is terminated in fittings listed for grounding
(d) all of the above

43. Where a supplemental grounding electrode is a "made" electrode, the bonding jumper between the supplemental electrode and the service equipment shall not be required to be larger than ____ copper.

(a) #10 (b) #8 (c) #6 (d) #4

44. A separate copper equipment grounding conductor run in flexible metal conduit for a 40 ampere circuit shall be not less than ____.

(a) #12   (b) #10   (c) #8   (d) #6

45. Given: A hand-held, motor-operated, cord-and-plug connected tool. Disregarding exceptions, the exposed non-current carrying metal parts must be grounded when ____.

(a) in residential occupancies
(b) in hazardous (classified) locations
(c) the power source is over 150 volts to ground
(d) all of the above

46. For any building, the service disconnecting means shall consist of not more than ____ switches or circuit breakers.

(a) 2   (b) 4   (c) 6   (d) 8

47. The ampacity of the branch circuit conductors and the rating or setting of the overcurrent protective device supplying fixed electric space-heating equipment consisting of resistance elements with or without a motor shall not be less than ____ of the total load of the motors and the heaters.

(a) 125%   (b) 100%   (c) 80%   (d) 40%

48. The size and number of conductors shall be that for which the cablebus is designed, and in no case smaller than ____ AWG.

(a) 500 Kcmil   (b) 750 Kcmil   (c) 250 Kcmil   (d) #1/0

49. Outlet boxes mounted in non-combustible walls or ceilings must be mounted so that they will be set back not more than a maximum of ____ from the finished surface.

(a) 1/8"   (b) 1/4"   (c) 1/2"   (d) 3/4"

50. Disregarding any exceptions, Type MI cables shall not be permitted to be used ____.

(a) where exposed to oil and gasoline
(b) where exposed to destructive corrosive conditions
(c) where embedded in plaster or concrete whether above or below grade
(d) In any of the above conditions

2020

JOURNEYMAN
OPEN
BOOK
EXAM #5

50 QUESTIONS
TIME LIMIT - 2 HOURS

TIME SPENT ☐ **MINUTES**

SCORE ☐ %

JOURNEYMAN OPEN BOOK EXAM #5   **Two Hour Time Limit**

1. Ground-fault protection that functions to open the service disconnecting means ____ protect(s) service conductors or the service disconnecting means.

(a) will   (b) will not   (c) adequately   (d) totally

2. Which of the following is a **false** statement?

(a) Direct buried conductors are required to be spliced in a splice box.
(b) Direct buried conductors are permitted to be soldered.
(c) Where wire connectors are used for splicing direct buried conductors, the connectors must be listed for such use.
(d) Where necessary to prevent physical damage, direct buried conductors shall be protected by raceways, boards sleeves, or other approved means.

3. The Code requires that heating panels be separated from outlet boxes that are to be used for mounting fixtures not less than ____ inches.

(a) 12   (b) 8   (c) 6   (d) 10

4. At least ____ inches of free conductor shall be left at each outlet and switch point.

(a) 4   (b) 6   (c) 8   (d) 12

5. It shall be permissible to apply a demand factor of 75% to the nameplate-rating load of 4 or more ____ fastened in place in a dwelling.

I. water heaters   II. dishwashers   III. clothes dryers

(a) I only   (b) II only   (c) I and II only   (d) I, II and III

6. Where outdoor lampholders have terminals that puncture the insulation and make contact with the conductors, they shall be attached only to ____.

(a) conductors with rubber insulation
(b) solid conductors
(c) conductors of the stranded type
(d) a #12 conductor

7. Lamp tie wires, mounting screws, clips, and decorative bands on glass lamps spaced not less than ____ inches from lamp terminals shall not be required to be grounded.

(a) 1 1/4   (b) 1 1/2   (c) 2   (d) 4

8. Class II locations are those that are hazardous because of _____.

(a) the presence of combustible dust
(b) over 8' depth of water
(c) flammable gases or vapors may be present in the air
(d) easily ignitible fibers are stored or handled

9. Where conduit is threaded in the field, a standard conduit cutting die with a ____ inch taper per foot shall be used.

(a) 1/2   (b) 3/4   (c) 1   (d) 1 1/4

10. Equipment grounding conductors, when installed, ____ be included when calculating conduit fill.

(a) should   (b) shall   (c) should not   (d) shall never

11. In a straight run of rigid nonmetallic conduit between securely mounted boxes, expansion joints are required where the computed length change due to thermal expansion or contraction is at least ___ inch or more.

(a) 1/8   (b) 1/4   (c) 3/8   (d) 1/2

12. The minimum feeder allowance for show window lighting expressed in volt-amps per linear foot shall be ____ va.

(a) 100   (b) 200   (c) 300   (d) 180

13. Angle pull dimensional requirements apply to junction boxes only when the size of conductor is equal to or larger than ____.

(a) #0   (b) #4   (c) #3/0   (d) #6

14. The maximum length of a bonding jumper on the outside of a raceway is ____.

(a) 3'   (b) 6'   (c) 8'   (d) none of these

15. Rigid nonmetallic conduit may be used ____.

(a) above ground in direct sunlight
(b) as a support for lighting fixtures
(c) as a grounding conductor
(d) all of these

16. MI cable has ____.

(a) solid copper conductors
(b) outer sheath to provide mechanical protection
(c) an adequate path for grounding purposes
(d) all of these

17. Which of the following may be used as a feeder from the service equipment to a mobile home?

I. A permanently installed feeder   II. One 50 amp power supply cord

(a) I only   (b) II only   (c) either I or II   (d) neither I nor II

18. Multispeed motors shall be marked with the code letter designating the locked-rotor ____ per horsepower for the highest speed at which the motor can be started.

(a) amps   (b) F.L.C.   (c) kva   (d) watts

19. The length of a type S cord connecting a trash compactor must not exceed ____.

(a) 18"   (b) 4'   (c) 36"   (d) 2'

20. Electrical installations in hollow spaces, vertical shafts and ventilation or air-handling ducts shall be so made that the possible spread of fire or products of combustion will not be ____.

(a) substantially increased   (b) allowed   (c) exposed   (d) under rated

21. Electric equipment shall be installed in a neat and ____ manner.

(a) efficient   (b) safe   (c) workmanlike   (d) orderly

22. The space measured horizontally above a show window must have at least one receptacle for each ____ linear feet.

(a) 12   (b) 10   (c) 8   (d) 6

23. Conductor overload protection is not required if ____.

(a) conductors are oversized by 125%
(b) conductors are part of a limited-energy circuit
(c) interruption of the circuit can create a hazard
(d) none of these

24. The distance between a cable or conductor entry and its exit from the box shall be not less than ____ times the outside diameter, over sheath, of that cable or conductor, 1000 volt system.

(a) 6   (b) 18   (c) 36   (d) 48

25. A thermal barrier shall be required if the space between the resistors and reactors and any combustible material is less than ____ inches.

(a) 4   (b) 6   (c) 8   (d) 12

26. An attachment plug connecting to a receptacle shall ____ the equipment grounding conductor.

(a) have conductors the same size as
(b) provide for first-make, last-break of
(c) provide a twist-lock connection for
(d) none of these

27. When more than one calculated or tabulated ampacity could apply for a given circuit length, the ____ value shall be used.

(a) lowest   (b) average   (c) highest   (d) none of these

28. Cable splices made and insulated by approved methods shall be permitted within a cable tray provided they are accessible and ____.

(a) have a hinged cover
(b) are crimped properly
(c) are not over 600 volt
(d) are permitted to project above the side rail where not subject to physical damage

29. Electronically actuated fuses may or may not operate in a current limiting fashion, depending on the ____.

(a) ambient temperature   (b) type of control selected
(c) listing   (d) torque

30. Connection by means of wire binding screws or studs and nuts having upturned lugs or equivalent shall be permitted for ____ or smaller conductors.

(a) #10   (b) #8   (c) #6   (d) none of these

31. Electrical nonmetallic tubing is permitted to be used in sizes up to ____.

(a) 1"   (b) 2"   (c) 2 1/2"   (d) 4"

32. Ampacity of fixture wire is determined ____.

(a) by referring to the ampacity Table 310.16
(b) by calculation, using the expected temperature rise of the fixture
(c) from a table in article 402 of the Code
(d) none of these

33. Wind electric systems can be interactive with other electrical power production sources or might be stand-alone systems. Wind electric systems can have____.

(a) ac or dc output   (b) with or without electrical energy storage
(c) such as batteries (d) all of these

34. Means shall be provided to ensure that the ____ is energized when the first heater circuit is energized.

(a) ballast   (b) fan circuit   (c) coil   (d) relay

35. A pool recirculating pump motor receptacle shall be permitted not less than ____ feet from the inside walls of the pool.

(a) 6   (b) 8   (c) 10   (d) 15

36. Fixtures shall be wired with conductors having insulation suitable for ____ to which the conductors will be subjected.

I. environmental conditions   II. current-voltage   III. temperature

(a) II only   (b) III only   (c) I, II and III   (d) II and III

37. What is the minimum working clearance on a circuit 120 volts to ground, exposed live parts on one side and no live or grounded parts on the other side of the working space?

(a) 3'   (b) 3 1/2'   (c) 4'   (d) 6'

38. The maximum weight of a light fixture that may be mounted on the screw shell of a brass socket is ____ pound(s).

(a) 1/2   (b) 1   (c) 6   (d) none of these

39. The grounded service conductor shall not be smaller than the required ____.

(a) as specified in T. 250.102(C1)   (b) largest phase conductor
(c) ungrounded service conductor   (d) largest equipment conductor

40. Type UF cable shall be permitted for interior wiring in _____ locations.

I. dry   II. wet   III. corrosive

(a) I only   (b) I or II   (c) I or III   (d) I, II or III

41. Type _____, a flat cable assembly, is an assembly of parallel conductors formed integrally with an insulating material web specifically designed for field installation in surface metal raceway.

(a) FCC   (b) FC   (c) TC   (d) SNM

42. For feeder and service calculations, a maximum of _____ of lighting track or fraction thereof shall be considered 150va.

(a) 2'   (b) 4'   (c) 5'   (d) 8'

43. Under the optional method of calculation "other loads" are permitted a demand factor from 220.82, the first 10 kva of "other load" @ 100% and the remainder of "other load" at 40%. "Other load" could consist of which of the following?

I. electric heat   II. electric range   III. air conditioning

(a) I only   (b) II only   (c) III only   (d) I, II and III

44. Reasonable efficiency of operation can be provided when _____ is taken into consideration in sizing the branch circuit conductors.

(a) mechanical strength   (b) ambient temperature   (c) voltage drop   (d) none of these

45. Voltage shall not exceed 600 volts between conductors on branch circuits supplying only ballasts for electric-discharge lamps in tunnels with a height of not less than _____ feet.

(a) 12   (b) 15   (c) 18   (d) 22

46. Conduit encased in a concrete trench is considered a _____ location.

(a) wet   (b) dry   (c) damp   (d) moist

47. The conductor between a lightning arrester and the line for installations operating at 1000 volts or more must be at least _____.

(a) #14 copper   (b) #6 copper   (c) #8 copper   (d) none of these

48. What is the nominal battery voltage for an alkali type battery per cell?

(a) 2.0 volt   (b) 6.0 volt   (c) 1.5 volt   (d) 1.2 volt

49. The conductors and equipment required or permitted by this Code shall be acceptable only if ____.

(a) approved   (b) identified   (c) labeled   (d) listed

50. Where multiple rod, pipe, or plate electrodes are installed, they shall be not less than ____ apart.

(a) 18"   (b) 6'   (c) 8'   (d) 10'

2020

JOURNEYMAN
OPEN
BOOK
EXAM #6

50 QUESTIONS
TIME LIMIT - 2 HOURS

TIME SPENT [   ] MINUTES

SCORE [   ] %

JOURNEYMAN OPEN BOOK EXAM #6   **Two Hour Time Limit**

1. The overhead service conductors from the last pole or other aerial support to and including the splices, if any, connecting to the service-entrance conductors at the building or other structure is called the ____.

(a) temporary service   (b) service lateral   (c) service drop   (d) service point

2. If a switch or circuit breaker serves as the disconnecting means for a permanently connected motor driven appliance of more than ___ horsepower, it shall be located within sight from the motor controller.

(a) 1/8   (b) 1/4   (c) 1/2   (d) 3/4

3. Overcurrent devices shall be enclosed in ___.

I. cabinets   II. cutout boxes

(a) I only   (b) II only   (c) I or II   (d) none of these

4. Where reduced heating of the conductors results from motors operating on duty-cycle, intermittently, or from all motors not operating at one time, the feeder conductors ____

(a) are not allowed to have the ampacity reduced
(b) may have an ampacity less than specified if acceptable to the authority having jurisdiction
(c) must be sized no smaller than 125% of the largest motor connected to the feeder
(d) must be sized not smaller than 125% of the largest motor plus other loads

5. Live parts of generators operated at more than ___ volts to ground shall not be exposed to accidental contact where accessible to unqualified persons.

(a) 30   (b) 50   (c) 120   (d) 150

6. A ___ is a circuit operating at 1000 volts, nominal, or less, between phases that connects two power sources or power supply points, such as the secondaries of two transformers.

I. branch circuit individual   II. branch circuit multiwire   III. secondary tie

(a) I only   (b) II only   (c) III only   (d) I and II only

7. Entrances to rooms and other guarded locations containing exposed live parts shall be marked with ___ warning signs forbidding unqualified persons to enter.

(a) yellow   (b) blue   (c) conspicuous   (d) orange

8. Overhead spans of open conductors and open multiconductor cables not over 600 volts shall have a vertical clearance of not less than ___ above the roof surface.

(a) 8' 6"   (b) 6'   (c) 4'   (d) 3'

9. Where single conductors #1/0 through 4/0 are installed in a ladder or ventilated trough cable tray, they shall be installed in no more than ___.

I. a depth of 4"   II. a depth of 6"   III. a single layer

(a) I only   (b) II only   (c) III only   (d) I or II only

10. Where flexible cords are permitted by the code to be permanently connected, it is permissible to omit ___ for such cords.

(a) switches   (b) receptacles   (c) grounding connections   (d) GFCI protection

11. Listed or labeled equipment shall be installed, used, or both, in accordance with ___ .

(a) the job specifications
(b) the plans
(c) the instructions given by the authority having jurisdiction
(d) the instructions included in the listing or labeling

12. A grounding electrode connection that is encased in concrete or directly buried shall ___.

(a) be made accessible   **(b) be made only by exothermic welding**
(c) be a minimum #4 bare   **(d) not be required to be accessible**

13. Wet niche or no niche lighting fixtures that are supplied by a flexible cord or cable shall have all exposed noncurrent carrying metal parts grounded by an insulated copper equipment grounding conductor not smaller than the supply conductors and not smaller than ___.

(a) #16   (b) #18   (c) #14   (d) #12

14. If laid in notches in wood studs, joists, rafters, or other wood members, ___ shall be protected against nails or screws by a steel plate at least 1/16" thick.

(a) EMT   (b) rigid nonmetallic conduit   (c) intermediate steel conduit   (d) flexible conduit

15. A two pole circuit breaker that may be used for protecting a 3 phase corner grounded delta circuit shall be marked ___.

(a) 1ø 120/240v   (b) 1ø — 3ø   (c) 1ø/2ø/3ø   (d) 480Y/277v

16. When installing a surge arrester at the service of less than 1000 volts, the grounding conductor shall be connected to ___.

I.   the grounded service conductor
II. the grounding electrode conductor
III. the grounding electrode for the service
IV. the equipment grounding terminal in the service equipment

(a) I and II only   (b) I and III only   (c) III and IV only   (d) I, II, III, or IV

17. A means shall be provided in each metal box over 100 cubic inches for the connection of an equipment grounding conductor. The means shall be permitted to be ___.

I. a tapped hole   II. the cover screw   III. a screw used to mount the box

(a) I only   (b) II only   (c) I and II only   (d) I, II, or III

18. A luminaire installed outdoors is permitted to be supported by ___.

I.   trees   II.   a metal pole   III. an outlet box

(a) I only   (b) II and III only   (c) II only   (d) I, II, or III

19. ___cable(s) used for remote-control signaling, or power-limited systems that supply critical circuits to ensure survivability for continued circuit operation for a specified time under fire conditions.

(a) Class 1   (b) XL   (c) CI   (d) RMC

20. A ___ shall be used to connect the equipment grounding conductors, the service equipment enclosures, and where the system is grounded, the grounded service conductor to the grounding electrode.

(a) busbar   (b) neutral conductor
(c) 5/8" ground rod   (d) grounding electrode conductor

21. For equipment rated 1200 amperes or more, and over 6 feet wide, containing overcurrent devices, switching devices, or control devices, there shall be one entrance not less than ___ inches wide and 6 1/2 feet high at each end.

(a) 24   (b) 30   (c) 36   (d) 48

22. Appliances that have ___ that are to be connected by (1) permanent wiring method or (2) by field installed attachment plugs and cords with three or more wires (including the equipment grounding conductor) shall have means to identify the terminal for the grounded circuit conductor (if any).

I. screw shell lampholders   II. single pole overcurrent device in the line   III. single pole switch

(a) I and II only   (b) I and III only   (c) II and III only   (d) I, II and III

23. Of the following, ___ box may be used for a floor receptacle.

(a) a 4 11/16" x 1 1/4" square metal box with device ring listed for the purpose
(b) a 3" x 2" x 2 1/2" metal device box with device ring listed for the purpose
(c) a box listed specifically for this application
(d) any of these

24. For a one family dwelling, at least one receptacle outlet, in addition to any provided for laundry equipment, shall be installed in each ___ .

I. basement   II. detached garage with electric power   III. attached garage

(a) I only   (b) II only   (c) I and III only   (d) I, II, and III

25. Where nonmetallic sheathed cable is used with boxes no larger than ___ mounted in walls or ceilings and where the cable is fastened within 8 inches of the box, securing the cable to the box shall not be required.

(a) 2 1/4" x 4"   (b) 2/12" x 4"   (c) 2" x 4"   (d) 1 1/4" x 4"

26. For swimming pool water heaters rated at more than ___ amperes that have specific instructions regarding bonding and grounding, only those parts designated to be bonded shall be bonded, and only those parts designated to be grounded shall be grounded.

(a) 50   (b) 40   (c) 30   (d) 20

27. A dormitory unit is a building or a space in a building in which group sleeping accommodations are provided for more than ____ persons who are not members of the same family.

(a) 10   (b) 12   (c) 16   (d) 20

28. A power system for facilities or parts of facilities that require continuous operation for the reasons of public safety, emergency management, national security, or business continuity is a/an _____.

(a) optional stand by system   (b) emergency system (EMS)
(c) dedicated emergency system   (d) critical operations power systems (COPS)

29. For AC adjustable voltage, variable torque drive motors, the ampacity of conductors, or ampere ratings of switches, circuit breakers or fuses and ground fault protection shall be based on the operating current marked on the nameplate. If the current does not appear on the nameplate, the ampacity determination shall be based on ___ of the values given in tables 430-149 and 430-150.

(a) 80%   (b) 100%   (c) 125%   (d) 150%

30. Which of the following is a **false** statement?

(a) **An accessible plug and receptacle shall be permitted to serve as the disconnecting means for a cord and plug connected appliance.**
(b) **For a household electric range, a plug and receptacle connection at the rear base is acceptable as the disconnect if it is accessible from the front by removal of a drawer.**
(c) **A counter mounted cooking unit shall be connected by a permanent wiring method.**
(d) **A switch with a marked off position that is a part of an appliance and disconnects all ungrounded conductors is permitted in a dwelling if the circuit is protected by a circuit breaker.**

31. Where a transformer vault is constructed with other stories below it, the floor shall have a minimum fire resistance of 3 hours unless ___.

(a) **the floors in contact with the earth not less than 3" thick**
(b) **protected with automatic sprinkler**
(c) **constructed of fire rated wallboard**
(d) **constructed of steel studs and fire rated wallboard**

32. For battery racks, there shall be a minimum clearance of ____ between a cell container and any wall or structure on the side not requiring access for maintenance. Battery stands shall be permitted to contact adjacent walls or structures, provided that the battery shelf has a free air space for not less than 90 percent of its length.

(a) 2"   (b) 1 1/2"   (c) 1"   (d) 1/2"

33. When calculating the conductor fill for strut-type channel raceway with internal joiners, the raceway shall be permitted to be filled to ___ percent of the cross-sectional area.

(a) 20   (b) 25   (c) 30   (d) 40

34. Which of the following wiring methods may be used inside the duct used for vapor removal and ventilation of commercial type cooking equipment?

(a) **nonmetallic sheathed cable**   (b) EMT   (c) rigid steel conduit   (d) none of these

35. Splices and taps shall be permitted in surface nonmetallic raceways having a removable cover that is accessible after installation. The conductors, including splices and taps, shall not fill the raceway to more than ___ percent of its area at that point.

(a) 31   (b) 40   (c) 53   (d) 75

36. Cabinets and cutout boxes shall be deep enough to allow the closing of the doors when ___ ampere branch circuit panelboard switches are in any position; when combination cutout switches are in any position; or when other single throw switches are opened as far as their construction will permit.

(a) 15   (b) 20   (c) 30   (d) 100

37. Underfloor flat-top raceways over 4 inches but not over 8 inches wide with a minimum of 1 inch spacing between raceways shall be covered with concrete to a depth of not less than ___.

(a) 3/4"   (b) 1"   (c) 1 1/2"   (d) 2"

38. Luminaires located in the same room and not directly associated with a hydromassage bathtub, shall be installed in accordance with the requirements covering the installation of that equipment in ___.

(a) swimming pool area   (b) kitchen   (c) exercise room   (d) bathrooms

39. The allowable fill for a 1 1/4 inch rigid schedule 40 PVC with more than 2 conductors is ___ sq. in.

(a) .794   (b) .333   (c) .495   (d) .581

40. Induction coils shall be prevented from inducing circulating currents in surrounding metallic equipment, supports, or structures by ___.

I. isolation   II. shielding   III. insulation of the current paths

(a) I only   (b) II only   (c) III only   (d) I, II or III

41. At least one receptacle shall be located a minimum of 5 feet from and not more than ___ feet from the inside wall of a spa or hot tub installed indoors.

(a) 6   (b) 10   (c) 12   (d) 20

42. An electronically actuated fuse generally consists of all of the following EXCEPT ____?

(a) a control module that provides current sensing
(b) electronically derived time-current characteristics
(c) an interrupting module that interrupts current when an overcurrent occurs
(d) a thermally sensitive part that is heated and severed by passage of overcurrent through it

43. An underground pull box used for circuits of over 600 volts shall have the cover locked, bolted or screwed on, or the cover is required to weigh over ____ pounds.

(a) 25   (b) 50   (c) 75   (d) 100

44. Given: On a circuit where a grounding means does not exist, a nongrounding-type receptacle is replaced with a ground-fault circuit-interrupter-type (GFCI) receptacle which supplies no other receptacles. This new GFCI receptacle shall be marked ____.

(a) "Not Grounded"   (b) "GFCI Protected"
(c) "No Equipment Ground"   (d) "No Grounded Conductor"

45. Plate electrodes shall be installed not less than ____ below the surface of the earth.

(a) 12"   (b) 2 1/2'   (c) 36"   (d) 42"

46. For dwelling units, all of the following are true EXCEPT ____.

(a) outdoor outlets are permitted to be supplied through the small appliance branch circuits
(b) the outlet for kitchen refrigeration equipment may be supplied by an individual 15 amp branch circuit
(c) bathroom receptacles shall be supplied by a 20 amp branch circuit which shall have no other outlets
(d) the clothes washer shall be supplied by a 20 amp branch circuit and outlets outside the laundry area are NOT permitted on this circuit

47. In a recreational vehicle park, tent sites equipped with only 20 ampere supply facilities shall be calculated on the basis of ___ per site.

(a) 180 va   (b) 300 va   (c) 360 va   (d) 600 va

48. Where GFCI protection is located in the power supply cord for an outdoor portable sign, the ground-fault circuit interrupter shall be located within ___ inches of the attachment plug.

(a) 6
(b) 12
(c) 18
(d) 24

49. Illumination shall be provided for working spaces containing battery systems. The lighting outlets shall not be controlled by automatic means only. Additional lighting outlets shall not be required where the work space is illuminated by an adjacent light source. The location of luminaires shall not ____.

I. expose personnel to energized battery components while performing maintenance on the luminaires in the battery space
II. create a hazard to the battery upon failure of the luminaire

(a) I only   (b) II only   (c) both I and II   (d) neither I nor II

50. Given: A metal underground water pipe is used as a grounding electrode and used to bond other electrodes together. The grounding electrode conductor is connected to the water pipe on the interior of the building. The connection of the grounding electrode conductor to the interior water pipe shall be made a maximum of ___ feet from the point where the water pipe enters the building.

(a) 3   (b) 5   (c) 8   (d) 10

2020

JOURNEYMAN
OPEN
BOOK
EXAM #7

50 QUESTIONS
TIME LIMIT - 2 HOURS

TIME SPENT ☐ **MINUTES**

SCORE ☐ %

JOURNEYMAN OPEN BOOK EXAM #7   Two Hour Time Limit

1. A 4-conductor, #12 Type SO flexible cord is used on a single-phase, 120/240 volt circuit. One conductor is a grounded neutral and one of the conductors is the equipment grounding. The allowable ampacity of the cord is ____ amperes.

(a) 15 (b) 20 (c) 25 (d) 30

2. Fixture wires shall not be smaller than ____ copper.

(a) #22 (b) #18 (c) #16 (d) #14

3. The maximum fixture weight that may be supported by the screw shell of a lampholder is ____ pounds.

(a) 2 (b) 3 (c) 5 (d) 6

4. A communication circuit run underground in a raceway, handhole or manhole containing electric light or power conductors shall be in a section separated from such conductors by means of ____.

(a) metallic partitions
(b) concrete
(c) a partition of 12" of air space
(d) a partition of nonmetallic conduit

5. The interiors of paint spray booths are considered ____.

(a) Class I, Division 1
(b) Class I, Division 2
(c) Class II, Division 1
(d) Class II, Division 2

6. Where a power-supply cord is used for a mobile home, the rating of the attachment plug cap and corresponding receptacle shall be ____ amperes.

(a) 30 (b) 35 (c) 40 (d) 50

7. Commercial buildings and commercial occupancies accessible to pedestrians shall be provided with not less than one outlet for sign or outline lighting use. The outlet shall be supplied by a ____ ampere branch circuit which supplies no other load.

(a) 15 (b) 20 (c) 25 (d) 30

8. A 240 volt to ground overhead service cable shall have a minimum clearance to a swimming pool diving platform of ____.

(a) 14.5'   (b) 17'   (c) 22.5'   (d) 25'

9. Aluminum cable trays shall not be used as equipment grounding conductors for circuits with ground-fault protection above ____ amperes.

(a) 600   (b) 800   (c) 1200   (d) 2000

10. Conductors of light and power systems of 1000 volts or less may occupy the same enclosure, without regard to whether the individual circuits are AC or DC, only where all conductors are ____.

(a) insulated for the maximum of 300 volts
(b) insulated for the maximum temperature within the enclosure
(c) insulated for the maximum voltage of any conductor within the enclosure
(d) none of the above

11. Of the types of conductors listed below, ____ is not permitted for use in wet locations.

(a) RHH   (b) XHHW   (c) THWN   (d) MI cable

12. Where direct buried conductors or cables emerge from the ground, they shall be protected by enclosures or raceways. In no case shall the protection be required to exceed ____ below finished grade.

(a) 12"   (b) 18"   (c) 24"   (d) 30"

13. The National Electrical Code defines continuous load as a load where the ____ current is expected to continue for three hours or more.

(a) continuous   (b) minimum   (c) maximum   (d) normal

14. Switches and circuit breakers used as switches shall be so installed that the center of the grip of the operation handle be not more than ____ above the floor.

(a) 5'   (b) 5' 6"   (c) 6' 6"   (d) 6' 7"

15. After a capacitor, 600 volts, nominal, and under, is disconnected from the source of supply, the residual voltage of the capacitor shall be reduced 50 volts or less within ____.

(a) 20 seconds
(b) 30 seconds
(c) 45 seconds
(d) 60 seconds

16. An insulated conductor used within a switchboard or switchgear shall be ____.

(a) Listed
(b) flame retardant
(c) rated not less than the voltage applied to it and to other conductors with which it may come into contact
(d) all of the above

17. The maximum length of a flexible cord used for a 240 volt room air conditioner is ____ feet.

(a) 3 (b) 4 (c) 6 (d) 10

18. Copper to aluminum snap switches are abbreviated as ____.

(a) CU/ALM (b) CO/AL (c) CU/AL (d) CO/ALR

19. A general-use switch rated at twice the full-load current shall be permitted as a disconnecting means for stationary motors rated at ____ horsepower or less.

(a) 1 1/2 (b) 2 (c) 3 (d) 7 1/2

20. Fixture studs that are not a part of outlet boxes, hickeys, tripods and crowfeet shall be made of ____.

(a) steel
(b) malleable iron
(c) other suitable material
(d) all of the above

21. #12 copper conductors which extend beyond a motor control equipment enclosure shall be permitted to be protected by the motor branch-circuit protective device if its rating is not more than ____ amperes.

(a) 25 (b) 30 (c) 50 (d) 60

22. Where nails are used to mount conductor supports for open wiring on insulators, they shall not be smaller than ____.

(a) 6d (b) 8d (c) 10d (d) 16c

23. Boxes that enclose utilization equipment supplied by #12 or #10 conductors shall have an internal depth that is not less than ____.

(a) 1/2" (b) 3/4" (c) 15/16" (d) 1 3/16"

24. Which type of cable shall be permitted to be securely supported at intervals not exceeding 6 feet?

(a) Armored cable.
(b) Concealed knob and tube wiring.
(c) Mineral-insulated metal sheathed cable.
(d) None of the above.

25. #12 NMC is fastened 1/2" from a nonmetallic box. The cable shall not require additional support within the box if the box is not larger than _____.

(a) 2" x 3"
(b) 2 1/4" x 4"
(c) 1 1/4" x 4 11/16"
(d) 2 1/8" x 4 11/16"

26. Bending of nonmetallic sheathed cable shall not be less than _____ the radius of the inner edge of the cable.

(a) 2 times the diameter of   **(b) 3 times the circumference of**
(c) 4 times the circumference of   **(d) 5 times the diameter of**

27. The individual conductors in a cablebus shall be supported not greater than _____ for vertical runs.

(a) 18"   (b) 3'   (c) 6'   (d) 12'

28. Type UF cable feeder conductor, where buried in the earth and not subject to any specific locations, shall be buried a minimum of _____.

(a) 6"   (b) 12"   (c) 1 1/2'   (d) 2'

29. Disregarding exceptions, wireways shall not contain more than _____ current-carrying conductors at any cross section of the wireway.

(a) 8   (b) 12   (c) 20   (d) 30

30. The ampacity of Type UF cable shall be that of _____ conductors.

(a) 60°C   (b) 75°C   (c) 85°C   (d) 90°C

31. Liquidtight flexible metal conduit may be used in _____.

(a) 5" trade size
(b) 4 1/2" trade size
(c) areas that are subject to physical damage
(d) areas that are both exposed and concealed

32. The total number of quarter bends allowed in one run of rigid nonmetallic conduit shall not exceed
_____.

(a) 3   (b) 4   (c) 6   (d) 8

33. Where rigid metal conduit is threaded in the field, a cutting die with ____ taper per foot shall be used.

(a) 1/4"   (b) 3/8"   (c) 5/8"   (d) 3/4"

34. Service conductors installed in a building shall be considered outside of the building if installed in a raceway enclosed by ____.

(a) 3/4" exterior grade plywood
(b) 5/8" fire rated gypsum board
(c) 2" of concrete
(d) none of the above

35. Where conductors are run in parallel in multiple raceways, the equipment grounding conductor shall be ____.

(a) run in parallel in each raceway
(b) run outside the raceways
(c) run in isolated raceways
(d) the same size as the circuit conductors

36. The screw shell of a plug-type fuse holder shall be connected to the ____ side of the circuit.

(a) line   (b) load   (c) grounded   (d) neutral

37. A grounding electrode conductor shall be permitted to be run along the surface of a building without protection if it is stapled to the building and free from exposure to physical damage, and is not smaller than ____.

(a) #8   (b) #6   (c) #4   (d) #2

38. Where an objectable flow of current occurs over a grounding conductor due to the use of multiple grounds, to correct the situation ____.

(a) increase the size of the grounding conductor
(b) change the locations of the grounding connections
(c) additional grounding connections shall be installed to take care of the overflow
(d) all of the above

39. A room air conditioner rated 3-phase or rated over 250 volts shall be connected ____.

(a) directly to a wiring method recognized in Chapter 3
(b) with a grounding plug
(c) with a 3-prong attachment plug
(d) with a 4-prong attachment plug

40. The minimum size conductor for bonding metallic parts of a swimming pool structure is ____ solid copper insulated, covered or bare.

(a) #10   (b) #8   (c) #6   (d) #4

41. The term "cabled" refers to a manufacturing process of twisting single conductors together and may also be referred to as ____.

(a) connected   (b) grouped   (c) plexed   (d) having continuity

42. All receptacles installed on 15 or 20 ampere branch circuits shall be of the ____ type.

(a) grounding   (b) nongrounding   (c) isolated ground   (d) GFCI

43. Individual open conductors and cables other than service entrance cables shall not be installed less than ____ feet from grade level.

(a) 8   (b) 10   (c) 15   (d) 18

44. Two-wire circuits of two or more ungrounded conductors shall be permitted to be tapped from the ungrounded conductors of circuits having ____.

(a) grounding conductors
(b) grounded neutral conductors
(c) both (a) and (b)
(d) neither (a) nor (b)

45. Disregarding any exceptions, the total connected load on fixed electric space heating loads shall be computed at ____.

(a) 70%   (b) 75%   (c) 100%   (d) 125%

46. Every dining room of a dwelling requires receptacle outlets be installed so that no point along the floor line in any wall space is more than ____ feet, measured horizontally, from an outlet.

(a) 6   (b) 8   (c) 10   (d) 12

47. Guest rooms and suites that are provided with ____ shall have branch circuits and outlets installed to meet the rules for dwelling units.

(a) electric heat   (b) air conditioning
(c) permanent provisions for cooking   (d) electric appliances

48. When only one receptacle for non-motorized equipment is installed on an individual branch circuit with a 30 ampere rating, the receptacle shall have a current rating of ____ amperes.

(a) 15   (b) 20   (c) 30   (d) 40

49. A branch circuit consisting of two or more ungrounded conductors having a potential difference between them and an identified grounded conductor having equal potential difference between it and each ungrounded conductor of the system is called ____ branch circuit.

(a) a general-purpose
(b) a multi-wire
(c) an individual
(d) an appliance

50. Ferrous raceways, boxes, fittings, etc., shall not be used outdoors or in wet locations if protected solely by ____.

(a) zinc
(b) PVC
(c) cadmium
(d) enamel

2020

JOURNEYMAN
OPEN
BOOK
EXAM #8

50 QUESTIONS
TIME LIMIT - 2 HOURS

TIME SPENT ☐ **MINUTES**

SCORE ☐ %

JOURNEYMAN OPEN BOOK EXAM #8   Two Hour Time Limit

1. For voltage of 1000 or less, individual open service conductors in dry locations should be separated by ____.

(a) 4 1/2"   (b) 3 1/2"   (c) 4"   (d) 2 1/2"

2. Where motors are provided with terminal housing, the housing shall be ____ and of substantial construction.

I. plastic   II. metal

(a) I only   (b) II only   (c) both I and II   (d) neither I nor II

3. A 1000 watt incandescent lamp shall have a ____ base.

(a) mogul   (b) standard   (c) admedium   (d) copper

4. Boxes that enclose utilization equipment that projects more than 1 7/8" rearward from the mounting plane of the box shall have a depth that is not less than the depth of the equipment plus ____.

(a) 1/4"   (b) 1/2"   (c) 7/8"   (d) 15/16"

5. Ground-fault circuit protection for personnel is required for all 120v single-phase, 15 and 20 ampere receptacles that are installed in a dwelling unit ____.

(a) attic   (b) garage   (c) bedroom   (d) living room

6. For dwelling unit(s), the computed floor area shall not include ____.

I. carports   II. garages   III. bathrooms   IV. open porches

(a) II and IV only   (b) I, III and IV only   (c) I, II and IV only   (d) I, II, III and IV

7. Which of the following is **not** true concerning the optional method for a dwelling unit?

(a) **The optional method of calculation is permitted if the service-entrance conductors have an ampacity of 200 or greater.**
(b) **The neutral would be determined by section 220.61.**
(c) **A demand of 40% of the nameplate rating(s) of electric space heating of four or more separately controlled units can be applied.**
(d) **A demand of 65% of the nameplate rating(s) of central electric space heating can be applied.**

8. Bonding all piping and ____ within the premises will provide additional safety.

(a) water heaters   (b) pumps   (c) metal air ducts   (d) none of these

9. Finished ceilings containing heating cables shall be permitted to be covered with ____.

I. wallpaper   II. plastic   III. paint   IV. wood

(a) I or III   (b) III or IV   (c) I, III or IV   (d) I, II, III or IV

10. Metal-enclosed busways over 600v shall be installed so that ____ from induced circulating currents in any adjacent metallic parts will not be hazardous to personnel or constitute a fire hazard.

(a) stray currents   (b) magnetic flux   (c) the impedance   (d) temperature rise

11. The largest conductor permitted in 3/8" flexible conduit is ____.

(a) #12   (b) #16   (c) #14   (d) #10

12. AC - DC general use snap switches may be used for control of inductive loads not exceeding ____ of the rating at the voltage.

(a) 50%   (b) 80%   (c) 100%   (d) 70%

13. No point along the floor line in any useable wall space in a dwelling may be more than ____ feet from an outlet.

(a) 6   (b) 6 1/2   (c) 8   (d) 10

14. ____ conductors shall be used for wiring on fixture chains and other moveable parts.

(a) Solid   (b) Covered   (c) Insulated   (d) Stranded

15. Overhead service drop conductors shall have a horizontal clearance not less than ____ feet from a pool.

(a) 8   (b) 10   (c) 15   (d) 20

16. The Code rules and provisions are enforced by ____.

(a) the electric utility company that provides the power
(b) the U.S. government
(c) government bodies exercising legal jurisdiction over electrical installations
(d) U.L.

17. Where permissible, the demand factor applied to that portion of the unbalanced neutral feeder load in excess of 200 amps is _____ percent.

(a) 40   (b) 80   (c) 70   (d) 125

18. Panelboards equipped with snap switches rated at 30 amps or less, shall have overcurrent protection not in excess of _____ amps.

(a) 150   (b) 300   (c) 100   (d) 200

19. For a feeder rated 100 through 400 amps, the feeder conductors supplying the entire load associated with a one-family dwelling, or the feeder conductors supplying the entire load associated with an individual dwelling unit in a two-family or multifamily dwelling, shall be permitted to have an ampacity not less than _____% of the feeder rating.

(a) 83   (b) 75   (c) 70   (d) 50

20. Parts that must be removed for lamp replacement shall be _____.

I. insulated   II. hinged   III. held captive

(a) I only   (b) II or III   (c) II only   (d) I, II or III

21. Flexible cord shall be permitted _____.

I. to facilitate the removal or disconnection of appliances
II. for connection of appliances to prevent the transmission of noise

(a) I only   (b) II only   (c) both I or II   (d) neither I nor II

22. Messenger wires used to support festoon wiring shall **not** be attached to any _____.

I. plumbing equipment   II. downspout   III. fire escape

(a) I only   (b) II only   (c) III only   (d) I, II and III

23. Flexible cords shall be connected to devices and to fittings so that tension will not be transmitted to joints or terminal screws. This shall be accomplished by _____.

(a) using support or strain-relief fittings
(b) winding with tape
(c) knot in cord
(d) all of these

24. Service heads for service conductors shall be _____.

(a) raintight   (b) weatherproof   (c) rainproof   (d) watertight

25. Open conductors run individually as service drops shall be _____.

I. insulated   II. bare   III. covered

(a) I only   (b) II only   (c) III only   (d) I or III

26. What length of nipple may utilize the 60% conductor fill?

(a) 12"   (b) 18"   (c) 24"   (d) all of these

27. A one-family dwelling unit that is at grade level shall have _____ outdoors.

(a) one receptacle at the back   (b) one receptacle at the front
(c) two receptacles at the back   (d) one receptacle at front and one at the back

28. The largest standard cartridge fuse rating is _____ amps.

(a) 6000   (b) 1200   (c) 1000   (d) 600

29. Surface metal raceways when extended through walls or floors must be in _____ lengths.

(a) 8 foot   (b) 3 foot   (c) 5 foot   (d) none of these

30. Conductors shall be _____ unless otherwise provided in the Code.

(a) lead   (b) stranded   (c) copper   (d) aluminum

31. What is the minimum size fixture wire?

(a) #16   (b) #18   (c) #20   (d) #22

32. The number of square feet that each plate electrode should present to the soil is _____ sq.ft.

(a) 4   (b) 3   (c) 2   (d) 1

33. Lighting systems operating at 30 volts or less shall be supplied from a maximum ___ ampere branch circuit.

(a) 15   (b) 20   (c) 25   (d) 30

34. The path to ground from circuits, equipment, and conductor enclosures shall ____.

I. have sufficiently low impedance to limit the voltage to ground and to facilitate the operation of the circuit protective devices in the circuit
II. shall be capable of safely carrying the maximum fault current likely to be imposed on it
III. be permanent and electrically continuous

(a) I only   (b) II only   (c) III only   (d) I, II and III

35. Receptacles on construction sites shall not be installed on branch circuits which ____.

(a) are over 15 amps   (b) supply temporary lighting
(c) are supplied with cords   (d) none of these

36. Where screws are used to mount knobs, or where nails or screws are used to mount cleats, they shall be of a length sufficient to penetrate the wood to a depth to at least ____ the height of the knob and the full thickness of the cleat.

(a) twice   (b) one-half   (c) one-quarter   (d) 3 times

37. FCC cable shall consist of ____ flat copper conductors, one of which shall be an equipment grounding conductor.

I. three   II. four   III. five

(a) I only   (b) II only   (c) III only   (d) I, II or III

38. The combined voltage drop of feeder and branch-circuit conductors shall not exceed ____ for circuits of sensitive electronic equipment.

(a) 2.5%   (b) 3%   (c) 4%   (d) 5%

39. When counting the number of conductors in a box, a conductor running through the box is counted as ____ conductor(s).

(a) one   (b) two   (c) zero   (d) none of these

40. You may install ____ #8 TW conductors in a 1 1/2" E.M.T. conduit.

(a) 13   (b) 22   (c) 18   (d) none of these

41. Service cables mounted in contact with a building shall be supported at intervals not exceeding ____ feet.

(a) 10   (b) 3   (c) 2 1/2   (d) 4 1/2

42. Expansion joints and telescoping sections of raceways shall be made electrically continuous by equipment ____ or other means approved for the purpose.

(a) grounding conductors   (b) grounded conductor
(c) bonding jumpers   (d) none of these

43. Conductors ____ and larger shall be stranded when installed in raceways.

(a) #10   (b) #8   (c) #6   (d) #4

44. For the kitchen small appliance branch circuit in a dwelling, the Code requires not less than which of the following?

(a) two 20 amp circuits   (b) one 15 amp circuit
(c) two 15 amp circuits   (d) one 20 amp circuit

45. In combustible walls or ceilings, the front edge of an outlet box or fitting may set back of the finished surface ____.

(a) 1/4"   (b) 1/8"   (c) 1/2"   (d) shall be flush

46. Lighting fixtures mounted on walls shall be installed with the top of the fixture lens at least ____ below the normal water level of the pool.

(a) 15"   (b) 3'   (c) 18"   (c) 12"

47. Which of the following may not be used in damp or wet locations?

(a) type AC armored cable   (b) open wiring
(c) electrical metal tubing   (d) rigid metal conduit

48. A grounding electrode conductor subject to severe physical damage shall be protected when:

I. #4 or larger   II. #6 or larger

(a) I only   (b) II only   (c) both I and II   (d) neither I nor II

49. Which of the following is **not** a standard size fuse?

(a) 110 amp   (b) 601 amp   (c) 75 amp   (d) 125 amp

50. Where the number of current-carrying conductors in a raceway or cable exceeds three, or where single conductors or multiconductor cables are installed without maintaining spacing for a continuous length longer than ____ and are not installed in raceways, the allowable ampacity of each conductor shall be reduced as shown in Table 310.15(B)(3)(a).

(a) 12"   (b) 18"   (c) 24"   (d) 30"

2020

JOURNEYMAN
OPEN
BOOK
EXAM #9

50 QUESTIONS
TIME LIMIT - 2 HOURS

TIME SPENT ☐ MINUTES

SCORE ☐ %

1. What is the area of square inches for a #14 RHW without outer covering?

(a) .0135   (b) .0209   (c) .0230   (d) .0327

2. The ampacities provided by this section do not take ____ into consideration.

(a) insulation   (b) AWG   (c) CMA   (d) voltage drop

3. Flexible cords shall be secured to the undersides of showcases so that ____.

I.   the free lead at the end of a group of showcases will have a female fitting not extending beyond the case
II. wiring will not be exposed to physical damage
III. a separation between cases not in excess of 2", nor more than 12" between the first case and the supply receptacle will be assured

(a) I only   (b) II only   (c) III only   (d) I, II and III

4. All heating elements that are ____, and part of an appliance shall be legibly marked with the ratings in volts and amperes, or in volts and watts, or with the manufacturer's part number.

I. replaceable in the field   II. rated over one ampere   III. over 150 volts

(a) II and III   (b) I and II   (c) I and III   (d) I, II and III

5. All conductors in a multiwire branch circuit shall originate from the same ____.

(a) feeder   (b) service   (c) panelboard   (d) receptacle

6. The parallel conductors in each phase or neutral shall ____.

I.   have the same insulation type and conductor material
II. be the same size in cma
III. be the same length and be terminated in the same manner

(a) I only   (b) II only   (c) III only   (d) I, II and III

7. Where nails are used to mount knobs, they shall not be smaller than ____ penny.

(a) 6   (b) 8   (c) 10   (d) 16

8. In computing the load of fluorescent fixtures, the computation shall be based on the _____ of the fixture.

(a) wattage of the ballast   (b) wattage of the lamps
(c) total ampere rating   (d) none of these

9. Open conductors on insulators must be covered when they are within _____ feet of a building.

(a) 10   (b) 12   (c) 15   (d) 25

10. No grounded interior wiring shall be electrically connected to a supply system unless the supply system contains a corresponding conductor which is _____.

(a) shielded   (b) bonded   (c) grounded   (d) low-voltage

11. All splices, joints and free ends of conductors are required to be covered with an insulation _____ the conductor.

(a) as thick as   (b) equivalent to   (c) thicker than   (d) larger than

12. Appliances fastened in place, connected to branch circuits with other loads shall not exceed _____ percent of the branch circuit rating.

(a) 40   (b) 50   (c) 70   (d) 80

13. Multioutlet assembly may be used _____.

(a) where concealed   (b) in storage battery rooms
(c) in dry locations   (d) in hoistways

14. A multiwire branch-circuit may supply _____.

(a) only one utilization equipment
(b) where all ungrounded conductors are opened simultaneously
(c) both (a) and (b)
(d) neither (a) nor (b)

15. Which of the following is **not** required on a motor nameplate?

(a) watts   (b) horsepower   (c) manufacturer's identification   (d) voltage

16. Conductors shall **not** be installed in locations where the operating temperature will exceed that specified for the type of _____ used.

(a) connectors   (b) protection   (c) insulation   (d) wiring

17. Where a service mast is used for the support of service drop conductors, it shall be of adequate strength or be supported by _____.

(a) studs   (b) braces or guys   (c) rigid conduit   (d) R.C. beams

18. Permanent ladders or stairways shall be provided to give safe access to the working space around electric equipment over 600 volts installed on _____ or in attic or roof rooms or spaces.

I. balconies   II. mezzanine floors   III. platforms

(a) I only   (b) II only   (c) III only   (d) I, II and III

19. The definition of a bathroom is an area including a _____ with one or more of the following: a toilet, a tub, or a shower.

(a) water heater   (b) sliding glass door   (c) spa   (d) basin

20. Open conductors shall be supported on glass or porcelain-knobs, _____.

I. strain insulators   II. brackets   III. racks

(a) I only   (b) II only   (c) III only   (d) I, II or III

21. Which of the following is **true** concerning type NM cable?

(a) it may be installed where exposed to corrosive fumes
(b) it may be fished in air voids in masonry block or tile walls
(c) it may be embedded in masonry, concrete, or plaster
(d) it may be covered with plaster, adobe, or similar finish

22. At least one 125-volt, single-phase, 15- or 20-ampere-rated receptacle outlet shall be installed within _____ of the electrical service equipment requiring servicing.

(a) 6'   (b) 10'   (c) 25'   (d) 50'

23. In dwelling units and guest rooms of hotels and motels, overcurrent devices shall not be located in ___.

(a) hallways   (b) bathrooms   (c) bedrooms   (d) kitchens

24. Means shall be provided to disconnect the _____ of all fixed electric space heating equipment from all ungrounded conductors.

I.   heater
II. motor
III. motor controllers
IV. supplementary overcurrent protective devices

(a) I and II only   (b) II and IV only   (c) I and IV only   (d) I, III and IV only

25. The grounded conductor (#1100 kcmil or less) brought to the service, shall _____ the minimum size grounding electrode conductor, sized from Table 250.66.

(a) not be more than   (b) not be less than   (c) be twice   (d) none of these

26. Open motors with commutators shall be located so sparks cannot reach adjacent combustible material, but this _____.

(a) is only required for over 600 volts
(b) shall not prohibit these motors on wooden floors
(c) does not prohibit these motors from Class I locations
(d) none of these

27. The maximum number of overcurrent devices that may be installed in a lighting panel is _____.

(a) 24   (b) 36   (c) 42   (d) 48

28. Where an AC system operating at _____ volts or less is grounded at any point, the grounded conductor shall be run to each service.

(a) 300   (b) 600   (c) 1000   (d) 1500

29. General-use snap switch suitable only for use on alternating-current circuits for controlling _____.

I.   resistive and inductive loads not exceeding the ampere rating of the switch
II. tungsten-filament lamp loads not exceeding the ampere rating of the switch
III. motor loads not exceeding 80% of the ampere rating of the switch

(a) I only   (b) III only   (c) I and II only   (d) I, II and III

30. Type FCC cable wiring system is designed for installations under _____.

(a) tile   (b) carpet   (c) carpet squares   (d) concrete

31. A residence has a front entrance on the north side of the house along with an attached garage with an 8' wide door, also a back entrance door on the south side of the house. How many lighting outlets are required for these outdoor entrances?

(a) 1 (b) 2 (c) 3 (d) none of these

32. Where required, drawings for feeder installations must be submitted before ____.

(a) completion of installation   (b) beginning of installation
(c) the use of feeders   (d) the use of branch-circuits

33. Nonmetallic sheath cable: If the attic is **not** accessible by stairs or permanent ladder, the cable needs to be protected only within ____ feet of a scuttle hole.

(a) 2 (b) 3 (c) 6 (d) 10

34. Transformer enclosures which extend directly to underwater pool light forming shells shall be provided with ____ grounding terminals.

(a) one
(b) two
(c) the number of conduit entries plus one
(d) a grounding bus for

35. Conductors other than service conductors shall not be installed in the same service raceway or service-entrance cable except ____.

I. grounding electrode conductors
II. load management control conductors having overcurrent protection

(a) I only (b) II only (c) both I and II (d) neither I nor II

36. A #6 copper conductor with one end bonded to the service raceway or equipment and with ____ inches or more of the other end made accessible on the outside wall of the dwelling is an example of the approved means for the external connection of a bonding, or grounding conductor to the service raceway or equipment.

(a) 6 (b) 12 (c) 24 (d) 36

37. Surge arresters shall be permitted to be located ____ and shall be made inaccessible to unqualified persons unless listed for installation in accessible location.

I. outdoors II. indoors

(a) I only (b) II only (c) either I or II (d) neither I nor II

38. Which of the following is NOT true concerning temporary wiring?

(a) All lamps shall be protected by a suitable fixture or guard.
(b) Handle ties are permitted to disconnect multiwire branch circuits.
(c) Tests shall be performed on cords and receptacles and plugs for correct attachment to the equipment grounding conductor.
(d) Temporary power for Christmas decorative lighting shall not exceed 60 days.

39. Where single conductors or multiconductor cables are stacked or bundled longer than _____ without maintaining spacing and are not installed in raceways, the ampacity of each conductor shall be reduced.

(a) 12"   (b) 18"   (c) 20"   (d) 2'

40. Boxes that enclose equipment supplied by #14 or smaller conductors shall have a depth that is not less than _____.

(a) 1/2"   (b) 7/8"   (c) 15/16"   (d) 1 1/16"

41. Where buildings exceed 3 stories or 50 feet in height, overhead lines shall be arranged, where practicable, so that a clear space (or zone) of at least _____ feet wide will be left either adjacent to the buildings or beginning not over 8 feet from them to facilitate the raising of ladders when necessary for fire fighting.

(a) 4   (b) 6   (c) 8   (d) 10

42. For uniform application of Articles 210, 215 and 220, a nominal voltage of _____ shall be used in computing the ampere load on a conductor.

(a) 110/220   (b) 115/230   (c) 120/240   (d) 125/250

43. When balancing a 3-wire circuit, single-phase 230/115 volt, the neutral conductor _____.

(a) is used only for grounding   (b) should carry the unbalance
(c) should carry the sum   (d) none of these

44. Range hoods shall be permitted to be cord-and-plug connected with a flexible cord identified as suitable for use on range hoods if the length of the cord is not less than _____ and not over _____.

(a) 12" - 24"   (b) 18" x 18"   (c) 16" - 36"   (d) 18" - 36"

45. When an outlet from an underfloor raceway is discontinued, the circuit conductors supplying the outlet ____.

(a) may be handled like abandoned outlets on loop wiring
(b) may be reinsulated
(c) may be spliced
(d) shall be removed from the raceway

46. If festoon lighting exceeds ____ feet, the conductors shall be supported by messenger wire.

(a) 15   (b) 20   (c) 25   (d) 40

47. A single receptacle shall have a rating of ____ percent of the branch-circuit rating.

(a) 70   (b) 80   (c) 100   (d) 125

48. An auxiliary gutter shall not extend a greater distance than ____ feet.

(a) 10   (b) 30   (c) 50   (d) 75

49. Solid dielectric insulated conductors operated above 2000 volts in permanent installations shall have ozone-resistant insulation and shall be ____.

(a) covered   (b) protected   (c) shielded   (d) surface mounted

50. Conductor sizes are given in AWG and ____.

(a) length   (b) numbers   (c) CM   (d) insulation

2020

JOURNEYMAN
OPEN
BOOK
EXAM #10

50 QUESTIONS
TIME LIMIT - 2 HOURS

TIME SPENT ☐ **MINUTES**

SCORE ☐ %

JOURNEYMAN OPEN BOOK EXAM #10   **Two Hour Time Limit**

1. In dwelling units and guest rooms of hotels, motels, and similar occupancies, the voltage shall not exceed 120 volts, between conductors that supply the terminals of ___.

I.   cord and plug connected loads 1440 volt amperes or less
II. cord and plug connected loads 1440 volt amperes or less, or less than 1/8 horsepower
III. luminaires

(a) I only   (b) I and II only   (c) I and III only   (d) I, II and III

2. Unless identified for use in the operating environment, no conductors or equipment shall be located in ____ having a deteriorating effect on the conductors or equipment.

I. damp or wet locations   II. where exposed to gases, fumes, vapors, liquids, etc.

(a) I only   (b) II only   (c) both I and II   (d) neither I nor II

3. Transformers of more than ____ kva rating shall be installed in a transformer room of fire-resistant construction.

(a) 35,000   (b) 87 1/2   (c) 112 1/2   (d) 75

4. Conduit bodies shall have a cross-sectional area at least ____ that of the largest conduit to which they are connected, #6 conductors and smaller.

(a) 100%   (b) twice   (c) 40%   (d) 75%

5. Type FCC cable shall be clearly and durably marked on both sides at intervals of not more than ____.

(a) 18"   (b) 2'   (c) 30"   (d) 3'

6. A system or circuit conductor that is intentionally grounded is a ____ conductor.

(a) grounding   (b) unidentified   (c) grounded   (d) none of these

7. The area of square inches for a #1/0 bare conductor is ____.

(a) .087   (b) .109   (c) .137   (d) .173

8. ____ plugs driven into holes in masonry, concrete, plaster, or similar materials shall not be used.

(a) Metal   (b) Plastic   (c) Leather   (d) Wooden

9. Thermal insulation shall not be installed within _____ inches of the recessed fixture enclosure.

(a) 3   (b) 4   (c) 6   (d) 8

10. Service entrance cables, where subject to physical damage, shall be protected in which of the following?

I. EMT   II. IMC   III. RMC

(a) III only   (b) II and III   (c) I, II and III   (d) I and III

11. Overhead conductors, not supported by messenger wires, for festoon lighting shall not be smaller than _____.

(a) #14   (b) #12   (c) #10   (d) #8

12. Which of the following is a standard size fuse?

(a) 75   (b) 95   (c) 601   (d) 1500

13. Where ungrounded conductors are increased in size, equipment grounding conductors, where required, shall be adjusted proportionally according to _____.

(a) diameter   (b) cross section area   (c) circular mil area   (d) circumference

14. Voltage between the hot (ungrounded) conductors on FCC cable shall not exceed _____ volts.

(a) 50   (b) 300   (c) 150   (d) 600

15. The work space required by the code for electrical equipment shall not be used for ___.

I. passageway   II. storage   III. panelboards

(a) I only   (b) II only   (c) III only   (d) I and II only

16. Cablebus framework, where _____, shall be permitted as the equipment grounding conductor for branch circuits and feeders.

(a) bonded as required by Article 250
(b) welded
(c) protected
(d) galvanized

17. According to the Code, metal enclosures for grounding electrode conductors shall be ____.

(a) not permitted   **(b) one continuous length**
(c) rigid conduit   **(d) none of these**

18. Feeders containing a common neutral shall be permitted to supply ____.

I. 2 or 3 sets of 3-wire feeders   II. 2 sets of 4-wire or 5-wire feeders

(a) I only   **(b) II only**   **(c) either I or II**   **(d) neither I nor II**

19. Operation at loads, and intervals of time, both of which may be subject to wide variation is the definition of ____.

(a) varying duty   **(b) demand factor**
(c) cycle   **(d) periodic duty**

20. Underground cable and conductors installed under a building shall be in a ____ that is extended beyond the outside walls of the building.

(a) sleeve   **(b) duct bank**   **(c) gutter**   **(d) raceway**

21. Where NM cable is used, the cable assembly, including the sheath, shall extend into the box no less than ____.

(a) 1/2"   **(b) 3/4"**   **(c) 1/4"**   **(d) 1"**

22. The current carried continuously in bare copper bars in sheet metallic auxiliary gutters shall not exceed ____ amperes per square inch.

(a) 560   **(b) 700**   **(c) 800**   **(d) 1000**

23. Under the optional method of calculation for a single-family dwelling, all "other load" beyond the initial 10 kva is to be assessed at ____ percent.

(a) 40   **(b) 50**   **(c) 60**   **(d) 75**

24. Metal conduit and metal piping within ____ feet of the inside walls of the pool and that are not separated from the pool by a permanent barrier are required to be bonded.

(a) 4   **(b) 5**   **(c) 8**   **(d) 10**

25. Suitable covers shall be installed on all boxes, fittings, and similar enclosures to prevent accidental contact with ____ parts or physical damage to parts or insulation. Over 600v nominal.

(a) energized   (b) mechanical
(c) electrical   (d) none of these

26. A unit of an electrical system which is intended to carry but not utilize electric energy would be a ____.

I. light bulb   II. snap switch   III. device   IV. receptacle

(a) I only   (b) III only   (c) I, II and IV   (d) II, III, and IV

27. Type ____ cable is a factory assembly of one or more conductors, each individually insulated and enclosed in a metallic sheath of interlocking tape, or a smooth or corrugated tube.

(a) MI   (b) AC   (c) MC   (d) MV

28. ____ boxes shall not be used where conduits or connectors requiring the use of locknuts or bushings are to be connected to the side of the box.

(a) Round   (b) Shallow   (c) Device   (d) Gang

29. Lampholders installed over highly combustible material shall be of the ____ type.

(a) porcelain   (b) low smoke   (c) switched   (d) unswitched

30. Nonconductive coatings (such as paint, lacquer, and enamel) on equipment to be grounded shall be removed from threads and other contact surfaces to _____.

(a) provide a water tight joint
(b) provide a sealed joint
(c) assure good electrical continuity
(d) lower inductance

31. UF cable installed to an outdoor post light on a residential branch circuit rated 15 amps, 115 volt would require a minimum burial depth of ____ inches.

(a) 24   (b) 18   (c) 12   (d) 6

32. The ampacity of types NM and NMC cable shall be that of ____ conductors.

(a) 60° C   (b) 75° C   (c) 90° C   (d) 140° C

33. When an outlet is removed from a cellular metal floor raceway, the sections of circuit conductors supplying the outlet shall be ____.

(a) taped   (b) dead-ended   (c) shorted together   (d) removed from the raceway

34. Bored holes in wood members for cable or raceway-type wiring shall be bored so that the edge of the hole is not less than ____ from the nearest edge.

(a) 1 1/4"   (b) 1 1/8"   (c) 1 1/2"   (d) 1 1/16"

35. Where practicable, dissimilar metals in contact anywhere in the system shall be avoided to eliminate the possibility of ____.

(a) hysteresis   (b) galvanic action   (c) specific gravity   (d) resistance

36. The radius of the inner edge of any bend shall not be less than ____ times the diameter of the metallic sheath of MI cable not more than 3/4" in external diameter.

(a) 5   (b) 3   (c) 8   (d) 10

37. A 500 ampere load supplied by a 120/240v feeder requires a feeder neutral with an ampacity of ____ amps.

(a) 410   (b) 340   (c) 280   (d) 350

38. A service drop over a residential driveway shall have a minimum height of ____ feet.

(a) 10   (b) 12   (c) 15   (d) 18

39. The grounded conductors of ____ metal-sheathed cable shall be identified by distinctive marking at the terminals during the process of installation.

(a) armored cable   (b) mineral-insulated   (c) copper   (d) aluminum

40. Electric heating appliances employing resistance-type heating elements rated more than ____ amperes shall have the heating elements subdivided.

(a) 60   (b) 50   (c) 48   (d) 35

41. What is the minimum size conductor permitted for general wiring under 600 volts?

(a) #12 copper   (b) #14 aluminum   (c) #14 copper   (d) #12 aluminum

42. Class III locations are those that are hazardous because of ____.

(a) the presence of combustible dust
(b) over 8' depth of water
(c) flammable gases or vapors may be present in the air
(d) the presence of easily ignitible fibers or flyings

43. The maximum number of quarter bends in one run of EMT is ____.

(a) two   (b) four   (c) five   (d) none of these

44. The conductors, including splices and taps in metal surface raceway shall not fill the raceway to more than ____ percent of its area at that point.

(a) 75   (b) 40   (c) 38   (d) 53

45. The minimum feeder load for a 40 foot long show window is ____ va.

(a) 4000   (b) 8000   (c) 10,000   (d) none of these

46. Type MC cable shall not be used where exposed to ____ conditions.

(a) wet   (b) destructive corrosive   (c) unsafe   (d) high-heat

47. Where MI cable terminates, a ____ shall be provided immediately after stripping to prevent the entrance of moisture into the insulation.

(a) bushing   (b) connector   (c) fitting   (d) seal

48. A nipple contains four #6 THW copper current-carrying conductors. The ampacity of each conductor would be ____ amperes.

(a) 65   (b) 52   (c) 39   (d) 55

49. The DC resistance @ 167° F for a #2/0 bare aluminum conductor would be ____ ohm per thousand feet of conductor.

(a) 0.0967   (b) 0.101   (c) 0.319   (d) 0.159

50. The approximate area of square inch for a #4/0 THW aluminum building wire is ____.

(a) .3288   (b) .3904   (c) .3267   (d) .2780

2020

JOURNEYMAN OPEN BOOK EXAM #11

50 QUESTIONS
TIME LIMIT - 2 HOURS

TIME SPENT [   ] MINUTES

SCORE [   ] %

JOURNEYMAN OPEN BOOK EXAM #11   **Two Hour Time Limit**

1. A code letter D is marked on a motor nameplate. What is its locked-rotor kva per horsepower?

(a) 0 - 3.14 kva   (b) 3.15 - 3.54 kva   (c) 3.55 - 3.99 kva   (d) 4.0 - 4.49 kva

2. A 240/120v three-wire feeder is to be installed underground from a dwelling unit to a detached garage on the same property. The feeder will be fed from a 90 amp circuit breaker in the dwelling unit panelboard and installed in rigid PVC conduit to the garage. Which of the following best describes Code requirements for installation of this feeder?

(a) It must terminate in not more than six disconnecting means.
(b) It must terminate in the garage in an overcurrent device.
(c) It must have an equipment grounding conductor.
(d) It must terminate in a single disconnecting means.

3. Flexible metal conduit shall be permitted for grounding purposes if _____.

(a) the total length does not exceed 6 feet
(b) the circuit is rated at 20 amps or less
(c) it is terminated in fittings listed for grounding
(d) all of the above

4. Which of the following is NOT an approved grounding electrode?

(a) 10' of bare #4 in the bottom of a footer   **(b) 10' of buried 3/4" copper water pipe**
(c) An 8' x 1/2" stainless steel rod   **(d) An 8' x 5/8" iron ground rod**

5. The Code definition of Nacelle is _____.

(a) a French charge controller
(b) a low temperature reading
(c) an adjustment factor in France
(d) an enclosure housing the alternator of a wind turbine

6. Built-in dishwashers and trash compactors intended for dwelling use are allowed to be cord and plug connected when _____.

(a) the receptacle is located in the same space or adjacent to
(b) the cord is 3 to 4 feet long and the receptacle is accessible
(c) the receptacle is located to avoid physical damage to the cord
(d) all of the above

7. When a continuous-duty motor rated one horsepower or more, but not marked with a service factor or temperature rise, is protected by a separate overload device, the device shall be selected to trip at no more than ____ of the motor nameplate rating.

(a) 100%   (b) 110%   (c) 115%   (d) 125%

8. ____ loads can increase heat in a transformer without operating its overcurrent protective device.

(a) Continuous   (b) Ground fault   (c) Nonlinear   (d) Intermittent

9. A 24" wide by 5' long island counter top shall have receptacles installed ____.

(a) so that at least one is provided   (b) every 24"
(c) only if the owner wants them   (d) every 12"

10. Fixtures installed in recessed cavities in walls or ceilings shall be installed so that adjacent combustible material will not be subjected to temperatures in excess of ____ Celsius.

(a) 60°   (b) 90°   (c) 110°   (d) 125°

11. The installation of outside wiring on surfaces of buildings shall be permitted for circuits not over 600 volts, nominal as ____.

(a) flexible metal conduit   (b) SE cable
(c) open wiring on insulators   (d) all of these

12. All switches and circuit breakers used as switches shall be located so that the center of the operating handle is not more than ____ off the floor or platform.

(a) 6' 3"   (b) 6' 4"   (c) 6' 6"   (d) 6' 7"

13. Heating assemblies employing resistance heating elements intended to heat nonmetallic pipelines or vessels may use the factory-installed attachment plug as the disconnecting means when ____ and the voltage is 150 volts or less.

(a) it is operating at 20 amps or less
(b) it is a ground-fault protected circuit
(c) it is operating at 30 amps or less and is GFI protected
(d) it is operating at 20 amps or less and is GFI protected

14. Receptacles shall NOT be required to be tamper-resistant ____.

(a) in guest rooms
(b) in child care facilities
(c) in dwelling units non-locking type
(d) where located 5 1/2' above the floor

15. Where connected to a 30 amp branch circuit supplying one receptacle, the receptacle shall have an ampere rating equal to 30 amps and a maximum load of ____ .

(a) 12 amps   (b) 16 amps   (c) 20 amps   (d) 24 amps

16. In industrial establishments, when single conductor cable, #1/0 or larger, is installed in ladder cable tray, the maximum allowable rung spacing shall be ____.

(a) 4"   (b) 6"   (c) 9"   (d) 12"

17. Which of the following 1/2" flexible metal raceways or 1/2" liquidtight flexible metal raceways are approved equipment grounding conductors?

(a) Two feet of liquidtight flex in a 60 amp circuit.
(b) Two 36" pieces of liquidtight flex in a 20 amp circuit.
(c) Two feet of flexible metal conduit in a 30 amp circuit.
(d) Two 42" pieces of flexible metal conduit in a 20 amp circuit.

18. A 300 foot run of 800 amp busway is installed in a commercial warehouse building. The last 20' of the busway run is reduced to a bus rating of 200 amps. Which of the following best describes requirements for installation of the smaller bus?

(a) This installation meets Code requirements.
(b) It must be protected by an overcurrent device.
(c) Busway is not permitted in commercial buildings.
(d) It must be at least 1/3 the ampere rating of the larger bus.

19. The minimum illumination permitted by Code about service equipment, switchgear, panelboards, etc. operating at less than 600 volts is ____.

(a) 20 foot-candles   (b) illumination is not required
(c) 50 foot-candles   (d) no minimum illumination

20. A vertical run of 4" rigid conduit is installed to a height of 250 feet. The conduit contains four #500 kcmil THHN copper conductors. How many conductor supports are required?

(a) none   (b) 3   (c) 4   (d) 5

21. Which of the following wiring methods may be installed in notches cut into wood framing members without being protected by a steel plate 1/16" thick?

(a) **Rigid nonmetallic conduit** (b) **Armored cable**
(c) **Nonmetallic sheathed cable** (d) **Metal clad cable**

22. A recessed incandescent fixture with a solid lens is installed in the ceiling of a clothes closet. This fixture must ____.

(a) **be installed a minimum of 12" from storage space**
(b) **be installed a minimum of 6" from storage space**
(c) **be installed a minimum of 24" from storage space**
(d) **A recessed fixture is not permitted in a clothes closet**

23. For a feeder supplying household electric ranges, wall-mounted ovens, counter mounted cooking units, and electric dryers, the maximum unbalanced load shall be considered as ____ of the load on the ungrounded conductors.

(a) **60%** (b) **70%** (c) **80%** (d) **125%**

24. How many outside receptacles, accessible at grade level, are required for a single-family dwelling?

(a) **1** (b) **2** (c) **3** (d) **4**

25. The identification of the grounded conductor in a flexible cord shall be permitted to be by ____.

(a) **any color braid with contrasting tracer**
(b) **a braid finished to show a blue color**
(c) **green insulation on the conductor**
(d) **black color on the conductor**

26. In which of the following locations would nonmetallic wireway not be permitted unless marked for the use?

(a) **Where subject to corrosive vapors.** (b) **In wet locations.**
(c) **Where exposed to sunlight.** (d) **In exposed locations.**

27. A surface metal raceway enclosure providing a transition from other wiring methods shall have a means for connecting ____.

(a) **a metal box to the raceway**
(b) **a nonmetallic box to the raceway**
(c) **an ungrounded conductor to the raceway**
(d) **an equipment grounding conductor**

28. If a building is provided with two sets of service drop conductors from the utility pole, and one service drop is 120/240v for lighting and receptacle loads, and the other service is 480v to supply motor loads. How many disconnecting means are permitted for this building?

(a) one   (b) two   (c) six   (d) twelve

29. The connection point between the facilities of the serving utility and the premises wiring is called the ____.

(a) service point   (b) service equipment   (c) metering point   (d) main disconnect

30. A wet bar is installed in the family room area of a dwelling unit with a wall receptacle installed within 6' of this wet bar. Which of the following best describes Code requirements for installation of this receptacle?

(a) It is not permitted within 6' of the wet bar.
(b) No other protection is required because it is in the family room.
(c) It must have GFCI protection even though it is in the family room.
(d) GFCI protection is required only if near kitchen and bathroom sinks.

31. Nonmetallic sheathed cable, NMC, must be supported at intervals not exceeding ____.

(a) 4'   (b) 4 1/2'   (c) 6'   (d) none of these

32. Snap switches rated ____ amps or less directly connected to aluminum conductors shall be listed and marked for CO/ALR.

(a) 10   (b) 20   (c) 30   (d) any ampere rating

33. A load connected to a diversion charge controller or diversion load controller, also known as a ____ load.

(a) static   (b) varying   (c) dump   (d) excitation

34. In general, rigid metal conduit shall be ____ of each outlet box, junction box, device box, cabinet, conduit body, or other conduit termination.

(a) securely fastened within 3'   (b) supported within 3'
(c) securely fastened within 5'   (d) supported within 5'

35. Which of the following wiring methods is **not** permitted to be installed as a "Messenger supported wiring" system?

(a) Multiconductor service entrance cable   (b) Metal-clad cable
(c) Power and control tray cable   (d) Nonmetallic sheathed cable

36. A flexible cord connection is made directly to the load end terminals of a busway plug-in device. The maximum length of this cord to a tension take-up device is _____ .

 (a) 3' (b) 4' (c) 5' (d) 6'

37. When sizing a pull box for a straight pull of # 4/3 Romex, the length of the box shall not be less than _____ times the trade diameter of the raceway.

(a) 4 (b) 6 (c) 8 (d) 10

38. When installing heating cables in plaster, a minimum of _____ of nonheating lead shall be embedded in plaster along with the splice between the heating cable and the nonheating lead.

(a) 3" (b) 4" (c) 6" (d) 8"

39. After being disconnected from the source of supply, the residual voltage of a capacitor operating at 600v or less, shall be reduced to _____ volts, nominal, or less, within 60 seconds.

(a) 24 (b) 30 (c) 50 (d) 100

40. When using BX, Armored cable, it shall be secured within _____ of every junction box, cabinet or outlet box.

(a) 3" (b) 6" (c) 8" (d) 12"

41. Fixed outdoor electric deicing and snow-melting equipment shall be protected by _____.

(a) ground-fault circuit-interrupter protection for personnel
(b) ground-fault circuit-interrupter protection for equipment
(c) being installed in rigid nonmetallic conduit for protection
(d) being installed in rigid metal conduit for protection

42. Horizontal installations of nonmetallic wireways shall be supported at distances not exceeding _____ unless listed for other support intervals.

(a) 2' (b) 3' (c) 4' (d) 5'

43. A #14 THHN copper conductor is used between a motor starter and a remote stop/start station. What is the maximum size circuit breaker permitted for the motor short-circuit ground-fault protection that will also protect the #14 conductor?

(a) 10 amp (b) 15 amp (c) 45 amp (d) 60 amp

44. A fault-sensing system can be accomplished by the use of two subtractive-connected donut-type current transformers installed to sense and signal when an unbalance occurs in the line current to the autotransformer of ____ or more of the rated current.

(a) 25%   (b) 50%   (c) 70%   (d) 80%

45. A #1/0 copper insulated grounding electrode conductor is installed in electrical metallic tubing to provide support for the ground wire. The EMT extends across the ceiling of a large structure from the service entrance equipment disconnecting means to a point where the underground metal water pipe enters the structure. Which of the following best describes Code requirements for this EMT raceway?

(a) It is used only for support so nothing special is required.
(b) It is considered to be a ground so nothing else is required.
(c) The ground wire is insulated so nothing special is required.
(d) It must be electrically bonded from the service to the water pipe.

46. Equipment that is intentionally connected to earth through a low impedance connection which has sufficient current-carrying capacity to prevent buildup of voltages that may result in undue hazards is considered to be _____.

(a) a grounding electrode conductor   (b) grounded
(c) a ground-fault circuit-interrupter   (d) effectively grounded

47. Appliance outlets installed in dwelling units for specific appliances shall be located within ____ of the intended location of the appliance.

(a) 2'   (b) 4'   (c) 6'   (d) 8'

48. A 14" wide 100 amp service equipment panelboard is installed on the wall in the basement of a building. The Code requires that a space of at least ____ be maintained about this panelboard.

(a) 14"   (b) 24"   (c) 30"   (d) 36"

49. Fixed electric space heating loads shall be computed at ____ of the total connected load.

(a) 60%   (b) 80%   (c) 100%   (d) 125%

50. The maximum overcurrent device permitted to protect a 208v, 5 kw water heater connected with #8 copper is ____ amps.

(a) 25   (b) 30   (c) 35   (d) 40

2020

JOURNEYMAN
OPEN
BOOK
EXAM #12

50 QUESTIONS
TIME LIMIT - 2 HOURS

TIME SPENT [   ] MINUTES

SCORE [   ] %

JOURNEYMAN OPEN BOOK EXAM #12   **Two Hour Time Limit**

1. Where used as switches in 120 volt and 277 volt fluorescent lighting circuits, circuit breakers shall be marked ____.

(a) UL   (b) SWD   (c) AMPS   (d) VA

2. The grounding electrode conductor shall be ____ and shall be installed in one continuous length without a splice or joint.

I. solid   II. solid or stranded   III. insulated, covered or bare

(a) I only   (b) I and III   (c) I, II, III   (d) III only

3. The disconnecting means for motor circuits rated 1000v, nominal, or less, shall have an ampere rating of what percent of the motor F.L.C.?

(a) 100%   (b) 125%   (c) 115%   (d) 140%

4. Recessed portions of enclosures for flush recessed fixtures shall be spaced from combustible material by at least ____.

(a) 1/4"   (b) 3/4"   (c) 1"   (d) 1/2"

5. Where it is impracticable to locate the service head above the point of attachment, the service head location shall be permitted no further than how many feet from the point of attachment?

(a) 1'   (b) 2'   (c) 3'   (d) 4'

6. For fixed multi-outlet assemblies where a number of appliances are likely to be used simultaneously, calculate a load of 180 volt-amps for each ____ ft.

(a) 1   (b) 2   (c) 3   (d) 5

7. Screw-type pressure terminals used with #14 or smaller copper conductors in motor controllers shall be torqued to a minimum of ____ pound-inches.

(a) 7   (b) 10   (c) 12   (d) 20

8. The identification of terminals to which a grounded conductor is to be connected shall be substantially ____ in color.

(a) brass   (b) copper   (c) green   (d) white

9. Branch circuits for lighting and for appliances, including ____ appliances, shall be provided to supply the loads calculated.

(a) portable   (b) motor-operated   (c) fixed   (d) stationary

10. Where an optical fiber cable is exposed to contact with electric light or power conductors and the cable enters the building, the non-current-carrying metallic members ____.

(a) shall be grounded
(b) or interrupted by an insulating joint
(c) the grounding or interruption shall be close as practicable to the point of entrance
(d) all of the above

11. Each electric appliance shall be provided with a nameplate, giving the identifying name and the rating in ____.

I. volts and watts   II. watts and amps   III. volts and amperes

(a) I only   (b) I or III   (c) I or II   (d) II or III

12. Ground-fault protection of equipment shall be provided for solidly grounded wye electrical services of more than 150 volts to ground, but not exceeding 1000 volts phase-to-phase for each service disconnecting means rated ____ amperes or more.

(a) 200   (b) 600   (c) 800   (d) 1000

13. For industrial establishments only, omission of overcurrent protection shall be permitted at points where busways are reduced in size, provided that the smaller busway does not extend more than ____ feet and has a current rating at least equal to ____ the rating or setting of the overcurrent device next back on the line.

(a) 30' ... 80%   (b) 50' ... 1/3   (c) 20' ... 1/2   (d) 40' ... 75%

14. When conduit nipples having a maximum length not to exceed 24" are installed between boxes ____.

I.   the nipple can be filled 75%   II.   note 8 derating does apply
III. note 8 derating does not apply   IV.   the nipple can be filled 60%

(a) I and II   (b) II and IV   (c) III and IV   (d) I and III

15. Compliance with the provisions of the Code will result in ____.

(a) good electrical service   (b) an efficient system   (c) freedom from hazard   (d) all of these

16. The total rating of a plug connected room air-conditioner where lighting units or other appliances are also supplied shall not exceed ____ percent.

(a) 80   (b) 70   (c) 50   (d) 40

17. What is the minimum number of overload units such as heaters, trip coils, or thermal cutouts allowed for a three-phase AC motor protection?

(a) 1   (b) 2   (c) 3   (d) none of these

18. All conductors the size below can be connected in parallel except ____.

(a) #250 kcmil   (b) #2/0   (c) #1   (d) #1/0

19. Where raceways are exposed to widely different temperatures, they shall be ____.

(a) sealed   (b) bonded   (c) grounded   (d) isolated

20. When installing rigid nonmetallic conduit ____.

I. all joints shall be made by an approved method
II. there shall be support within 2 feet of each box, cabinet
III. all cut ends shall be trimmed inside and outside to remove rough edges

(a) I, II and III   (b) I and III   (c) I and II   (d) II and III

21. The minimum size copper equipment grounding conductor required on a motor branch circuit with a 30 amp circuit breaker and #12 copper conductors is ____.

(a) #10   (b) #8   (c) #12   (d) #14

22. A raceway including the end fitting shall not use more than ____ inches into a panel containing 42 spaces for overcurrent devices.

(a) 8   (b) 2   (c) 10   (d) 3

23. Junction boxes for pool lighting shall not be located less than ____ feet from the inside wall of a pool unless separated by a fence or wall.

(a) 3   (b) 4   (c) 6   (d) 8

24. The unit lighting load for dwellings expressed in va per square foot is ____ va.

(a) 2 (b) 5 (c) 3 (d) none of these

25. Metal plugs or plates used with non-metallic boxes shall be recessed ____.

(a) 3/8" (b) 1/2" (c) 1/4" (d) 1/8"

26. Supplementary overcurrent devices shall ____.

(a) not be required to be readily accessible
(b) be used as a substitute for branch-circuit overcurrent devices
(c) be readily accessible
(d) rated not over 15 amp

27. Mats of insulating rubber or other suitable floor insulation shall be provided for the operator where the voltage to ground exceeds ____ on live-front switchboards.

(a) 50 (b) 100 (c) 120 (d) 150

28. A unit or assembly of units or sections, and associated fittings, forming a rigid structural system used to support cables and raceways would be the definition of ____.

(a) wireway (b) multi-outlet assembly (c) cable tray system (d) FCC

29. A pliable raceway is a raceway which can be bent ____ with a reasonable force, but without other assistance.

(a) with heat (b) without heat (c) by hand (d) easily

30. What is the demand factor for five household clothes dryers?

(a) 70% (b) 85% (c) 50% (d) 100%

31. Article 242 Part III is for surge arresters over ____ volts.

(a) 240 (b) 480 (c) 600 (d) 1,000

32. Busways shall be securely supported, unless otherwise designed and marked at intervals not to exceed ____ feet.

(a) 10 (b) 5 (c) 3 (d) 8

33. Where it is unlikely that two dissimilar loads will be in use simultaneously, it shall be permissible to ____ of the two in computing the total load of a feeder.

(a) omit both   (b) omit the larger
(c) omit the smaller   (d) omit neither

34. Which of the following electrodes must be supplemented by an additional electrode?

(a) metal underground water pipe   (b) metal frame of a building
(c) ground ring   (d) concrete encased

35. In judging equipment, considerations such as the following shall be evaluated:

I. mechanical strength   II. cost   III. arcing effects   IV. guarantee

(a) I only   (b) I and II   (c) II and IV   (d) I and III

36. For the use of nonmetallic surface extensions the building _____.

I.   cannot exceed three floors
II. is occupied for office purposes
III. is occupied for residential purposes

(a) I only   (b) II only   (c) II and III   (d) I, II and III

37. When a flat cable assembly is installed less than ____ feet from the floor, it shall be protected by a metal cover identified for the use.

(a) 8   (b) 10   (c) 12   (d) 15

38. Pendant conductors longer than ____ shall be twisted together where not cabled in a listed assembly.

(a) 12"   (b) 18"   (c) 2'   (d) 3'

39. Cablebus shall be permitted to be used for ____.

I. services   II. feeders   III. branch circuits

(a) I only   (b) II only   (c) II and III   (d) I, II and III

40. Each vented cell shall be equipped with a ____ designed to prevent destruction of the cell.

(a) gas arrester   (b) insulator   (c) flame arrester   (d) electrolyte

41. Thermoplastic insulation may stiffen at temperatures colder than minus ____ degrees C, requiring care be exercised during installation.

(a) 5   (b) 10   (c) 15   (d) 30

42. Flexible cords shall **not** be used in all but one of the following:

(a) substitute for fixed wiring
(b) where run through holes in walls
(c) where attached to the building surface
(d) for pendants wiring fixtures, portable lamps, elevator cables

43. The minimum ampacity for a 120/240v service entrance conductors one circuit is ____ amps.

(a) 15   (b) 30   (c) 60   (d) 100

44. A fixture that exceeds ____ inches in any dimension shall not be supported by the screw shell of a lampholder.

(a) 8   (b) 10   (c) 12   (d) 16

45. Lighting track which operates at 30 volts or higher shall be installed at least ___ feet above the finished floor.

(a) 3   (b) 5   (c) 8   (d) 10

46. Which of the following is the maximum number of current-carrying conductors that can be used at any cross-section of a wireway?

(a) 100   (b) 30   (c) 50   (d) 40

47. The following letter suffixes shall indicate the following:

____ -for two insulated conductors laid parallel within an outer nonmetallic covering.

(a) D   (b) M   (c) R   (d) N

48. The means of identification of each ungrounded conductor of a branch circuit supplied from more than one nominal voltage system, wherever accessible, may be by ____.

I.   tagging, or other equally effective means
II. marking tape
III. separate color coding

(a) I only   (b) II only   (c) III only   (d) I, II or III

49. For dwelling units, the computed floor area at 3va per square foot does NOT include ____.

I. bathrooms   II. garages   III. open porches

(a) I and III only   (b) II and III only   (c) I and II only   (d) I, II and III

50. The screw shell contact of lampholders in grounded circuits shall be connected to the ____ conductor.

(a) green   **(b) grounding**
(c) ungrounded   **(d) grounded**

2020

JOURNEYMAN OPEN BOOK EXAM #13

50 QUESTIONS TIME LIMIT - 2 HOURS

TIME SPENT [ ] **MINUTES**

SCORE [ ] %

JOURNEYMAN OPEN BOOK EXAM #13

1. Exposed vertical risers of IMC for industrial machinery or fixed equipment can be supported at intervals not exceeding _____ feet if the conduit is made up with threaded couplings, firmly supported at the top and bottom of the riser, and no other means of support is available.

(a) 12 (b) 15 (c) 20 (d) 25

2. Equipment listed by a qualified electrical testing laboratory is not required to have the factory-installed _____ wiring inspected at the time of installation except to detect alterations or damage.

(a) internal (b) external (c) associated (d) low-voltage

3. Where _____ conductors are run in separate raceways or cables, the same number of conductors must be used in each raceway or cable.

(a) aluminum (b) control (c) parallel (d) communication

4. In multiwire circuits, the continuity of the _____ conductor must not be dependent upon the device connections.

(a) red (b) black (c) ungrounded (d) grounded

5. Conductors must have their ampacity determined using the _____°C column of Table 310.16 for circuits rated 100 amps or less or marked #14 through #1 conductors, unless the equipment terminals are listed for use with higher temperature rated conductors.

(a) 60 (b) 75 (c) 90 (d) 110

6. What is the minimum cover requirement for UF cable supplying power to a 120 volt, 15 amp GFCI protected circuit outdoors under a driveway of a one-family dwelling?

(a) 6" (b) 12" (c) 18" (d) 24"

7. A bare #4 copper conductor installed near the bottom of a concrete footing that is in direct contact with earth may be used as a grounding electrode conductor when the conductor is at least _____ in length.

(a) 10' (b) 15' (c) 20' (d) 25'

8. Service cables must be equipped with a _____ listed for use in a wet location.

(a) cover (b) conduit (c) service head (d) coupling

9. Overcurrent protection devices must be ____.

(a) inaccessible to unauthorized personnel   (b) visible
(c) accessible (as applied to equipment)   (d) readily accessible

10. A single receptacle is a single contact device with no other contact device on the same ____.

(a) equipment   (b) yoke   (c) circuit   (d) run

11. Ground-fault protection that functions to open the service disconnect ____ protect(s) service conductors or the service equipment on the line side.

(a) adequately   (b) completely   (c) will   (d) will not

12. When the opening to an outlet, junction, or switch point is less than 8" in any dimension, each conductor must be long enough to extend at least ____ outside the opening of the enclosure.

(a) 2"   (b) 3"   (c) 4"   (d) 6"

13. Circuit breakers must be marked with their ____ rating in a manner that will be durable and visable after installation.

(a) type   (b) AIC   (c) torque   (d) ampere

14. Metal raceways, cable armor, and other metal enclosures for conductors shall be ____ joined together to form a continuous electrical conductor.

(a) permanently   (b) continuously   (c) electrically   (d) metallically

15. Where flexible cord is used in listed extension cord sets, the conductors are considered protected against overcurrent when used within ____.

(a) indoor installations   (b) the extension cord's listing
(c) non-hazardous locations   (d) 75' of the panelboard

16. Conductors smaller than #1/0 can be connected in parallel to supply control power, provided ____.

(a) they are all contained within the same raceway or cable
(b) each parallel conductor has the ampacity sufficient to carry the entire load
(c) the circuit overcurrent protection device rating does not exceed the ampacity of any individual parallel conductor
(d) all of these

17. A _____ is an accommodation that combines living, sleeping, sanitary, and storage facilities.

(a) dwelling unit   (b) single-family dwelling   (c) guest suite   (d) guest room

18. Many terminations and equipment are marked with _____.

(a) a removable label   (b) a tightening torque   (c) a stencil   (d) a logo

19. The feeder conductor ampacity must not be less than that of the service-entrance conductors where the feeder conductors carry the total load supplied by service-entrance conductors with an ampacity of _____ or less.

(a) 55 amps   (b) 60 amps   (c) 100 amps   (d) 150 amps

20. Receptacles, polarized attachment plugs, and cord connectors for plugs and polarized plugs must have the terminal intended for connection to the grounded conductor identified. Identification must be by a metal or metal coating that is substantially _____ in color, or by the word white or the letter "W" located adjacent to the identified terminal.

(a) white   (b) gray   (c) yellow   (d) a or b

21. A device that, by insertion in a receptacle, establishes a connection between the conductors of the attached flexible cord and the conductors connected permanently to the receptacle(s) is called a(n) _____.

(a) plug   (b) plug cap   (c) attachment plug   (d) any of these

22. Unguarded live parts operating at 30,000 volts located above a working space must be elevated at least _____ above the working space.

(a) 9.6"   (b) 12.5'   (c) 24'   (d) 30'

23. For a one-family dwelling, at least one receptacle outlet is required in each _____.

(a) attached garage   (b) detached garage with power   (c) basement   (d) all of these

24. All electrical connections in marinas and boatyards must be located _____.

(a) not below the electrical datum plane
(b) at least 12" above the deck of a floating pier
(c) not less than 12" above the deck of a fixed pier
(d) all of these

25. The bonding bar shall be connected to the grounding electrode with a minimum _____ copper conductor.

(a) #6   (b) #4   (c) #2   (d) #1/0

26. When the building disconnecting means is a power-operated switch or circuit breaker, it must be able to be opened by hand in the event of a ____.

(a) power failure   (b) short circuit   (c) ground fault   (d) power surge

27. A ____ is a building or portion of a building in which one or more self-propelled vehicles can be kept for use, sale, storage, rental, repair, exhibition, or demonstration purposes.

(a) garage   (b) commercial garage   (c) residential garage   (d) service garage

28. ____ shall be provided to give safe access to the working space around equipment over 600 volts installed on platforms, balconies, mezzanine floors, or in attic or roof rooms or spaces.

(a) Openings   (b) Platforms or ladders   (c) Ladders   (d) Permanent ladders or stairways

29. Panelboards shall not be permitted to be reconditioned. In the event the replacement has not been listed for the specific enclosure and the available fault current is greater than ____ amperes, the completed work shall be field labeled.

(a) 10,000   (b) 7,500   (c) 5,000   (d) 2,500

30. A ____ switch is a manually operated device used in conjunction with a transfer switch to provide a means of directly connecting load conductors to a power source, and of disconnecting the transfer switch.

(a) transfer   (b) motor-circuit   (c) bypass isolation   (d) safety

31. Equipment such as raceways, cables, wireways, cabinets, panels, etc. can be located above or below other electrical equipment when the associated equipment does not extend more than ____ from the front of the electrical equipment.

(a) 3"   (b) 4"   (c) 6"   (d) 12"

32. The minimum size service-drop conductor permitted is a # ____ copper or # ____ aluminum.

(a) 8, 8   (b) 8, 6   (c) 6, 8   (d) 6, 6

33. Cables or raceways installed using directional boring equipment shall be ____ for this purpose.

(a) listed   (b) approved   (c) marked   (d) labeled

34. Any current in excess of the rated current of equipment, or the ampacity of a conductor, is called ____ current.

(a) over   (b) faulted   (c) shorted   (d) trip

35. Additional services are permitted for different voltages, frequencies, or phases, or for different uses such as for ____.

(a) hospitals   (b) aircraft hangers   (c) special events   (d) different rate schedules

36. The service disconnecting means must plainly indicate whether it is in the ____ position.

(a) tripped   (b) correct   (c) up or down   (d) open or closed

37. Agricultural buildings where excessive dust and dust with water may accumulate, are defined as including all areas of ____ confinement systems, where litter dust or feed dust, including mineral feed particles may accumulate.

(a) fish   (b) livestock   (c) poultry   (d) all of these

38. An 8" x 8" x 4" deep junction box requires 6" of free conductor, measured from the point in the box where the conductors enter the enclosure. The 3" of conductor outside-the-box rule ____.

(a) could apply   (b) does apply   (c) does not apply   (d) often applies

39. ____ is a qualifying term indicating that there is a purposely-introduced delay in the tripping action of the circuit breaker, which decreases as the magnitude of the current increases.

(a) Time delay   (b) Controller   (c) Inverse-time   (d) Adverse-time

40. The rating of the branch circuit is determined by the rating of the ____.

(a) branch-circuit overcurrent protection   (b) total load of appliances
(c) total lighting load   (c) conductor size

41. Surrounded by a case, housing, fence, or wall(s) that prevents persons from accidentally contacting energized parts is called ____.

(a) protected   (b) guarded   (c) isolated   (d) enclosed

42. Conductor overload protection is not required where the interruption of the ____ would create a hazard, such as in a material-handling magnet circuit or fire-pump circuit. However, short-circuit protection is required.

(a) service   (b) phase   (c) line   (d) circuit

43. Conduit installed underground or encased in concrete slabs that are in direct contact with the earth is considered a _____ location.

(a) damp   (b) wet   (c) dry   (d) moist

44. _____ in dwelling units must supply only loads within that dwelling unit or loads associated only with that dwelling unit.

(a) Branch circuits   (b) Feeders   (c) The service   (d) The GFCI

45. Each disconnecting means must be legibly marked to indicate its purpose unless located and arranged so _____.

(a) they are not readily accessible   (b) that they can be locked and tagged out
(c) the purpose is evident   (d) that they operate at less than 300 volts to ground

46. Service cables mounted in contact with a building must be supported at intervals not exceeding _____ .

(a) 30"   (b) 48"   (c) 52"   (d) 6'

47. When one electrical circuit controls another circuit through a relay, the first circuit is called a _____.

(a) signal circuit   (b) control circuit   (c) controller circuit   (d) remote-control circuit

48. Bends in ITC cable must be made _____.

(a) using listed bending tools   (b) not less than 4 times the diameter of the cable
(c) not to exceed 30°   (d) so as not to damage the cable

49. Utilization equipment weighing not more than 6 pounds shall be permitted to be supported on other boxes or plaster rings that are secured to ther boxes, provided the equipment or its supporting yoke is secured to the box with no fewer than two _____ or larger screws.

(a) #10   (b) #8   (c) #6   (d) #4

50. The ampacity of ungrounded (phase) conductors from the generator terminals to the first overcurrent protection devices must not be less than _____ of the nameplate rating of the generator.

(a) 80%   (b) 100%   (c) 115%   (d) 125%

2020

JOURNEYMAN
OPEN
BOOK
EXAM #14

50 QUESTIONS
TIME LIMIT - 2 HOURS

TIME SPENT [   ] MINUTES

SCORE [   ] %

JOURNEYMAN OPEN BOOK EXAM #14   **Two Hour Time Limit**

1. Where devices containing a disconnecting means are mounted out of reach, suitable means shall be provided to operate the disconnecting means from the floor on a busway. Which of the following is permitted?

(a) devices cannot be mounted out of reach
(b) ladders
(c) sticks
(d) no method is permitted

2. Transformers shall have a secondary short circuit current of not more than _____ mA if the open circuit voltage is over 7500 volts.

(a) 150   **(b) 200**   **(c) 300**   **(d) 500**

3. Ground-fault circuit-interrupters shall be installed in the branch circuit supplying underwater pool lighting fixtures operating at more than _____ volts.

(a) 12   **(b) L.V. contact limit**   **(c) 24**   **(d) 50**

4. Each transformer shall be provided with a nameplate giving the name of the manufacturer; rated kv; frequency; primary and secondary voltage; impedance of transformers _____ kva and larger.

(a) 112 1/2   **(b) 25**   **(c) 33**   **(d) 50**

5. _____ is defined as properly localizing a fault condition to restrict outages to the equipment affected, accomplished by choice of the selective and installation fault protective devices.

(a) Monitoring   **(b) Coordination**   **(c) Choice selection**   **(d) Fault device**

6. Two-wire DC circuits and AC circuits of two or more ungrounded conductors shall be permitted to be tapped from the ungrounded conductors of circuits having _____.

(a) a properly sized tap conductor
(b) less than 50 volts
(c) a balanced neutral system
(d) a grounded neutral conductor

7. Application of demand factors to small appliance and laundry loads in dwellings are permitted in Table _____.

(a) 220.12   **(b) 220.42**   **(c) 220.71**   **(d) 220.80**

8. Conductors for festoon lighting shall be of the _____ type.

I. thermoplastic   II. thermoset   III. shielded

(a) I only   (b) I or II only   (c) II or III only   (d) I, II, or III

9. Not more than one conductor shall be connected to the grounding electrode by a single clamp or fitting unless the clamp or fitting is _____.

(a) cast bronze or brass
(b) listed for multiple conductors
(c) 0.043" in thickness
(d) none of these

10. FCC cable can have individual branch circuits with a rating not exceeding _____ amperes.

(a) 15   (b) 20   (c) 25   (d) 30

11. Auxiliary equipment for electric-discharge lamps shall be _____ and treated as sources of heat.

(a) enclosed in noncombustible cases
(b) thermally protected
(c) weatherproof
(d) ventilated

12. Where used outside, aluminum or copper-clad aluminum grounding conductors shall not be installed within _____ inches of earth.

(a) 24   (b) 18   (c) 30   (d) 36

13. If equipment has been damaged by fire, or products of combustion, or water, it shall be specifically evaluated by its manufacturer or _____ prior to being returned to service.

(a) an AHJ   (b) by an electrical engineer
(c) a qualified testing laboratory   (d) a qualified maintenance electrician

14. Time switches, flashers, and similar devices where mounted so they are accessible only to qualified persons and so located in an enclosure that any energized parts within _____ of the manual adjustment or switch are covered by suitable barriers.

(a) 4"   (b) 6"   (c) 12"   (d) 18"

15. What size rigid PVC conduit schedule 40 is required for eight #6 XHHW conductors?

(a) 3/4"   (b) 1"   (c) 1 1/4"   (d) 1 1/2"

16. The minimum radius for a bend of 1" rigid conduit with three #10 TW conductors is _____ inches. (one shot bender)

(a) 6   (b) 11   (c) 5 3/4   (d) none of these

17. No parts of cord-connected luminaires, chain-, cable-, or cord-suspened luminaires' lighting track, pendants, or ceiling-suspended (paddle) fans shall be located within a zone measured 3' horizontally and ___ vertically from the top of the bathtub rim or shower stall threshold.

(a) 6'   (b) 8'   (c) 10'   (d) 12'

18. Receptacles located _____ feet above the floor are not counted in the required number of receptacles along the wall.

(a) 4   (b) 6   (c) 5 1/2   (d) none of these

19. Pool-associated motors shall be connected to an equipment grounding conductor not smaller than # _____.

(a) 14   (b) 12   (c) 10   (d) 8

20. RTRC larger than size _____ shall not be used.

(a) 2   (b) 4   (c) 6   (d) 10

21. What is the area of square inch for a #12 RHW without outer covering?

(a) .0353   (b) .0293   (c) .182   (d) .026

22. Metal enclosures used to protect _____ from physical damage shall not be required to be grounded.

(a) service conductors   (b) feeders   (c) cable assemblies   (d) none of these

23. Connection devices or fittings must **not** connect grounding conductors to equipment by means of _____.

(a) pressure connections
(b) solder
(c) lugs
(d) approved clamps

24. A bare #4 conductor may be concrete encased and serve as the grounding electrode when at least ____ feet in length.

(a) 10   (b) 12   (c) 20   (d) 15

25. Which of the following is **not** a standard classification for a branch circuit supplying several loads?

(a) 20 amp   (b) 25 amp   (c) 30 amp   (d) 50 amp

26. Underfloor raceways may be occupied up to ____ percent of the area.

(a) 55   (b) 30   (c) 40   (d) 38

27. The volume per #14 conductor required in a box is ____ cubic inch.

(a) 2.25   (b) 2   (c) 3   (d) 2.5

28. What size copper grounding electrode conductor is required for a #1500 kcmil copper service conductor?

(a) #2/0   (b) #3/0   (c) #0   (d) #2

29. Electrical nonmetallic tubing shall be clearly and durably marked at least every ____ feet.

(a) 3   (b) 6   (c) 8   (d) 10

30. Vertical and horizontal spacing between supported cablebus conductors shall not be less than ____ at the points of support.

(a) 1"   (b) 1 1/2"   (c) 2"   (d) one conductor diameter

31. ____ switches shall be used for capacitor switching.

(a) Isolation   (b) Group-operated   (c) Shunt   (d) High-voltage

32. Switching devices shall be located at least ____ horizontally from the inside walls of the pool.

(a) 18"   (b) 2'   (c) 4'   (d) 5'

33. The secondary circuits of wound-rotor AC motors, including conductors, controllers, resistors, etc. shall be considered as protected against overload by the ____.

(a) disconnect
(b) controller
(c) breaker
(d) motor-overload device

34. Enclosures for overcurrent devices in damp or wet locations shall be identified for use in such locations and shall be mounted so there is at least ____ inch air space between the enclosure and the wall.

(a) 1/4   (b) 3/8   (c) 3/4   (d) 1

35. Which of the following is required for temporary wiring?

(a) Flexible cords shall be protected from accidental damage.
(b) All branch circuits shall originate in an approved panelboard.
(c) All conductors shall be protected as provided in article 240.
(d) All of these.

36. Nonmetallic surface extensions with one or more extensions shall be permitted to be run in any direction from an existing outlet, but not on the floor or within ____ inches from the floor.

(a) 6   (b) 4   (c) 3   (d) 2

37. Water heaters having a capacity of ____ gallons or less shall have a branch circuit rating not less than 125% of the rating of the water heater.

(a) 60   (b) 75   (c) 90   (d) 120

38. A spacing of not less than ____ shall be maintained between neon tubing and the nearest surface, other than its support.

(a) 1/4"   (b) 1/2"   (c) 3/8"   (d) 5/16"

39. An autotransformer starter shall provide ____.

I. an "off position"   II. a running position   III. at least one starting position

(a) I only   (b) II only   (c) I and II   (d) I, II and III

40. A metal elbow installed underground in a run of nonmetallic conduit is not required to be grounded, if it is isolated by a minimum over of at least ____ inches to any part of the elbow.

(a) 6   (b) 12   (c) 18   (d) 24

41. Temporary wiring shall be removed ____ upon completion of construction or purpose for which the wiring was installed.

(a) 30 days   (b) immediately   (c) A.S.A.P.   (d) 60 days

42. Type MV cables shall **not** be used unless identified for the use ____.

I. in cable trays   II. where exposed to direct sunlight

(a) I only   (b) II only   (c) both I and II   (d) neither I nor II

43. In completed installations each outlet box shall have a ____.

(a) receptacle   (b) switch   (c) cover   (d) fixture

44. Which of the following shall be provided where necessary to assure electrical continuity?

(a) Grounding   (b) Bonding   (c) Jumpers   (d) Shunts

45. A continuous white or gray covering on a conductor shall be used only for the ____ conductor.

(a) grounding   (b) ungrounded   (c) hot   (d) grounded

46. Grounding of a metal raceway used to protect Romex is required if the raceway is ____ feet or over, or within reach of ground or grounded metal.

(a) 6   (b) 8   (c) 10   (d) 25

47. A single electrode consisting of a ____ which does not have a resistance to ground of 25Ω or less shall be augmented by one additional electrode.

I. rod   II. pipe   III. plate

(a) I only   (b) II only   (c) III only   (d) I, II or III

48. What is the va input of a fully loaded 5 hp 230 volt single-phase motor?

(a) 746   (b) 3730   (c) 6440   (d) 12,880

49. The minimum size of a copper equipment grounding conductor required for equipment connected to a 40 amp circuit is _____.

(a) #12   (b) #14   (c) #8   (d) #10

50. 2" rigid metal conduit shall be supported every _____ feet.

(a) 10   (b) 12   (c) 14   (d) 16

2020

JOURNEYMAN
OPEN
BOOK
EXAM #15

50 QUESTIONS
TIME LIMIT - 2 HOURS

TIME SPENT ☐ MINUTES

SCORE ☐ %

JOURNEYMAN OPEN BOOK EXAM #15   **Two Hour Time Limit**

1. Type P conductors shall be of tinned copper. Conductors shall employ flexible stranding. The minimum conductor size shall be ____.

(a) 18 AWG   (b) 16 AWG   (c) 14 AWG   (d) 12 AWG

2. The current carried continuously in bare aluminum bars in auxiliary gutters shall not exceed ____ amperes per square inch.

(a) 560   (b) 700   (c) 800   (d) 1000

3. Type UF cable shall be permitted for ____.

(a) service entrance cable   (b) embedded in concrete
(c) direct burial   (d) hoistways

4. Soldered splices must be ____ so as to be electrically secure before soldering.

(a) tinned   (b) joined mechanically   (c) taped   (d) insulated

5. No conductor larger than ____ shall be installed in a cellular concrete floor raceway without special permission.

(a) #2   (b) #4   (c) #1/0   (d) #1

6. In general, the voltage limitation between conductors in surface metal raceways is ____ volts.

(a) 300   (b) 500   (c) 600   (d) 1000

7. Luminaires located within the actual outside dimensions of the bathtub or shower to a height vertically of ____ from the top of the bathtub rim or shower threshold shall be marked suitable for damp locations or marked suitable for wet locations.

(a) 6'   (b) 8'   (c) 10'   (d) 12'

8. Conduit used to protect direct buried cable shall be provided with a ____ where the cable leaves the conduit underground.

(a) seal   (b) clamp   (c) bushing   (d) connector

9. Temporary electrical power and lighting installations shall be permitted ____.

I.   for developmental work
II. for permanent wiring
III. during emergencies and for tests

(a) I only   (b) II only   (c) I and II only   (d) I and III only

10. The ampacity of a 60°C #22 AWG copper conductor located in a permanent amusement attraction where the ambient temperature is 30°C is ____.

(a) 0.8   (b) 2   (c) 3   (d) 5

11. An autotransformer which is used to raise the voltage to more than ____ volts, as part of a ballast for supplying lighting units, shall be supplied only by a grounded system.

(a) 300   (b) 150   (c) 125   (d) 50

12. ____ is a system in which heat is generated on the inner surface of a ferromagnetic envelope embedded in or fastened to the surface to be heated.

(a) Duct heaters   (b) Electrode-type boilers   (c) Space heating   (d) Skin effect heating

13. The service disconnecting means shall plainly indicate ____.

(a) its voltage rating   (b) the maximum horsepower rating
(c) the maximum fuse size   (d) whether it is in the open or closed position

14. Using the optional method of calculation for a single-dwelling unit, the central space heating would be calculated at ____ percent.

(a) 40   (b) 50   (c) 65   (d) 100

15. Using the general method of calculation, what is the minimum demand for a household clothes dryer?

(a) 4 kw   (b) 4.5 kw   (c) 5 kw   (d) 6 kw

16. Type THW insulation has a ____ degree C rating for use in wiring through fixtures.

(a) 60   (b) 75   (c) 85   (d) 90

17. Fixture wire shall be considered as protected by a 20 amp branch circuit breaker up to 50' if it is a ____ AWG.

(a) #14   (b) #20
(c) #18   (d) #16

18. Supply bonding jumpers must be sized ____.

(a) according to the fuse size   (b) same as the largest service conductor
(c) 1/3 as large as the service conductor   (d) according to Table 250.102(C)(1)

19. Unless specified otherwise, live parts of electrical equipment operating at ____ volts or more shall be guarded.

(a) 32   (b) 50   (c) 115   (d) 150

20. The frame of an electric range may be grounded by being connected to the grounded conductor of the 120/240v branch circuit, if the grounded conductor is not less than a ____ copper.

(a) #10   (b) #8   (c) #6   (d) none of these

21. The Code ____.

(a) is not intended for a design specification
(b) is not intended for an instruction manual for untrained persons
(c) is not necessarily efficient
(d) all of the above

22. Bathroom receptacle outlets shall be supplied by ____ .

I. ground fault protection for personnel   II. at least one 20 amp branch circuit

(a) I only   (b) II only   (c) both I and II   (d) neither I nor II

23. The circular mil area of a #12 conductor is ____.

(a) 10380   (b) 26240   (c) 6530   (d) 6350

24. A panelboard contains six 3-pole circuit breakers and eight 2-pole circuit breakers. The maximum allowable number of single-pole breakers permitted to be added in this panelboard is ____.

(a) 8   (b) 16   (c) 28   (d) 42

25. A 50 hp 208v, three-phase squirrel cage motor has a full-load current of ____ amps.

(a) 130   (b) 143   (c) 162   (d) 195

26. Where conductors of different systems are installed in the same raceway, one system shall have a neutral having an outer covering of white or natural gray and each other system having a neutral shall have an outer covering of ____.

(a) white with green stripe
(b) white or gray
(c) blue
(d) white with colored stripe (other than green) or distinguished by other suitable means

27. A feeder tap in a raceway terminating in a single circuit breaker with an ampacity 1/3 of the feeder conductors may extend not over ____ feet.

(a) 6   (b) 10   (c) 25   (d) 50

28. For general motor application, the motor branch circuit fuse size must be determined from ____.

(a) motor nameplate current   (b) NEMA standards
(c) NEC Tables   (d) Factory Mutual

29. Minimum and maximum sizes of EMT are ____ except for special installations.

(a) 5/16" to 3"   (b) 3/8" to 4"   (c) 1/2" to 3"   (d) 1/2" to 4"

30. Locations of lamps for outdoor lighting shall be ____.

I. below all energized conductors   II. below all transformers

(a) I only   (b) II only   (c) both I and II   (d) neither I nor II

31. The number and size of conductors in any raceway shall not be more than will permit ____.

I. ready installation or withdrawal of the conductors without damage to the conductors or to their insulation
II. dissipation of the heat

(a) I only   (b) II only   (c) both I and II   (d) neither I nor II

32. Type MV cables shall be permitted for use on power systems rated up to ____ volts.

(a) 600   (b) 4160   (c) 2300   (d) 35,000

33. Handles or levers of circuit breakers, and similar parts which may move suddenly in such a way that persons in the vicinity are likely to be injured by being struck by them, shall be ____.

I. concealed   II. isolated   III. guarded

(a) I or II only   (b) II or III only   (c) I or III only   (d) I, II or III

34. In a dwelling, the minimum feeder neutral for a 5 kva clothes washer/dryer would be ____ kva.

(a) 5   (b) 4.3   (c) 3.5   (d) 3.0

35. The grounding electrode shall be installed such that ____ of length is in contact with the soil.

(a) 6'   (b) 7'   (c) 7' 6"   (d) 8'

36. All switchboards and panelboards supplied by a feeder in other than one-or-two family dwellings shall be marked to indicate the ____ where as the power supply originates.

I. device
II. equipment
III. device or equipment

(a) I only   (b) II only   (c) III only   (d) I, II and III

37. Connection from any grounding conductor of the type FCC cable shall be made to the shield system at each ____.

(a) receptacle   (b) outlet   (c) switch   (d) junction

38. Where a metal lampholder is attached to a flexible cord, the inlet shall be equipped with an insulating bushing which, if threaded, shall not be smaller than nominal ____ inch pipe size.

(a) 1/4   (b) 3/8   (c) 1/2   (d) 5/8

39. The connection of a grounding electrode conductor to a driven ground rod shall be ____.

(a) visible   (b) accessible   (c) readily accessible   (d) not required to be accessible

40. A thermal protector is intended to protect a motor against ____.

(a) dangerous overheating   **(b) short circuit**
(c) ground fault   **(d) none of these**

41. A 3" x 2" x 2" device box is how many cubic inches?

(a) 12   (b) 14   (c) 10   (d) 8

42. The power supply cord to a mobile home must not be longer than ____ feet.

(a) 21   (b) 26 1/2   (c) 36 1/2   (d) 50

43. Which of the following statements about the protection of nonmetallic sheathed cable from physical damage is/are correct?

I. When passing through a floor, the cable shall be enclosed in a pipe or conduit extending at least 6 inches above the floor.
II. When run across the top of the floor joists in an accessible attic, the cable shall be protected by guard strips.

(a) I only   (b) II only   (c) both I and II   (d) neither I nor II

44. The minimum clearance for service drops, not exceeding 600 volts, over commercial areas subject to truck traffic is ____ feet.

(a) 10   (b) 12   (c) 15   (d) 18

45. Plug fuses of the Edison-base type shall be used ____.

(a) where overfusing is necessary
(b) only for 50 amps and above
(c) as a replacement for type S fuses
(d) only as a replacement item in existing installations

46. In each kitchen and dining area, a receptacle outlet shall be installed at each counter space ____ inches or wider.

(a) 12   (b) 24   (c) 36   (d) 48

47. Straight runs of 1 1/4" rigid metal conduit may be secured at not more than ____ intervals.

(a) 5'   (b) 10'   (c) 12'   (d) 14'

48. Unless part of listed decorative lighting assemblies, pendant conductors shall not be smaller than ____ for mogul-base or medium-base screw shell lampholders or smaller than 18 AWG for intermediate or candelabra-base lampholders.

(a) 20 AWG   (b) 18 AWG   (c) 16 AWG   (d) 14 AWG

49. When determining the load on the "volt-amps per square foot" basis, the floor area shall be computed from the ____ dimensions of the building.

(a) inside   (b) outside   (c) midpoint   (d) any of these

50. Insulated conductors shall be a thermoset type identified for use in Type P cable. All conductors shall be suitable for wet conditions. The minimum wall thickness shall be ____ mils.

(a) 26   (b) 30   (c) 35   (d) 37

2020

JOURNEYMAN
OPEN
BOOK
EXAM #16

50 QUESTIONS
TIME LIMIT - 2 HOURS

TIME SPENT ☐ **MINUTES**

SCORE ☐ %

JOURNEYMAN OPEN BOOK EXAM #16   **Two Hour Time Limit**

1. When using the interior metal water piping system for the grounding electrode, the connection of the grounding electrode to the water piping system must be made ____.

(a) in the garage or carport
(b) in the basement or crawl space
(c) at any accessible place near the panelboard
(d) within the first five feet entering the building

2. Pendant conductors longer than ____ shall be twisted together where not cabled in a listed assembly.

(a) 18"   (b) 20"   (c) 24"   (d) 36"

3. The working clearance in front of a 2300 volt switchboard to a wooden wall is ____.

(a) 30"   (b) 36"   (c) 42"   (d) 48"

4. The terminal bar in a panelboard is connected to the neutral bar only when the panelboard is used as ____.

(a) fire alarm circuits   (b) service equipment   (c) sign lighting   (d) pool equipment

5. Wire terminals located in panelboards shall be arranged ____.

(a) so they are not readily accessible
(b) so they may not be tampered with or changed
(c) so the installer must reach across ungrounded lines
(d) so it will not be necessary for service personnel to reach across or beyond an uninsulated ungrounded line bus to make connections

6. The minimum allowed rating for the service disconnect of a single circuit installation is ____.

(a) 15 amps   (b) 20 amps   (c) 25 amps   (d) 30 amps

7. The service grounding electrode conductor is sized by the rating of the ____.

(a) load to be served
(b) supply transformer
(c) overcurrent protective device
(d) service-entrance conductors

8. The maximum distance that a SE cable strap can be from the meter base or service head is _____.

(a) 6" (b) 12" (c) 18" (d) 24"

9. Each patient bed location shall be provided with a minimum of _____ receptacles.

(a) 6 (b) 8 (c) 12 (d) 16

10. The maximum size rigid metal conduit allowed for electrical construction is _____.

(a) 4" (b) 6" (c) 8" (d) 12"

11. Appliance outlets installed for a specific appliance shall be installed within _____ of the intended location of the appliance.

(a) 3' (b) 4' (c) 6' (d) 12'

12. Type NMC cable may be used in _____.

(a) dry or moist locations   (b) theaters, auditoriums or similar places of assembly
(c) storage battery rooms   (d) hazardous (classified) locations

13. MI cable is prohibited _____.

(a) for residential branch circuits
(b) where exposed to low temperature
(c) where exposed to excessive moisture
(d) where exposed to destructive corrosive conditions

14. The maximum overcurrent protection for a #14 copper THHN wire installed in a raceway is _____ amperes.

(a) 12 (b) 15 (c) 16 (d) 20

15. Conductors that are paralleled, are _____.

(a) joined their full length
(b) electrically connected at one end only
(c) electrically joined at both ends to double the resistance
(d) electrically joined at both ends

16. Temporary wiring used on a construction project shall be removed ____.

(a) immediately upon completion of the construction
(b) one week before final inspection of construction
(c) 15 days before final inspection of construction
(d) one week after final inspection of construction

17. When receptacles are connected to circuits having different voltages, frequencies, or types of current (AC or DC) on the same premises, _____.

(a) each receptacle must be tagged for the intended use
(b) the attachment plugs must be of a design so they are not interchangeable
(c) none of the receptacles are allowed to be used without proper supervision
(d) one type must have a means of disconnection from the circuit when another type is used

18. The maximum voltage allowed to supply listed electric-discharge lighting in residences, hotels, motels and similar occupancies is ____.

(a) 120 volts (b) 208 volts (c) 240 volts (d) 277 volts

19. When outside overhead wiring is used, with no messenger cable, the minimum size copper wire allowed for spans up to 50 feet is ____.

(a) #12 (b) #10 (c) #8 (d) #6

20. For the purpose of calculating branch-circuit and feeder loads, _____ is **not** a nominal system voltage.

(a) 115/230 (b) 120/240 (c) 480Y/277 (d) 600Y/347

21. Which of the following are NOT considered electric vehicles?

(a) Industrial trucks (b) Vans (c) Buses (d) Trucks

22. A 125 volt, 15 or 20 amp receptacle shall be installed for the servicing of heating, air conditioning and refrigeration equipment in _____.

(a) commercial buildings   **(b) one and two family dwellings**
(c) all apartment buildings   **(d) all locations**

23. Cable tray systems shall not be used ____.

(a) in hoistways   **(b) for power and control applications**
(c) for signal cables **(d) for service-entrance systems**

24. Wall-switch controlled receptacles in dwelling units in lieu of lighting outlets are allowed in all habitable rooms except ____.

(a) bedrooms   (b) kitchen and bath   (c) living and family   (d) basement and attic

25. Receptacles installed in a guest room of a motel ____.

(a) must be spaced as a dwelling
(b) are not subject to Code spacing
(c) may be located conveniently for permanent furniture layout
(d) may be installed only if prior approval is given by the local inspector

26. Dry-type transformers must be readily accessible except for ____.

(a) those with a full-load current rating of 125 amps or less
(b) those with a full-load current rating of 250 amps or less
(c) those rated at 1000 volts or less and located in the open walls, columns, or structures
(d) those rated at 601 volts or more and located in the open walls, columns, or structures

27. When a capacitor contains ____ of flammable liquid, it shall be enclosed in a vault or an outdoor fenced enclosure.

(a) over 2 gallons   (b) over 3 gallons   (c) over 4 gallons   (d) over 5 gallons

28. The maximum voltage between conductors for lighting fixtures in a swimming pool is ____.

(a) 115 volts   (b) 120 volts   (c) 125 volts   (d) 150 volts

29. When the following condition(s) are met ____, a room air conditioner is considered to be a single motor unit in determining its branch circuit requirements.

(a) it is cord and plug connected and its rating is not more than 40 amps and 250 volt, 1 ø
(b) total rated-load current is shown on the room air-conditioner nameplate rather than individual motor currents
(c) the rating of the branch-circuit short-circuit and ground-fault protective device does not exceed the ampacity of the branch-circuit conductors or the rating of the receptacle, whichever is less
(d) All of the above

30. The function of the motor overcurrent protective device is ____.

(a) to interrupt fault currents   (b) to interrupt overloads
(c) both (a) and (b)   (d) (a) only

31. A _____ is a compartment or chamber to which one or more air ducts are connected and which forms part of the air distribution system.

(a) duct   (b) triplex   (c) plenum   (d) tap

32. _____ must not be allowed to come in contact with interior parts of electrical equipment.

(a) Insulators   (b) Busbars   (c) Terminals   (d) Abrasives

33. Branch circuits in multifamily dwellings for the purpose of alarm, signal, communications, central lighting, or other needs for public or commercial areas shall _____.

(a) be rated over 60 amps
(b) not be supplied from a dwelling unit's panelboard
(c) terminate in one of the dwelling unit's panelboards
(d) be rated over 30 amperes for any application or purpose

34. The smallest aluminum or copper-clad conductor permitted for service-entrance is _____.

(a) #10   (b) #8   (c) #6   (d) #4

35. The rating or setting of an overcurrent protective device used on each ungrounded conductor for each capacitor bank 600 volts or less shall be rated _____.

(a) 125% of the full-load rating   (b) 80% of the discharge rating
(c) as high as practicable   (d) as low as practicable

36. When counting the number of conductors in a box, a conductor running through the box with an unbroken loop not less than twice the minimum length required for free conductors is counted as _____ conductor(s).

(a) one   (b) two   (c) four   (d) not counted

37. Flat cable assemblies are suitable to supply tap devices for _____ loads. The maximum branch circuit rating is 30 amps.

(a) small appliance   (b) small power   (c) lighting   (d) all of these

38. Type SE cables are permitted for use for branch circuits or feeders where the insulated conductors are used for circuit wiring and the uninsulated conductor is used only for _____.

(a) equipment grounding   (b) remote control and signaling
(c) the grounded neutral   (d) none of these

39. Use of Type FCC systems in damp locations _____.

(a) are not permitted   (b) must be approved by the AHJ
(c) are permitted   (d) are permitted in a raceway embedded in 2" of concrete

40. Lighting outlets can be controlled by occupancy sensors equipped with a _____ that will allow the sensor to function as a wall switch.

(a) photo cell   (b) time delay   (c) resistor   (d) manual override

41. Horizontal runs of RMC supported by openings through _____ at intervals not exceeding 10' and securely fastened within 3' of termination points are permitted.

(a) concrete walls   (b) framing members   (c) rafters   (d) trusses

42. HDPE is not permitted where it will be subjected to ambient temperatures in excess of _____.

(a) 194°F   (b) 167°F   (c) 140°F   (d) 122°F

43. Each run of nonmetallic extension must terminate in a fitting that covers the end of the _____.

(a) assembly   (b) device   (c) box   (d) extension

44. An AFCI is an _____.

(a) alternate fire collector interrupter   (b) ampere faulting capacitor insulator
(c) appliance-fixture circuit identifier   (d) arc-fault circuit-interrupter

45. Which of the following shall be installed at or near equipment requiring servicing such as attics and underfloor spaces, utility rooms and basements?

(a) Lighting fixture with pull-chain switch
(b) Three receptacles with GFCI protection
(c) At least one switch-controlled lighting outlet
(d) Low-voltage transformer to service control components

46. Which using 2 1/2" rigid steel conduit for a through-the-roof 120/240 volt service mast, the minimum distance the conduit can protrude above the roof is _____.

(a) 12"   (b) 18"   (c) 24"   (d) 30"

47. A single made electrode with a resistance to ground of more than 25Ω is approved as a grounding electrode system if _____.

(a) the made electrode is constructed of copper
(b) the made electrode is constructed of aluminum
(c) the ground rod is driven into the earth 8 feet or more
(d) it is supplemented by one or more additional electrodes

48. An overcurrent device shall be located in a circuit _____.

(a) on the line side of the meter
(b) at the last outlet on the circuit
(c) at the first connector in the circuit
(d) at the point where the conductor receives its supply

49. Which of the following may not be used as a grounding electrode?

(a) Driven ground rod
(b) Metallic cold-water pipe
(c) Underground metallic gas pipe
(d) A grounding ring consisting of a #2 bare copper

50. When pendant conductors are longer than _____, they shall be twisted together.

(a) 12"   (b) 18"   (c) 24"   (d) 36"

2020

JOURNEYMAN
OPEN
BOOK
EXAM #17

50 QUESTIONS
TIME LIMIT - 2 HOURS

TIME SPENT [   ] **MINUTES**

SCORE [   ] %

JOURNEYMAN OPEN BOOK EXAM #17   **Two Hour Time Limit**

1. Where a ____ supplies continuous loads or any combination of continuous and noncontinuous loads, the rating of the overcurrent device shall not be less than the noncontinuous load plus 125% of the continuous load.

(a) load   (b) branch-circuit   (c) demand   (d) conductor

2. Type USE service entrance cable, identified for underground use in a cabled assembly, may have a ____ concentric conductor applied.

(a) bare copper   (b) covered metal
(c) bare aluminum   (d) covered

3. Throughout the Code, the voltage considered shall be that at which the circuit ____.

(a) is grounded   (b) feeds   (c) operates   (d) drops

4. Conductors shall be considered outside a building ____.

I.   when installed in a raceway
II. where installed within a building in a raceway enclosed by 2" of brick
III. where installed under not less than 2" of concrete beneath a building

(a) II only   (b) III only   (c) II and III only   (d) I, II and III

5. The ampacity of capacitor circuit conductors shall not be less than ____ percent of the rated current of the capacitor.

(a) 100   (b) 115   (c) 135   (d) 150

6. The temperature rating of a conductor is the maximum temperature, at any location along its length, that the conductor can withstand over a prolonged time period without ____.

(a) tripping the breaker   (b) serious degradation
(c) short circuiting   (d) a ground fault

7. All boxes and conduit bodies, covers, extension rings, plaster rings, and the like shall be durably and legibly with the ____ or trademark.

(a) weight   (b) cubic inch capacity   (c) Listing   (d) manufacturer's name

8. Branch circuits in dwelling units shall supply only loads within that dwelling unit or loads associated only with that dwelling unit. Branch circuits required for the purpose of lighting, ____, or other needs for public or common areas shall not be supplied from a dwelling unit panelboard.

I. communications   II. signal   III. central alarm

(a) I only   (b) II only   (c) III only   (d) I, II and III

9. A #16 fixture wire is considered protected by a 20 amp overcurrent device up to ____ feet.

(a) 25   (b) 50   (c) 75   (d) 100

10. A/An ____ is a room in a building for living, sleeping, eating or cooking , but excluding bathrooms, toilet rooms, closets, hallways, storage or utility spaces and similar areas.

(a) guest room   (b) guest suite   (c) RV tent space   (d) habitable room

11. The ampacity of type UF cable shall be that of ____ conductors.

(a) 60°F   (b) 75°C   (c) 140°C   (d) 60°C

12. Each fitting attached to a heavy-duty lighting track shall ____.

(a) have individual overcurrent protection
(b) have double lock nuts
(c) be raintight
(d) not be over 3' in length

13. What is the cross sectional area of a 1 1/2" rigid metal conduit?

(a) 2.071   (b) .829   (c) 3.408   (d) 1.624

14. Unless identified as suitable for use with infrared heating lamps, screw-shell lampholders shall not be used with infrared lamps over ____ watts rating.

(a) 150   (b) 300   (c) 5000   (d) none of these

15. What is the minimum thickness of metal for a 6" x 4" x 3 1/4" box?

(a) .0625"   (b) .0747"   (c) 15 MSG   (d) 16 MSG

16. A receptacle which is secured solely by a single screw, installed in a raised cover on a four square box ___.

(a) is prohibited in all cases
(b) is allowed without exception
(c) is allowed only for a box cover listed for such use
(d) is allowed only when the raised cover is installed on a nonmetallic box

17. A circuit containing #12 THHN conductors is a ____ rated circuit when protected by a 15 amp rated circuit breaker.

(a) 25 amp   (b) 20 amp   (c) 15 amp   (d) 30 amp

18. A switch or circuit breaker should disconnect all grounded conductors of a circuit ____.

(a) before it disconnects the ungrounded conductors
(b) after it disconnects the ungrounded conductors
(c) simultaneously as it disconnects the ungrounded conductors
(d) none of these

19. Fixed appliances rated at not over ____ volt-amperes or 1/8 hp, the branch-circuit overcurrent device shall be permitted to serve as the disconnecting means.

(a) 240   (b) 300   (c) 400   (d) 480

20. What is the ampacity of a #8 XHHW copper conductor in a wet location?

(a) 55 amps   (b) 50 amps   (c) 45 amps   (d) 40 amps

21. Flexible metal conduit shall be secured by approved means at intervals not exceeding ____ feet and within 12" on each side of every outlet box.

(a) 2   (b) 4   (c) 4 1/2   (d) 8

22. The floors of vaults in contact with the earth shall be of concrete that is not less than ____ thick for equipment over 600 volts.

(a) 2"   (b) 4"   (c) 6"   (d) 8"

23. At what angle does a header attach to a floor duct?

(a) reverse   (b) parallel   (c) right angle   (d) none of these

24. Loop wiring for underfloor raceways shall not be considered ____.

(a) a splice   (b) a tap   (c) both (a) and (b)   (d) neither (a) nor (b)

25. Induction heating coils that operate or may operate at a voltage greater than 30 volts AC shall be _____ to protect personnel in the area.

I. isolated
II. made inaccessible by location
III. enclosed in a nonmetallic enclosure
IV. enclosed in a split metallic enclosure

(a) I or III only   (b) I, II or III only   (c) I, II or IV only   (d) I, II, III or IV

26. An office building has a 24 volt branch circuit installed for landscape lighting around the front of the building. The circuit was installed in UF cable which requires a minimum burial depth of _____ inches for this circuit.

(a) 6   (b) 8   (c) 12   (d) 24

27. Plaster, drywall or plasterboard surfaces that are broken or incomplete shall be repaired so there will be no gaps or open spaces greater than _____ inch at the edge of the fitting or box.

(a) 1/16   (b) 1/8   (c) 3/16   (d) 1/4

28. Concealed knob-and-tube wiring shall be permitted to be used only for extensions of existing installations and elsewhere only by special permission under the following conditions _____.

I. in unfinished attic and roof spaces when such spaces are insulated by loose or rolled insulating material
II. in the hollow spaces of walls and ceilings
III. in unfinished attic and roof spaces as provided in section 394.23

(a) I only   (b) I and II only   (c) II and III only   (d) I, II and III

29. Raceways shall be installed _____ between outlet, junction or splicing points prior to the installation of conductors.

(a) partially   (b) complete   (c) straight   (d) tightly

30. Flexible cords to portable electrically heated appliances rated at more than _____ watts shall be approved for heating cords.

(a) 50   (b) 100   (c) 300   (d) 500

31. A single grounding electrode is permitted when the resistance to ground does not exceed _____ ohms.

(a) 5   (b) 10   (c) 15   (d) 25

32. What is the area of square inches for a #12 RHH with an outer covering?

(a) .212   (b) .0353   (c) .0437   (d) .0293

33. At least one receptacle outlet shall be provided for the first _____,sq.ft. or fraction thereof, of the countertop or work surface.

(a) 6   (b) 9   (c) 10   (d) 12

34. The _____, or other descriptive marking by which the organization responsible for the product may be identified, shall be placed on all electric equipment.

I. trademark   II. cost   III. manufacturer's name

(a) I only   (b) I and II only   (c) I and III only   (d) I, II and III

35. The interior metal water piping system shall be bonded to the _____.

(a) grounded conductor at the service
(b) grounding electrode conductor
(c) service equipment enclosure
(d) all of these

36. Rigid schedule 80 PVC shall have a minimum burial depth of _____ inches.

(a) 6   (b) 10   (c) 18   (d) 24

37. Which of the following statements about FCC cable is **not** true?

(a) a bottom shield shall be installed beneath all type FCC cable, connectors, and insulating ends
(b) FCC cable can cross over or under flat telephone cable
(c) an FCC system with a height above floor level exceeding 0.090 inches shall be tapered
(d) receptacles and connections need not be polarized

38. Type AC cable shall be permitted for branch circuits and feeders in _____.

I. concealed work   II. exposed work   III. hazardous locations

(a) I, II and III   (b) II and III only   (c) I and III only   (d) I and II only

39. Except by special permission, no conductor larger than _____ shall be installed in cellular metal floor raceways.

(a) #1/0   (b) #2/0   (c) #250 kcmil   (d) #500 kcmil

40. Electrical continuity at service equipment shall be assured by _____.

I.   threadless couplings and connectors made up tight for rigid metal conduit, IMC and EMT
II. threaded couplings and threaded bosses on enclosures with joints shall be made up wrenchtight where rigid metal conduit and IMC are involved
III. standard locknuts or bushings

(a) I or III only   (b) II or III only   (c) I or II only   (d) I, II or III

41. The principal determinants of operating temperature are _____.

I.   heat generated internally in the conductor as the result of load current flow
II. the rate at which generated heat dissipates into the ambient medium
III. adjacent load-carrying conductors
IV. ambient temperature

(a) II and IV only   (b) I and IV only   (c) I, II and IV   (d) I, II, III and IV

42. The color _____ may have been used in the past as an ungrounded conductor. Care should be taken when working on existing systems.

(a) green   (b) white   (c) gray   (d) orange

43. Circuit breakers shall be so located or shielded so that persons _____.

(a) will not be burned or otherwise injured by their operation
(b) other than the authority cannot locate them
(c) cannot operate them without a key
(d) other than the authority cannot remove them

44. For other than a totally enclosed switchboard or switchgear, a space of not less than _____ shall be provided between the top of the switchboard and any combustible ceiling, unless a noncombustible shield is provided between the switchboard and the ceiling.

(a) 18"   (b) 2'   (c) 30"   (d) 36"

45. Equipment intended to interrupt current at fault levels shall have an ____ rating at nominal circuit voltage sufficient for the current that is available at the line terminals of the equipment.

(a) operating   (b) interrupting   (c) ampacity   (d) temperature

46. Heavy-duty lampholders shall have a rating not less than ____ watts of the admedium type, and not less than ____ watts of any other type.

(a) 750 ... 750   (b) 1000 ... 750   (c) 660 ... 750   (d) 660 ... 1000

47. The minimum feeder-circuit conductor size, before the application of any adjustment or correction factors, shall have an allowable ampacity equal to or greater than the noncontinuous load plus ____ percent of the continuous load.

(a) 100   (b) 125   (c) 80   (d) 75

48. Conductive materials enclosing electrical conductors are grounded to ____.

I.   prevent surges of voltage
II. prevent surges of lightning
III. to facilitate overcurrent device operation in case of ground faults

(a) I only   (b) II only   (c) III only   (d) all of these

49. ____ cable shall be flame-retardant, moisture-resistant, fungus-resistant, and corrosion-resistant.

(a) MI   (b) USE   (c) NMC   (d) NM

50. Circuit breakers shall not be located in the vicinity of easily ignitible material such as in ____.

(a) hallways   (b) laundry rooms   (c) clothes closets   (d) basements

2020

JOURNEYMAN
OPEN
BOOK
EXAM #18

50 QUESTIONS
TIME LIMIT - 2 HOURS

TIME SPENT [   ] MINUTES

SCORE [   ] %

JOURNEYMAN OPEN BOOK EXAM #18   **Two Hour Time Limit**

1. An electric pump installed in a pond may be supplied by a Type _____ flexible cord.

(a) TPT or TS   (b) SRD or SRDT   (c) SP-1 or SPE-1   (d) SO or ST

2. An AC transformer and DC rectifier arc welder with a 70% duty cycle, the ampacity of the supply conductors shall be calculated by multiplying the nameplate current by a factor of _____.

(a) .78   (b) .84   (c) .89   (d) .95

3. The circuit conductor that is defined as being intentionally grounded is the _____ conductor.

(a) equipment grounding   (b) grounding   (c) grounded   (d) grounding electrode

4. The motor nameplate full-load current rating is used for sizing the _____.

(a) branch circuit conductors
(b) motor disconnecting device
(c) branch circuit short circuit fuse
(d) motor overload protection device

5. Temperature controlled switching devices which do not have an "off" position shall _____.

(a) not be required to open all ungrounded conductors
(b) not be permitted to serve as the disconnecting means
(c) (b) only
(d) both (a) and (b)

6. The disconnecting means serving a hermetic refrigerant motor-compressor shall be selected on the basis of the nameplate rated-load current or branch-circuit selection current of the motor-compressor. The ampere rating shall be at least _____ of the nameplate rated-load current.

(a) 75%   (b) 80%   (c) 100%   (d) 115%

7. The ampacity of conductors that connect a capacitor to the terminals of a motor shall not be less than _____ of the ampacity of the motor circuit conductors.

(a) 33%   (b) 50%   (c) 75%   (d) 80%

8. Branch circuit conductors within 3 inches of a ballast within the ballast compartment shall have an insulation temperature rating not lower than _____.

(a) 60°C   (b) 75°C   (c) 85°C   (d) 90°C

9. Splices or taps shall be permitted within gutters when they are accessible. The conductors, including splices and taps, shall not fill the gutter to more than ____ of its area.

(a) 20%   (b) 40%   (c) 75%   (d) 80%

10. According to the National Electrical Code, electrical junction boxes shall be installed so that the wiring contained in the box ____.

(a) cannot be removed
(b) is visible at all times
(c) is always readily accessible
(d) can be rendered accessible without removing any part of the building or structure

11. Busways shall be supported at intervals not to exceed ____ unless otherwise designed and marked.

(a) 3'   (b) 5'   (c) 6'   (d) 8'

12. Rigid metal conduit shall be supported at least every ____ feet and shall be fastened in place within ____ feet of each box, outlet, cabinet or fitting, unless structural members interfere.

(a) 5;2
(b) 10;3
(c) 10;2
(d) 8;3

13. Screw-shell lampholders shall be wired so that the ____ conductor is connected to the screw-shell.

(a) bare   (b) ungrounded   (c) grounded   (d) grounding

14. Autotransformers are permitted in branch circuits when ____.

(a) transforming 240v, three-phase to single phase 120v
(b) transforming 480v to 120v
(c) transforming 208v to 240v
(d) not permitted by the Code

15. In determining load on the volt-amperes per square foot basis, the ____ the building shall be used.

(a) number of rooms in
(b) height of
(c) outside dimensions of
(d) inside dimensions of

16. Where feeder conductors originate in the same panelboard, and each feeder terminates in a single disconnecting means, not more than ____ feeders shall be permitted.

(a) 2 (b) 3 (c) 4 (d) 6

17. In a hospital General Care Area, each patient bed location shall be provided with a minimum of ____ receptacles.

(a) 3 single
(b) 2 single or 1 duplex
(c) 2 duplex or 4 single
(d) 4 duplex or 8 single

18. If practicable, the minimum distance allowed between overhead communication cables and lightning conductors is ____.

(a) 3' (b) 6' (c) 10' (d) 12'

19. The maximum allowable voltage permitted for Class 1 remote-control and signaling circuits is ____ volts.

(a) 12 (b) 24 (c) 300 (d) 600

20. Except where otherwise allowed, underwater lighting fixtures in the walls of permanently installed pools shall have the top of the fixture lens at least ____ below the normal water level of the pool.

(a) 6" (b) 12" (c) 18" (d) 24"

21. For general wiring in Class I, Division 1 locations, it is permissible to use ____.

(a) rigid metal conduit
(b) flexible metallic tubing
(c) electrical metallic tubing
(d) rigid non-metallic conduit

22. The National Electrical Code requires at least two small appliance branch circuits for dwellings. Either or both of these two circuits shall be permitted to supply circuits in which of the following four rooms?

(a) Kitchen, dining room, recreation room and breakfast room
(b) Kitchen, dining room, breakfast room and living room
(c) Kitchen, pantry, breakfast room and dining room
(d) Kitchen, pantry, breakfast room and hallway

23. An outside feeder conductor having an overhead span of 45 feet shall be not less than ____ copper.

(a) #14   (b) #12   (c) #10   (d) #8

24. Service conductors shall have a clearance of not less than ____ from the sides of openable windows.

(a) 24"   (b) 30"   (c) 36"   (d) 48"

25. For equipment grounding, exposed non-current carrying metal parts of fixed equipment likely to be energized shall be grounded where ____.

(a) in electrical contact with metal
(b) located in a damp or wet location and not isolated
(c) equipment operates with any terminal at more than 150 volts to ground
(d) all of the above

26. A panelboard for a residence shall not be installed in ____.

(a) a garage
(b) a basement
(c) an uncovered patio
(d) a clothes closet or bathroom

27. Each electrode of one grounding system shall not be less than ____ feet from any other electrode of another grounding system.

(a) 3   (b) 6   (c) 8   (d) 12

28. Round access openings in a manhole shall not be less than ____ in diameter.

(a) 16"   (b) 18"   (c) 24"   (d) 26"

29. Electric sign and outline lighting system equipment shall be at least 4.3 m or ____ above areas accessible to vehicles unless protected from physical damage.

(a) 10 ft   (b) 12 ft   (c) 14 ft   (d) 24 ft

30. Unless protected by ground-fault circuit-interrupter protection for personnel, the secondary winding of the isolation transformer connected to the pipeline or vessel being heated shall not have an output voltage greater than ____ volts ac.

(a) 10   (b) 25   (c) 30   (d) 35

31. Adjustable Speed Drive Systems: the incoming branch circuit or feeder to power conversion equipment included as a part of an adjustable-speed drive system shall be based on the rated input to the power conversion equipment. Where the power conversion equipment is marked to indicate that overload protection is included, additional _____ protection shall not be required.

(a) lockout   (b) overload   (c) disconnect   (d) fuses

32. DC motors operating from a rectifier bridge of the single-phase half-wave power supply, the conductors between the field wiring terminals of the rectifier and the motor shall have an ampacity of not less than ____ of the motor full-load current rating.

(a) 120%   (b) 125%   (c) 150%   (d) 190%

33. An inverse time circuit breaker that is used as both controller and disconnecting means is permitted to be operated by ___ attachment to the handle or lever.

(a) power   (b) manual   (c) actuator   (d) a or b

34. Single-phase cord-and-plug-connected room air conditioners shall be provided with factory-installed LCDI or AFCI protection. The LCDI or AFCI protection shall be an integral part of the attachment plug or be located in the power supply cord within 300 mm or ____ in. of the attachment plug.

(a) 12   (b) 14   (c) 20   (d) 30

35. A receptacle to supply electric power to a recreational vehicle shall be which of the following configurations.

(a) 50-ampere — 125/250-volt, 50-ampere, 3-pole, 4-wire grounding type for 120/240-volt systems
(b) 30-ampere — 125-volt, 30-ampere, 2-pole, 4-wire grounding type for 120-volt systems
(c) 20-ampere — 125-volt, 20-ampere, 3-pole, 4-wire grounding type for 120-volt systems
(d) 15-ampere — 125-volt, 15 ampere, 2 pole, 4-wire grounding type for 120-volt systems

36. When installing ventilation system electrical controls, they shall be arranged so the airflow can be _____.

(a) vented   (b) reversed   (c) looped   (d) prevented

37. When wiring a dwelling's bathroom you shall install at least one receptacle no less than ____ feet of the outside edge of the basin.

(a) 6   (b) 5   (c) 3   (d) 2

38. For raceways or cables exposed to direct sunlight on or above rooftops to the bottom of the raceway or cable is less than 7/8", a temperature adder of _____ shall be added to the outdoor temperature to determine the applicable ambient temperature for application of correction factors.

(a) 30°F   (b) 60°C   (c) 30°C   (d) 60°F

39. Where a single equipment grounding conductor is run with multiple circuits in the same raceway or cable, it shall be sized for the _____ over current device protecting conductors in the raceway or cable.

(a) least   (b) total   (c) largest   (d) average

40. GFCI protection is required for personnel _____.

(a) for boat houses
(b) for the kitchen
(c) laundry areas
(d) all of these

41. Cabinets and cutout boxes shall have sufficient space to accommodate _____ conductors installed in them without crowding.

(a) all   (b) large   (c) low voltage   (d) small

42. Types NM, NMC, and NMS cables shall **NOT** be used as follows _____.

(a) in exposed work   **(b) as service-entrance cable**
(c) fished in voids in masonry blocks   **(d) on the outside walls of masonry block or tile**

43. The largest rigid metallic conduit permitted to be used is a _____ trade size.

(a) 4   (b) 6   (c) 8   (d) 12

44. Which of the following conditions apply to receptacle cover plate's NEC regulation _____?

(a) Metal faceplate shall be of ferrous metal not less than 1.2 mm (0.040 in.) in thickness and/ or of nonferrous metal not less than 0.76 mm (0.030 in.) in thickness.
(b) Metal faceplate shall be ungrounded.
(c) Faceplate of insulating material shall be noncombustible and not less than 2.54 mm (0.010 in.) in thickness but shall be permitted to be less than 2.54 mm (0.010 in.) in thickness if formed or reinforced to provide adequate mechanical strength considered suitable for damp locations.
(d) all of the above

45. Delta breakers shall not be installed in a/an _____.

(a) buss   (b) box   (c) enclosure   (d) panelboard

46. The secondary winding of the isolation transformer connected to impedance heating elements shall not have an output voltage greater than ____ volts ac.

(a) 25   (b) 30   (c) 60   (d) 80

47. A metal underground water pipe, in direct contact with the earth for at least 10 feet, has traditionally been a preferred grounding electrode. For all new construction, a metal underground water pipe is ____.

(a) no longer accepted as a grounding electrode
(b) still the preferred grounding electrode, by itself, when available
(c) accepted as the only grounding electrode when buried at least 3 feet below the surface
(d) still an acceptable grounding electrode, but it must be supplemented by at least one additional grounding electrode

48. In readily accessible locations, turbine output circuits that operate at voltages greater than ____ shall be installed in raceways.

(a) 12v   (b) 20v   (c) 24v   (d) 30v

49. Cables buried directly in earth for residential branch circuits rated 120 volts or less with GFCI protection and maximum protection of 20 amps shall be permitted with a minimum cover of ____.

(a) 6"   (b) 12"   (c) 18"   (d) 24"

50. Of the following, ____ is not permitted for installation in cable trays.

(a) nonmetallic sheathed cable
(b) multiconductor service entrance cable
(c) single conductor smaller than #1/0
(d) multiconductor underground feeder and branch circuit cable

2020

JOURNEYMAN
OPEN
BOOK
EXAM #19

50 QUESTIONS
TIME LIMIT - 2 HOURS

TIME SPENT [　　　] **MINUTES**

SCORE [　　　] %

1. Conductors used exclusively for control or instrumentation smaller than 18 AWG, but not smaller than 22 AWG for single conductor and 26 AWG for multiconductor cable are secured within _____ inches of termination.

(a) 10   (b) 12   (c) 18   (d) 24

2. The minimum size copper equipment grounding conductor required on a motor branch circuit with a 30 amp circuit breaker and #12 copper conductors is _____.

(a) #10   (b) #8   (c) #12   (d) #14

3. Type 3 SPD connection shall be a minimum ___ feet of conductor distance from the service or separately derived system disconnect.

(a) 10   (b) 15   (c) 25   (d) 30

4. Mats of insulating rubber or other suitable floor insulation shall be provided for the operator where the voltage to ground exceeds _____ on live-front switchboards.

(a) 50   (b) 100   (c) 120   (d) 150

5. Cables shall be permitted to be applied where the system is provided with relay protection such that ground faults will be cleared as rapidly as possible but, in no case, within _____.

(a) 60 seconds   (b) one-half minute   (c) 40 seconds   (d) 2 minutes

6. Plug-in-type overcurrent protection devices or plug-in-type main lug assemblies that are _____ shall be secured in place by an additional fastener that requires other than a pull to release the device from the mounting means on the panel.

(a) three-phase only   (b) 480v   (c) back fed   (d) none of these

7. Unguarded live parts above working space shall be maintained at an elevation of _____ for 4160 volts.

(a) 8'   (b) 8' 6"   (c) 9'   (d) 10'

8. #0 copper conductors in vertical raceway shall be supported at intervals not exceeding _____ feet.

(a) 50   (b) 75   (c) 100   (d) 125

9. The nominal gas pressure for IGS cable insulation shall be ____ pounds per square inch gage.

(a) 5   (b) 10   (c) 15   (d) 20

10. Where installed in a metal raceway, all conductors of all feeders using a common neutral shall be ____.

(a) insulated for 600 volt   (b) enclosed within the same raceway
(c) shielded   (d) none of these

11. Liquidtight flexible conduit shall **not** be permitted ____.

(a) in hazardous locations
(b) where subject to physical damage
(c) in exposed and concealed work
(d) where installations requires flexibility or protection from liquids, vapors or solids

12. Adjacent load-carrying conductors have the dual effect of raising the ____ and impeding heat dissipation.

(a) insulation rating   (b) heat above 86°F   (c) ambient temperature   (d) skin effect

13. According to the Code, conductors on poles, where not placed on racks or brackets, shall be separated not less than ____ inches.

(a) 6   (b) 12   (c) 18   (d) 24

14. The minimum insulation level for neutral conductors in solidly grounded systems is ____ volts.

(a) 250   (b) 600   (c) 1000   (d) 1200

15. The branch circuit breaker device shall protect all ____.

(a) fittings   (b) branch circuit loads   (c) appliances   (d) conductors and equipment

16. Which of the following is **NOT** an acceptable method of mounting electrical equipment to a masonry wall?

(a) With screws driven into wooden plugs in the wall.
(b) With bolts through the wall supported by metal plates on the back side.
(c) With lag bolts screwed into lead masonry anchors.
(d) With molly bolts through holes drilled entirely through the wall.

17. Plug fuses and fuseholders shall **NOT** be used between conductors and the grounded neutral in circuits exceeding how many volts?

(a) 50 volts   (b) 100 volts   (c) 115 volts   (d) 150 volts

18. An all-electric home has a laundry area located in a kitchen closet. What is the **MINIMUM** number of branch circuits serving this kitchen?

(a) 2   (b) 3   (c) 4   (d) 5

19. Coatings on which of the following shall be removed at threads, contact points, and contact surfaces or be connected by means of fittings so designed as to make such removal unnecessary in bonding other enclosures for grounding?

(a) Zinc   (b) Enamel   (c) Copper   (d) Aluminum

20. What is the **MINIMUM** size underground service lateral for a copper-clad aluminum single-branch circuit serving a controlled water heater?

(a) #14   (b) #12   (c) #10   (d) #8

21. A single receptacle on an individual branch circuit shall have a **MINIMUM** rating of what percentage of the branch circuit's rating?

(a) 50%   (b) 70%   (c) 80%   (d) 100%

22. What is the **MINIMUM** size copper grounding conductor required to serve a multisection motor control center equipped with a 300-amp overcurrent device?

(a) #8 AWG   (b) #6 AWG   (c) #4 AWG   (d) #2 AWG

23. The effective grounding path to ground from circuits, equipment and metal equipment enclosures shall **NOT** ____.

(a) have sufficiently low impedance to limit the voltage to ground
(b) use earth as the sole equipment-grounding conductor
(c) have the capacity to conduct safely any fault currents to ground
(d) be permanent and continuous

24. Where cable assemblies with nonmetallic sheathes are used, the sheath shall extend not less than ____ inside the box.

(a) 6"   (b) 3"   (c) 1/2"   (d) 1/4"

25. What color must be used to identify an insulated #6 or smaller grounded conductor?

(a) Red   (b) Blue   (c) Green   (d) Gray

26. Which of the following colors indicates an equipment grounding conductor in a flexible cord?

(a) White   (b) White with blue stripe
(c) Green with a yellow stripe   (d) Green with gray stripe

27. What is the **MINIMUM** voltage rating for the insulation on a grounded conductor in a solidly grounded neutral system of over 1 kV?

(a) 240 volts   (b) 480 volts   (c) 600 volts   (d) 1000 volts

28. A device intended for the protection of personnel that functions to de-energize a circuit or portion thereof within an established period of time when a current to ground exceeds the values established for a Class A device is called a _____.

(a) limit switch   (b) circuit breaker   (c) ground-fault interrupter   (d) fuse

29. What is the **MAXIMUM** allowable AWG size for a solid conductor installed in a raceway?

(a) #14   (b) #12   (c) #10   (d) #8

30. What is the **MAXIMUM** allowable electrical potential for low-voltage equipment in frequent contact with patient's bodies?

(a) 6 volts   (b) 8 volts   (c) 10 volts   (d) 12 volts

31. Where are conduit seals **NOT** required in a Class I installation?

(a) Where metal conduit passes completely through the Class I area with no fittings less than 12" outside any classified area.
(b) Where a conduit less than 36" in length connects two enclosures.
(c) Where the conduit enters an explosion-proof motor
(d) Where the conduit exits the Class I area.

32. When combinations of conductors enter a box, which conductor size shall be used when utilizing the volume deductions permitted for fittings and devices?

(a) Total   (b) Smallest   (c) Largest   (d) Average

33. What protective device protects a motor against dangerous overheating and is assembled as an integral part of a motor or motor-compressor?

(a) Power cutout   (b) Current-release element   (c) Thermal protector   (d) Integral fuse

34. How much space is occupied by a #350 kcmil RHW grounding conductor without an outer covering?

(a) 0.5958 sq.in.   (b) 0.7870 sq.in.   (c) 0.8710 sq.in.   (d) 1.0010 sq.in.

35. A 2 hp motor has a service factor of 1.15. What is the MAXIMUM percentage rating for the overload protection?

(a) 115%   (b) 125%   (c) 130%   (d) 140%

36. After normal power fails, what is the **MAXIMUM** delay permitted in a legally required emergency standby system before emergency power is available?

(a) 30 seconds   (b) one minute   (c) 2 minutes   (d) 3 minutes

37. Listed nonmetallic raceways are permitted for all of the following uses **EXCEPT** ____.

(a) where subject to physical damage   (b) in exposed work
(c) where subject to corrosive vapors   (d) in wet locations

38. What special provision is required for all hospital bed locations?

(a) At least two branch circuits   (b) Tamper-resistant receptacles
(c) Explosion-proof receptacles   (d) A patient equipment-grounding point

39. Which of the following receptacle outlets in a mobile home requires GFCI protection?

(a) An outdoor receptacle
(b) A dishwasher receptacle
(c) A receptacle within 6' of a lavatory
(d) All of these

40. Communication wires and cables shall be separated at least ___ from conductors of any electric light or power circuits, Class 1, or non power-limited fire alarm circuits, or medium power network powered broadband communications circuits.

(a) 0"   (b) 2"   (c) 4"   (d) 6"

41. What is the MAXIMUM rung spacing for ladder cable trays carrying single conductor #4/0 AWG cable?

(a) 4"   (b) 6"   (c) 9"   (d) 12"

42. Conductors that supply one or more welders shall be protected by an overcurrent device rated or set at not more than ___ of the conductor rating.

(a) 80%   (b) 125%   (c) 150%   (d) 300%

43. Use of UF cable is permitted ____.

(a) where embedded in poured concrete   (b) in theaters
(c) for wiring in wet locations   (d) as service entrance conductors

44. What is the classification of a location where ignitible concentrations of flammable gas are likely to be present during normal operations?

(a) Class I, Division 1   (b) Class I, Division 2
(c) Class II, Division 1   (d) Class III, Division 1

45. A transformer is installed in an industrial plant to reduce a 1,200 volt supply to 480. The transformer is rated at 7.5% impedance. The location is unsupervised. What is the MAXIMUM setting for the overcurrent device on the secondary side?

(a) 125% of the transformer rating   (b) Equal to the transformer rating
(c) 225% of the transformer rating   (d) 250% of the transformer rating

46. Low-voltage fuseholders and low-voltage nonrenewable fuses shall not be ____.

(a) reconditioned   (b) used in dwellings   (c) 300 volt rating   (d) classified

47. The SPD shall be an integral part of the service equipment or shall be located ____.

(a) within 12'   (b) immediately adjacent thereto   (c) within 2"   (d) within sight

48. The attachment plug on a table lamp outfitted with a line-connected single-pole switch wired with a flat 2-conductor cord must be replaced. What type of attachment plug must be used?

(a) Twist lock   (b) Polarized   (c) Grounding   (d) Nonpolarized

49. A Class 1 power-limited circuit shall be supplied from a source having a rated output of not more than 30 volts and ___ volt amperes.

(a) 1000   (b) 1200   (c) 1500   (d) 2000

50. Luminaires recessed in ceilings, floors, or walls shall not be used to access outlet, pull, or junction boxes or conduit bodies, unless the box is ____.

(a) an integral part of the listed luminaire   (b) listed as a pull box
(c) a double gang box   (d) listed conduit body

2020

JOURNEYMAN
OPEN
BOOK
EXAM #20

50 QUESTIONS
TIME LIMIT - 2 HOURS

TIME SPENT [   ] **MINUTES**

SCORE [   ] %

JOURNEYMAN OPEN BOOK EXAM #20   **Two Hour Time Limit**

1. Where the number of current-carrying conductors in a raceway is seven, the individual ampacity of each conductor shall be reduced ____.

(a) to 70% due to the number of conductors
(b) to 80% if they are continuous loads
(c) to both (a) and (b) if both conditions exist
(d) neither apply if the ambient temperature is below 30° C or 86° F

2. Insulated bushings are required on conduit entering boxes, gutters, etc. if the conduit contains conductors as large as ____.

(a) #2   (b) #4   (c) #0   (d) #6

3. Flexible cables, as identified in Article 400, in sizes ____ and larger shall be permitted within the battery enclosure from the battery terminals to a nearby junction box where they will be connected to an approved wiring method.

(a) 6 AWG   (b) 4 AWG   (c) 1/0 AWG   (d) 2/0 AWG

4. Fluorescent lighting fixtures may be used as raceways if ____.

(a) they are connected by a conduit wiring method
(b) they are wired so that conductors are not closer than 3" from the ballast
(c) listed for use as a raceway
(d) none of these

5. When supplying a nominal 120v rated air-conditioner, the length of the flexible supply cord shall not exceed ____ feet.

(a) 4   (b) 6   (c) 8   (d) 10

6. Lighting equipment identified for horticultural use shall not be installed as lighting for general illumination unless such use is ____.

(a) approved   (b) listed   (c) identified   (d) is indicated in the manufacturer's instructions

7. The number of #12 THW conductors allowed in a 3/4" IMC conduit will be ____ the number of #12 TW conductors allowed in a 3/4" conduit.

(a) equal to   (b) greater than   (c) less than   (d) none of these

8. When connections are made in the white wire in a multiwire circuit at receptacles, they are required to be made ____.

(a) connected to the silver terminal on the duplex
(b) to the brass colored terminal
(c) with a pigtail to the silver terminal
(d) none of these

9. The splice connection between the nonheating lead and heating element, within concrete, masonry, or asphalt, shall be located no less than 1" and no more than ____ from the metal raceway.

(a) 2" (b) 4" (c) 6" (d) 8"

10. Which of the following is **not** true?

(a) The receptacle outlet spacing in a motel room can be more than 12' from outlet to outlet.
(b) A two-family dwelling requires at least one receptacle outlet outdoors for each dwelling unit at grade level.
(c) A vehicle door in an attached garage is not considered as an outdoor entrance.
(d) A vehicle door in an attached garage is considered as an outdoor entrance.

11. Service-drop conductors shall have ____.

I. adequate mechanical strength
II. sufficient ampacity to carry the load as computed in accordance with Article 220

(a) I only (b) II only (c) both I and II (d) neither I nor II

12. The frame of a clothes dryer shall be permitted to be grounded to the grounded circuit conductor if ____.

I. the grounded conductor is insulated
II. the grounded conductor is not smaller than #10 copper
III. the supply circuit is 120/240v single-phase

(a) I only (b) II only (c) III only (d) I, II and III

13. A 20 ampere rated branch circuit serves four receptacles. The rating of the receptacles must not be less than ____ amperes.

(a) 20 (b) 15 (c) 25 (d) none of these

14. When the voltage to a building is 480/277, and the service drop runs not more than four feet past the edge of the overhang of the roof, how high must it be above the roof?

(a) 18"   (b) 3'   (c) 4'   (d) 8'

15. The industrial control panel does not include the ____.

(a) relays   (b) timers   (c) disconnect   (d) controlled equipment

16. Where the calculated number of conductors, all of the same size, includes a decimal fraction, the next higher whole number shall be used if ____.

(a) .5 and larger   (b) .6 and larger   (c) .7 and larger   (d) .8 and larger

17. The height of a circuit breaker used as a switch shall not exceed ____ above the floor.

(a) 4'   (b) 4 1/2'   (c) 5'   (d) 6' 7"

18. The number of #12 conductors permitted in a 3" x 2" x 1 1/2" deep device box is ____.

(a) 6   (b) 5   (c) 4   (d) 3

19. What is the minimum height of a service drop attachment to a building?

(a) 8 feet   (b) 10 feet   (c) 12 feet   (d) 15 feet

20. Heating cables shall be furnished with nonheating leads at least ____ in length.

(a) 7'   (b) 8'   (c) 10'   (d) 12'

21. In a dwelling, which appliance shall be grounded?

(a) toaster   (b) can opener   (c) blender   (d) aquarium

22. Accessible conductive parts bonded together to reduce voltage gradients is a/an ____.

(a) datum plane   (b) equipotential plane   (c) effective ground point   (d) island mode

23. Rigid conduit buried in an area subject to heavy vehicular traffic shall have a minimum cover of ____ inches.

(a) 6   (b) 12   (c) 18   (d) 24

24. A single-family dwelling contains a 200 amp single-phase service panel supplied with #2/0 THW conductors. The minimum size bonding jumper for this service is ____.

(a) #6 aluminum   (b) #6 copper   (c) #4 aluminum   (d) #4 copper

25. A 1 1/2" rigid metal nipple with three conductors can be filled to an area of ____ square inches.

(a) .98   (b) 1.07   (c) 1.2426   (d) 1.34

26. Grounding electrode conductors smaller than #6 shall be in ____.

I. EMT   II. IMC   III. rigid PVC   IV. rigid metal conduit

(a) I and IV only   (b) I, II and IV only   (c) II and IV only   (d) I, II, III and IV

27. Generators with greater than ____ rating shall be provided with a remote emergency stop switch to shut down the prime mover.

(a) 5 kW   (b) 7.5 kW   (c) 10 kW   (d) 15 kW

28. Type SE service-entrance cables shall be permitted in interior wiring systems where all of the circuit conductors of the cable are of the ____ type.

I. thermoset   II. thermoplastic   III. metal

(a) I and II only   (b) II only   (c) II and III only   (d) I, II and III

29. Elevator traveling cables for operating ____ circuits shall contain nonmetallic fillers as necessary to maintain concentricity.

I. signal   II. control

(a) I only   (b) II only   (c) both I and II   (d) neither I nor II

30. Low probability of damage other than slight swelling of the capacitor case, as identified by the ____ of the capacitor.

(a) color   (b) case rupture curve   (c) residual voltage   (d) inrush current

31. For household ranges rated ___ or more rating, the minimum branch circuit rating shall be 40 amperes.

(a) 4 kW   (b) 6 kW   (c) 8 kW   (d) 8 3/4 kW

32. Receptacles located within ____ feet of the inside walls of a pool shall be protected by a ground-fault circuit-interrupter.

(a) 8   (b) 10   (c) 15   (d) 20

33. Portable appliances used on 15 or 20 amp branch circuits, the rating of any one portable appliance shall not exceed ____ percent of the branch circuit rating.

(a) 60   (b) 100   (c) 80   (d) 50

34. All fixtures installed in damp locations shall be marked ____.

(a) waterproof   (b) suitable for wet locations   (c) damp locations   (d) weatherproof

35. What kind of lighting loads does the Code say there shall be no reduction in the size of the neutral conductor?

(a) dwelling unit   (b) hospital   (c) nonlinear   (d) motel

36. How would you seal unused ko's in panels and boxes?

(a) cardboard   (b) duct seal   (c) tape   (d) metal plugs and plates

37. Electrodes of steel or iron shall have a diameter of at least ____.

(a) 1/2"   (b) 3/4"   (c) 1"   (d) 5/8"

38. A permanent and legible single-line diagram of the local switching arrangements, clearly identifying each point of connection to the ____ section, shall be provided within sight of each point of connection.

(a) service   (b) feeder   (c) high-voltage   (d) switch-gear

39. In closed construction in a manufactured building, cables shall be permitted to be secured only at cabinets, boxes, or fittings where ____ or smaller conductors are used and protected as required.

(a) #2 AWG   (b) #10 AWG   (c) #2/0 AWG   (d) #250 kcmil

40. The maximum length of exposed cord in a fountain shall be ____ feet.

(a) 3   (b) 4   (c) 6   (d) 10

41. Fixture studs that are not part of outlet boxes, _____ shall be made of steel, malleable iron, or other material suitable for the application.

I. crowfeet   II. hickeys   III. tripods

(a) I only   (b) II only   (c) III only   (d) I, II and III

42. A garbage disposal in the kitchen of a residence provided with a type SO three-conductor cord terminated with a grounding-type attachment plug shall be permitted where all of the following conditions are met _____.

I.   the receptacle shall be readily accessible
II.   the receptacle shall be located to avoid physical damage to the flexible cord
III. the receptacle shall be accessible
IV. the length of the cord shall not be less than 18" and not over 36"

(a) I, II and IV   (b) I, II and III   (c) II, III and IV   (d) III and IV

43. The minimum radius of the inside of a bend for a 3/4" flexible metallic tubing used for flexing is _____ inches.

(a) 17 1/2   (b) 12 1/2   (c) 10   (d) 5

44. Battery systems shall be permitted to serve as the _____ for all or parts of an essential electrical system.

(a) stand alone system   (b) back feed   (c) standby   (d) alternate source

45. Cables of the AC type, except ACL, shall have an internal bonding strip of _____ in intimate contact with the armor for its entire length.

I. aluminum   II. copper

(a) I only   (b) II only   (c) either I or II   (d) neither I nor II

46. A factory-assembled structure or structures transportable in one or more sections that are built on a permanent chassis and designed to be used as other than a dwelling unit without a permanent foundation is the definition of a/an _____.

(a) RV   (b) mobile home   (c) manufactured building   (d) relocatable structure

47. Where two or more relocatable structures are structurally connected to form a single unit, it shall be permissible to install one communication system bonding jumper with a minimum _____ copper.

(a) 10 AWG   (b) 8 AWG   (c) 6 AWG   (d) 4 AWG

48. Fixtures shall be supported independently of the outlet box where the weight exceeds _____ pounds.

(a) 60   (b) 50   (c) 40   (d) 30

49. Every circuit breaker having an interrupting rating other than _____ amperes, shall have its interrupting rating shown on the breaker.

(a) 1000   (b) 2000   (c) 5000   (d) 7500

50. Hoistway is a _____ in which an elevator or dumbwaiter is designed to operate.

(a) shaftway   (b) hatchway   (c) well hole   (d) all of these

2020

JOURNEYMAN
OPEN
BOOK
EXAM #21

50 QUESTIONS
TIME LIMIT - 2 HOURS

TIME SPENT [　　　] **MINUTES**

SCORE [　　　] %

JOURNEYMAN OPEN BOOK EXAM #21   **Two Hour Time Limit**

1. Where extensive metal in or on buildings or structures may become energized and is subject to personal contact _____ will provide additional safety.

(a) adequate bonding and grounding   **(b) bonding**
(c) suitable ground detectors   **(d) none of these**

2. Single conductor cables shall be _____ or larger and shall be of a type listed for use in cable trays.

(a) #1   (b) #1/0   (c) #4/0   (d) #250 kcmil

3. The grounded conductor, when insulated, shall have insulation _____.

I.   rated not less than 300 volts for solidly grounded neutral systems of 1 kv and over as described in section 250.184
II. which is suitable, other than color, for any ungrounded conductor of the same circuit on circuits of less than 1000 volts

(a) I only   (b) II only   (c) either I or II   (d) neither I nor II

4. Which of the following is **not** true regarding rigid nonmetallic conduit?

(a) Extreme cold may cause some nonmetallic conduits to become brittle and therefore more susceptible to damage from physical contact.
(b) Can be used to support luminaires.
(c) All cut ends shall be trimmed inside and outside to remove rough edges.
(d) Expansion joints shall be provided to compensate for thermal expansion and contraction.

5. Lighting track conductors shall be a minimum _____ AWG or equal, and shall be copper.

(a) #16   (b) #14   (c) #12   (d) #10

6. RTRC conduit 2" in size shall be securely fastened within 3' of each box and horizontally a maximum of _____ between supports.

(a) 5'   (b) 6'   (c) 7'   (d) 10'

7. Cablebus shall be installed only for _____ work.

(a) exposed   (b) commercial   (c) concealed   (d) hazardous

8. Knife switches rated for more than 1200 amperes at 250 volts ____.

(a) are used only as isolating switches
(b) should be placed so that gravity tends to close them
(c) should be opened slowly under load
(d) should be connected so blades are not dead in open position

9. A transverse metal raceway for electrical conductors, furnishing access to predetermined cells of a precast cellular concrete floor, which permits installation of conductors from a distribution center to the floor cells is called ____.

(a) an underfloor raceway   **(b) a header**
(c) a cellular raceway   **(d) a mandrel**

10. Because aluminum is not a magnetic metal, there will be no heating due to ____.

(a) electrolysis   (b) hysteresis   (c) hermetic   (d) galvanic action

11. Luminaires shall be so constructed, or installed, or equipped with shades or guards that combustible material will not be subjected to temperatures in excess of ____.

(a) 90°F   (b) 86°F   (c) 30°C   (d) 90°C

12. Overhead track and hoist system for moving material around the boatyard or moving or launching boats is the definition of a ___.

(a) monorail   (b) boat lift   (c) track hoist   (d) boat jack

13. All cut ends of rigid conduit shall be ____.

(a) threaded   (b) electrically continuous   (c) reamed   (d) cut square

14. What size conductor shall be connected between the ground grid and all metal parts of swimming pools?

(a) #8   (b) #10   (c) #6   (d) #4

15. Unsupported runs of armored cable shall be permitted to be unsupported where the cable is not more than ____ inches at terminals where flexibility is necessary.

(a) 24   (b) 30   (c) 36   (d) 48

16. A cabinet or cutout box if constructed of sheet steel, the metal thickness shall not be less than _____ inch uncoated.

(a) 0.053   (b) 0.503   (c) 0.040   (d) 0.373

17. The minimum headroom of working spaces about control centers shall be _____.

(a) 3' 6"   (b) 5"   (c) 6' 4"   (d) 6' 6"

18. Conductors of AC or DC circuits rated 600 volt or less, shall be permitted to occupy the same conduit if _____.

(a) all conductors shall have an insulation voltage rating equal to the maximum circuit voltage rating of any conductor in the conduit
(b) all conductors shall have a 600 volt insulation rating
(c) conductors must have a dividing barrier in the raceway
(d) AC and DC are not permitted in the same raceway

19. Where the service disconnecting means does not _____ the grounded conductor from the premises wiring, other means shall be provided for this purpose in the service equipment.

(a) shut off   (b) trip   (c) isolate   (d) disconnect

20. Low ambient conditions require special consideration. Explosionproof or dust-ignitionproof equipment may not be suitable for use at temperatures lower than _____ unless they are identified for low-temperature service.

(a) -13°F   (b) 20°C   (c) 10°F   (d) 15°F

21. Which of the following is true?

(a) The loads of outlets serving switchboards and switching frames in telephone exchanges shall be counted in branch-circuit computations.
(b) A multiple receptacle shall be considered at not less than 420va for computations of other outlets.
(c) The minimum general lighting load for a restaurant is 3 va per sq.ft.
(d) An electric clock may be connected to a small appliance branch circuit.

22. Cable or raceway that is installed through bored holes in wood members, holes shall be bored so that the edge of the hole is not less than 1 1/4" from the nearest edge of the wood member. Where this distance cannot be maintained, the cable or raceway shall be protected from penetration by nails and screws by a steel plate or bushing, at least _____ inch thick, and of appropriate length and width installed to cover the area of the wiring.

(a) 1/16   (b) 1/8   (c) 3/16   (d) 1/4

23. Except where fire stops are required, it shall be permissible to extend cablebus vertically through dry floors and platforms, provided the cablebus is totally enclosed at the point where it passes through the floor or platform and for a distance of _____ feet above the floor or platform.

(a) 6   (b) 8   (c) 10   (d) 4

24. Minimum headroom shall be provided for all working spaces about service equipment, switchboards, panelboards, or motor control centers except in service equipment or panelboards in dwelling units that do not exceed _____ amperes.

(a) 150   (b) 200   (c) 175   (d) 300

25. Fixtures which require aiming or adjusting after installation shall not be required to be equipped with an attachment plug or cord connector provided the exposed cord is _____.

I. not longer than that required for maximum adjustment
II. hard usage or extra-hard usage type

(a) I only   (b) II only   (c) both I and II   (d) neither I nor II

26. _____ or larger conductors supported on solid knobs shall be securely tied thereto by tie wires having an insulation equivalent to that of the conductor.

(a) #12   (b) #10   (c) #8   (d) #6

27. _____ is defined as the shortest distance measured between a point on the top surface of any direct buried conductor, cable, conduit, or other raceway and the top surface of finished grade.

(a) Depth   (b) Cover   (c) Gap   (d) Soil

28. Electric vehicle cable type EVJ _____.

I. comes in sizes #18-#500 kcmil   II. is for extra hard usuage   III. has thermoset insulation

(a) I only   (b) II only   (c) III only   (d) I, II and III

29. In land areas subject to tidal fluctuation, the electrical datum plane shall be a horizontal plane that is _____ above the highest tide level for the area occurring under normal circumstances based on the the highest tide level.

(a) 24"   (b) 3'   (c) 42"   (d) 4'

30. Tap conductors in a metal raceway for recessed fixture connections shall be limited to ____ feet in length.

(a) 2   (b) 4   (c) 6   (d) 10

31. Where a permanent barrier is installed in a pull box, each section is considered as _____.

(a) permanent barriers are not allowed   (b) a separate box
(c) 60% of the box   (d) the same box

32. Vending machines shall include a GFCI as an integral part of the attachment plug or located in the power supply cord within ____ of the attachment plug.

(a) 12"   (b) 16"   (c) 18"   (d) 24"

33. Underground service conductors carried up a pole must be protected from mechanical injury to a height of at least ____ feet.

(a) 12   (b) 8   (c) 15   (d) 9

34. Boxes that enclose utilization equipment supplied by #8, #6, or #4 conductors shall have an internal depth that is not less than ____.

(a) 7/8"   (b) 1 1/16"   (c) 1 3/16"   (d) 2 1/16"

35. Wall-mounted ovens and counter-mounted cooking units complete with provisions for mounting and for making electrical connections, shall be permitted to be ____.

I. plug and cord connected   II. permanently connected

(a) I only   (b) II only   (c) either I or II   (d) neither I nor II

36. Receptacles connected to circuits having different ____ on the same premises shall be of such design that the attachment plugs used on these circuits are not interchangeable.

I. current (AC or DC)   II. frequencies   III. voltages   IV. wattages

(a) I and III only   (b) I and II only   (c) I, II and III only   (d) I, II, III and IV

37. Electric vehicle power export equipment and electric vehicle supply equipment are sometimes contained in one piece of equipment, sometimes referred to as ____ EVSE.

(a) Class 1   (b) single unit   (c) bidirectional   (d) one circuit

38. Which of the following is **not** true?

(a) **A demand factor from Table 220.55 could be applied to a household counter-mounted cooking unit of 1760 watts.**
(b) **Ten household clothes dryers have a demand factor of 50%.**
(c) **A demand factor from Table 220.55 could be applied to a 1 3/4 kw wall-mounted oven.**
(d) **Table 220.55 is permitted for a branch circuit to a household range.**

39. Where the service overcurrent devices are locked or sealed, or otherwise not readily accessible, branch-circuit overcurrent devices shall be ____.

I.   of lower ampere rating than the service overcurrent device
II. mounted in an readily accessible location
III. installed on the load side

(a) I only   (b) II only   (c) III only   (d) I, II and III

40. Grounding conductors and bonding jumpers shall be connected by ____ or other listed means.

I. listed clamps   II. listed pressure connectors   III. exothermic welding

(a) I only   (b) II only   (c) III only   (d) I, II or III

41. Cable trays shall ____.

I.   have side rails or equivalent structural members
II. not present sharp edges or burrs
III. have suitable strength and rigidity

(a) I only   (b) I and II only   (c) III only   (d) I, II and III

42. A raceway containing 30 current carrying conductors, the ampacity of each conductor shall be reduced ____ percent.

(a) 80   (b) 70   (c) 45   (d) 50

43. The Code requires all conductors that attach to a cablebus to be in the same raceway because ____.

(a) of less voltage drop   (b) the cost is less   (c) it is easier to service   (d) of inductive current

44. A splash pad is a fountain with a pool depth of ____ or less, intended for recreational use by pedestrians.

(a) 1"   (b) 3"   (c) 5"   (d) 6"

45. Nonmetallic sheath cable must be supported within ____ of a metal box.

(a) 6"   (b) 12"   (c) 24"   (d) 48"

46. The temperature limitation of MI cable is based on the ____.

(a) ambient temperature   (b) conductor insulation
(c) insulating materials used in the end seal   (d) none of these

47. All electric equipment, including power supply cords used with storable pools shall be protected by ____.

(a) GFCI   (b) fuses   (c) circuit breakers   (d) current limiting fuses

48. Service conductors shall be attached to the disconnecting means by pressure connectors, clamps or other approved means, except connections that depend on ____ shall not be used.

(a) solder   (b) tension   (c) bolts   (d) pressure

49. Which of the following wiring methods is permitted through an air conditioning duct?

(a) electrical metallic tubing   (b) PVC
(c) no wiring method is permitted in an A/C duct   (d) romex

50. Conductors run above the top level of a window shall be permitted to be less than the ____ requirement for clearance from a window.

(a) 2'   (b) 3'   (c) 4'   (d) 8'

2020

JOURNEYMAN
OPEN
BOOK
EXAM #22

50 QUESTIONS
TIME LIMIT - 2 HOURS

TIME SPENT ☐ **MINUTES**

SCORE ☐ %

JOURNEYMAN OPEN BOOK EXAM #22   **Two Hour Time Limit**

1. HDPE conduit larger than trade size _____ shall not be used.

(a) 3   (b) 4   (c) 5   (d) 6

2. A system in which heat is generated in a pipeline or vessel wall by inducing current and hysteresis effect in the pipeline or vessel wall from an external isolated ac field source is called a/an _____ heating system.

(a) integrated   (b) induction   (c) impedance   (d) direct

3. Working space for equipment operating at 600 volts, nominal, or less to ground and likely to require examination, adjustment, servicing, or maintenance with exposed live parts on one side shall be _____ inches wide or the width of the panel or enclosure allowing the door(s) to open 90 degrees.

(a) 12   (b) 24   (c) 30   (d) 36

4. Where the transformer supplying the service is located outside the building, at least _____ additional grounding connection shall be made from the grounded service conductor to a grounding electrode, either at the transformer or elsewhere outside the building.

(a) one   (b) two   (c) three   (d) four

5. The dirt used to back fill a trench shall not contain _____ that could cause damage to raceways or cables.

(a) large rocks   (b) paving materials   (c) corrosive materials   (d) all of these

6. Wiring inside luminaires shall be arranged so they are not subject to ___ above those for which they are rated.

(a) temperatures   (b) insulations   (c) mounting heights   (d) moisture

7. Receptacles shall be listed for the purpose and marked with the _____ or identification and voltage and ampere.

(a) wire size   (b) manufacturer's name   (c) frequency   (d) type

8. A wall switch marked with the _____ shall completely disconnect all ungrounded conductors to the load it controls.

(a) off position (b) voltage (c) amps (d) horsepower

9. Which of the following would you find on a electrode type boilers legend plate _____.

(a) manufacturer's name
(b) normal rating in volts, amperes, and kilowatts
(c) electrical supply required, frequency, phase, number of wires
(d) all of the above

10. A Non-power limited fire alarm (NPLFA) circuits shall not be more than ____ volts.

(a) 12 (b) 24 (c) 115 (d) 600

11. The floors of vaults constructed with a vacant space or other stories below it, the floor shall have adequate structural strength for the load imposed on it and a minimum fire resistance of ___ hrs.

(a) 3 (b) 4 (c) 5 (d) 6

12. The grounded conductor of Type FC cable shall be identified throughout its length by means of a distinctive and durable _____ marking.

(a) white or gray (b) black (c) blue (d) green

13. Where pull and junction boxes are used, one or more sides of any pull box shall be _____.

(a) blocked (b) solid (c) welded (d) removable

14. Electrical systems that are grounded shall be connected to _____ in a manner that will limit the voltage imposed by lightning, line surges, or unintentional contact with higher-voltage lines and that will stabilize the voltage to earth during normal operation.

(a) structure (b) case (c) earth (d) metal

15. When installing fuses over 1000v, they must be installed in ____ with each ungrounded conductor.

(a) parallel (b) series (c) group (d) line

16. The neutral conductor of an impedance grounded neutral system shall be _____.

(a) unmarked (b) smaller (c) insulated (d) none of these

17. Type TC cables with metallic shielding shall have a minimum bending radius of not less than ___ times the cable overall diameter.

(a) ten   (b) twelve   (c) twenty four   (d) thirty six

18. The branch-circuit conductors supplying one or more units of a data processing system shall have an ampacity not less than _____ of the total connected load.

(a) 75%   (b) 100%   (c) 110%   (d) 125%

19. Tubular, strip, and immersion heaters are all types of _____ heaters.

(a) resistance   (b) induction   (c) impedance   (d) integrated

20. A motor controller that includes motor overload protection suitable for group motor application shall be marked with the motor ____ for such applications.

(a) overload protection   (b) kVA   (c) watts   (d) manufacturer

21. Elevators shall have a single means for disconnecting car light, receptacle(s) and ventilation power supply. This disconnect shall be _____ to correspond to the specific elevator car number whose power it controls.

(a) mounted   (b) located   (c) numbered   (d) fused

22. At least ____ receptacle outlet shall be installed outdoors. A receptacle outlet located in a compartment accessible from the outside of the park trailer shall be considered an outdoor receptacle.

(a) one   (b) two   (c) three   (d) none required

23. Switches, circuit breakers, relays, contactors, fuses and current-breaking contacts for bells, horns, sirens, and other devices in which sparks or arcs may be produced shall be provided with enclosures identified for ____ location.

(a) Class I   (b) Class II   (c) Class III   (d) Class IV

24. Over 1000v, mechanical ____ shall be provided in the housing to prevent the complete withdrawal of the circuit breaker from the housing when the stored energy mechanism is in the fully charged position, unless a suitable device is provided to block the closing function of the circuit breaker before complete withdrawal.

(a) relay   (b) lever   (c) interlocks   (d) reset

25. Where a branch circuit supplies a continuous and noncontinuous load, the rating of the overcurrent device shall be not less than the sum of the noncontinuous load plus ____ of the continuous load.

(a) 70%   (b) 75%   (c) 100%   (d) 125%

26. The maximum voltage permitted for operation of a lighting fixture installed in a swimming pool is ____ volts.

(a) 120   (b) 150   (c) 277   (d) 300

27. Sign circuits that supply signs and outline lighting systems containing incandescent, fluorescent and high-intensity discharge forms of illumination shall be rated not to exceed ____ amperes.

(a) 15   (b) 20   (c) 25   (d) 30

28. The ampacity of a conductor is defined by the National Electrical Code to be the current in amperes a conductor can carry continuously under the conditions of use without exceeding ____.

(a) the allowable voltage drop limitations
(b) its temperature rating
(c) its rated voltage
(d) its melting point

29. Transformers rated ____ kVA or larger are required to have their impedance marked on the nameplate.

(a) 7.5   (b) 12   (c) 15   (d) 25

30. Conductors and cables shall be routed to avoid wiring closer than ____ from the outer edge or any portion of the yard that can be used for mounting vessels or stepping or unstepping masts.

(a) 20'   (b) 30'   (c) 50'   (d) 100'

31. Splices and taps shall be permitted within wireways provided they are ____. The conductors, including splices and taps, shall not fill the wireway to more than ____ of its area at that point.

(a) sealed; 60%
(b) soldered; 50%
(c) accessible; 75%
(d) copper conductors only; 80%

32. The branch circuit rating for flat cable assemblies shall not exceed ____ amperes.

(a) 15   (b) 20   (c) 25   (d) 30

33. Disregarding any exceptions, Type UF cable shall be permitted to be ____.

(a) used in hoistways
(b) used as service entrance cable
(c) used in storage battery rooms
(d) buried directly in the earth for use underground

34. For general wiring, ____ type cable containing one or more conductors is approved for direct burial in earth.

(a) THW   (b) USE   (c) THHW   (d) THHN

35. The maximum number of overcurrent devices (other than those provided for in the mains) in a single cabinet of a lighting and appliance panelboard shall be ____.

(a) 24   (b) 32   (c) 36   (d) 42

36. In each attached garage and in each detached garage with electric power, at least one receptacle outlet shall be installed in each vehicle bay and not more than ____ above the floor.

(a) 5'   (b) 5.5'   (c) 6'   (d) 6.5'

37. A ridge on the exterior of a flexible cord is used to mark ____.

(a) high potential conductors
(b) the grounding conductor
(c) the grounded conductor
(d) the ungrounded conductor

38. A fixture that weighs more than ____ pounds shall be supported independently of the outlet box.

(a) 15   (b) 25   (c) 35   (d) 50

39. Two types of conductors allowed within 3 inches of a ballast within the ballast compartment of a fluorescent lighting fixture are ____.

(a) RH or RHW
(b) UF or THWN
(c) THW or THHN
(d) T or TW

40. The receptacle used for the EVPE outlet shall be rated 250 volts maximum, single phase, _____ amperes maximum.

(a) 30   (b) 45   (c) 50   (d) 60

41. Thermal insulation shall not be installed within _____ of a recessed light fixture enclosure unless the recessed light fixture is identified as suitable for direct contact with insulation.

(a) 1/2"   (b) 2"   (c) 3"   (d) 6"

42. Unless identified specifically for that use, screw-shell lampholders shall not be used with infrared lamps rated over _____ watts.

(a) 50   (b) 100   (c) 150   (d) 300

43. An insulated conductor larger than #6 shall, at the time of installation, be permitted to be permanently identified as a grounded conductor by _____.

(a) stripping the insulation from the entire exposed length
(b) coloring the exposed insulation green
(c) a distinctive white marking at its terminations
(d) none of the above meets the Code

44. According to the National Electrical Code, _____ shall not be used to mount electrical equipment onto a masonry wall.

(a) toggle bolts   (b) wooden plugs   (c) lead anchors   (d) lag bolts

45. Each multiwire branch circuit shall be_____ at the point where the branch circuit originates.

(a) run in the same raceway
(b) restricted to the same floor of the dwelling
(c) provided with a means to simultaneously disconnect all ungrounded conductors
(d) provided with a disconnecting means one standard size larger than normally required

46. What type of lampholder is required in a branch circuit in excess of 20 amperes?

(a) Brass
(b) Porcelain coated
(c) Shall not be of the interchangeable type
(d) Heavy duty

47. Electrical connections shall be located at least ____ above the deck of a floating pier.

(a) 6"   (b) 8"   (c) 10"   (d) 12"

48. When installing a new totally enclosed light fixture over an indoor swimming pool with ground fault protection, the minimum height shall be ____ above the maximum water level.

(a) 12'   (b) 10'   (c) 7 1/2'   (d) 6'

49. A grounding conductor for a communications system shall not be smaller than ____.

(a) #16   (b) #14   (c) #6   (d) #8

50. Tightening torque values for terminal connections shall be indicated on equipment or in installation instructions provided by the manufacturer. A/an ____ shall be used to achieve the indicated torque value.

(a) shelf life   (b) maintenance schedule   (c) warranty   (d) approved means

2020

JOURNEYMAN
OPEN
BOOK
EXAM #23

50 QUESTIONS
TIME LIMIT - 2 HOURS

TIME SPENT [   ] **MINUTES**

SCORE [   ] %

JOURNEYMAN OPEN BOOK EXAM #23   **Two Hour Time Limit**

1. Where is the #8 solid copper bonding conductor used with in-ground swimming pools, required to terminate?

(a) At the service equipment.
(b) At the grounding electrode.
(c) At the ground terminal of the remote panelboard.
(d) Shall not be required to be extended or attached to remote panelboards.

2. A dwelling has five 2-wire branch circuits supplying the total load. The electrician installed a 60 amp service using #6 service entrance conductors. Would this meet the Code?

(a) Yes, this service would handle seven 120 volt circuits.
(b) No, the Code requires a 100 amp service for a dwelling.
(c) No, three 120 volt, 15 amp circuits plus the two small appliance circuits might all be on at one time exceeding the 60 amps.
(d) Yes, three 15 amp circuits, plus the two-20 amp small appliance circuits, divided by 2, would only be 42.5 amps. A 60 amp service would be adequate.

3. Neutral conductors shall NOT be used for more than one _____ unless specifically permitted elsewhere in this Code.

(a) set of ungrounded feeder conductors
(b) multiwire branch circuit
(c) branch circuit
(d) all of these

4. The minimum working space in front of a 480 volt panel to a concrete wall is _____.

(a) 24"   (b) 30"   (c) 42"   (d) 48"

5. The main overcurrent protective device that feeds the floating building shall have ground-fault protection not exceeding _____ mA.

(a) 6   (b) 25   (c) 50   (d) 100

6. Means must be provided in the service equipment to disconnect the grounded conductor. Is this true even when the service equipment disconnects the ungrounded conductors?

(a) No, the grounded conductor is the neutral and it must never be disconnected.
(b) Yes, the Code has this requirement and it shall be followed.
(c) No, disconnecting the neutral during normal operations would create a hazard.
(d) Yes, whenever the ungrounded conductors are disconnected they also open the grounded.

7. You are installing two disconnecting means for motor operation: One for disconnecting the motor and motor controller from the circuit, and one for disconnecting a separate motor control circuit from the power supply. Where does the Code require the control circuit disconnect to be located?

(a) Next to the motor(s).   **(b) Adjacent to one another.**
(c) Outside for easy access.   **(d) "In Sight From" each other.**

8. The minimum clearance between luminaires installed in clothes closets and the nearest point of a closet storage space shall be ____ for surface-mounted incandescent or LED luminaires with a completely enclosed light source installed on the wall above the door or on the ceiling and ____for surface-mounted fluorescent luminaires installed on the wall above the door or on the ceiling.

(a) 6"; 6"
(b) 12"; 6"
(c) 6"; 12"
(d) 12"; 12"

9. General use receptacles used only by carnival personnel for the repair of carnival rides must ____.

(a) only be accessible by carnival personnel   **(b) be of the twist lock configuration**
(c) be GFCI protected and 20 amp in size   **(d) be GFCI protected**

10. Every motor controller must be capable of starting and stopping a motor. It must also be capable of ____.

(a) providing overcurrent protection
(b) providing ground-fault protection
(c) detecting variances in the circuit voltage
(d) interrupting the locked rotor current of the motor

11. Indoor installations of dry-type transformers greater than 112.5 kVA must be in an approved transformer room unless the transformer(s) ____.

(a) is rated at 75°C or lower
(b) primary is 2100 volts or less
(c) is rated at more than 35,000 volts
(d) is rated with Class 155 insulation or higher and separated from combustibles with appropriate barriers

12. Branch circuits feeding neon tubing installations must not be rated in excess of ____ amperes.

(a) 12   (b) 15   (c) 24   (d) 30

13. The Health care facility power source is a normal source consisting of generating units on the _____ the alternate source shall be either another generating set or an external utility service.

(a) premises   (b) remote location   (c) 3' from main   (d) vaulted room

14. Which of the following are recognized types of phase converters?

(a) Split-phase   (b) Compound-wound   (c) Static and rotary   (d) Shaded-pole

15. The minimum size disconnecting means allowed for a hermetic refrigerant motor-compressor is _____ of its nameplate rated-load current.

(a) 100%   (b) 115%   (c) 125%   (d) 130%

16. Motor-starter rheostats for DC motors operated from a constant voltage supply must be equipped with automatic devices that will interrupt the power supply before the speed of the motor falls to _____ its normal value.

(a) 1/3   (b) 1/2   (c) 2/3   (d) 3/4

17. The following must be provided in locations where electrical equipment would be exposed to physical damage:

(a) Working space   (b) Warning signs   (c) Enclosures or guards   (d) Sufficient headroom

18. Which of the following is an approved method for protecting the leads for heating cables as they leave a concrete surface?

(a) Rigid metal conduit   (b) Rigid nonmetallic conduit
(c) Intermediate metal conduit   (d) All of these

19. A device which, by insertion in a receptacle, establishes connection between the conductor of the attached flexible cord and the conductors connected permanently to the receptacle is a _____.

(a) controller   (b) attachment plug   (c) female plug   (d) male insert plug

20. In general, feeder and branch-circuit conductors must be protected by overcurrent devices connected _____.

(a) within 2' of the point where the conductors receive their supply
(b) within 3' of the point where the conductors receive their supply
(c) within 6' of the point where the conductors receive their supply
(d) at the point where the conductors receive their supply

21. Agricultural buildings housing animals and livestock rquire ____.

(a) no equipment grounding means
(b) grounding per hazardous location restrictions
(c) grounding only when water is used to wash livestock
(d) the equipment grounding conductor run underground to be insulated

22. A housing for a motor controller located in a corrosive environment must have a ____ type enclosure.

(a) 3S or 4X   (b) 4X and 3R   (c) 4X or 6P   (d) 3R or 3S

23. Underground wiring within ____ horizontally from the inside of the pool shall be permitted.

(a) 5'   (b) 6'   (c) 8'   (d) 10'

24. The maximum rating or setting of Time delay fuses (dual element) (branch circuit and ground fault device) shall not exceed ____ of AC single phase motor values.

(a) 175%   (b) 250%   (c) 300%   (d) 800%

25. The working space or clearance in front of a 120/208 volt panel to the front of a 277/480 volt panel on the other side of a hallway is ____.

(a) 24"   (b) 30"   (c) 36"   (d) 48"

26. The locked rotor kVA per HP rating for a code letter design "E" motor shall be ____.

(a) 3.2 - 3.9   (b) 4.5 - 4.99   (c) 2.2 - 2.6   (d) 6.0 - 6.5

27. When installing a ground ring, the installation must be installed a minimum of ____ feet deep and the length must be at least ____ feet long.

(a) 2.5', 10'   (b) 2', 20'   (c) 2.5', 20'   (d) 3', 30'

28. In general, controller enclosures shall be grounded if the voltage exceeds ____.

(a) 150 volts   (b) 300 volts   (c) regardless of voltage   (d) no grounding is required

29. A wall, screen, or fence must be ____ tall that encloses an outdoor electrical installation over 1000 volts to deter access by unqualified persons.

(a) 5'   (b) 6'   (c) 7'   (d) 8'

30. The smallest standard size plug-fuse rating for use on a residential 120 volt branch circuit is ____ amperes.

(a) 10   (b) 12   (c) 15   (d) 20

31. What is the required minimum headroom for electrical equipment that exceeds 6 1/2 feet in height?

(a) 6" higher than the height of the equipment
(b) 12" higher than the height of the equipment
(c) 3 feet higher than the height of the equipment
(d) Not less than the height of the equipment

32. Which of the following is not permitted to identify a #6 or smaller grounded conductor?

(a) Gray outer finish   (b) Natural gray outer finish
(c) White outer finish   (d) Three white stripes on other than green insulation

33. Which of the following areas are branch-circuit overcurrent devices not permitted?

(a) In residential unfinished basements   (b) In motel utility rooms
(c) In shops containing motor-driven tools (d) In residential or motel bathrooms

34. In a recreational vehicle, the maximum distance the supply may run inside the vehicle before it must have overcurrent protection is ____.

(a) 18"   (b) 3'   (c) 6'   (d) 12'

35. A circuit breaker with a slash rating of 120/240 is rated for what voltage to ground?

(a) 115 volts to ground   (b) 120 volts to ground
(c) 240 volts to ground   (d) Any voltage up to 240

36. Constant voltage generators, except AC generator exciters, must be protected from overloads by ____.

(a) circuit breakers   (b) fuses   (c) inherent design   (d) any of these

37. A mobile home disconnecting means shall be located not less than ____ above the finished grade or working platform.

(a) 2'   (b) 3'   (c) 4'   (d) 4 1/2'

38. Direct-current carrying conductors used in electroplating systems shall be protected by ____.

(a) fuses or circuit breakers
(b) other approved means
(c) a current-carrying device that operates a disconnecting means
(d) any of these

39. Overcurrent devices in an autotransformer shall **not** be installed ____.

(a) in series with the shunt winding   **(b) in parallel with the output conductors**
(c) in series with the output conductors   **(d) in parallel with the shunt winding**

40. The maximum overcurrent device rating for each resistance welder connected to an electrical system is ____.

(a) not over 350% of the rated primary current of the welder
(b) not over 300% of the rated primary current of the welder
(c) not over 150% of the rated primary current of the welder
(d) not over 100% of the rated primary current of the welder

41. A feeder tap less than 25' long does not require overcurrent protection at the tap if the ampacity of the tap is at least ____.

(a) 20% of the feeder conductor   **(b) 33 1/3% of the feeder conductor**
(c) 40% of the feeder conductor   **(b) 50% of the feeder conductor**

42. Feeder and branch circuit conductors that are installed on piers shall be provided with ground-fault protection not exceeding ____ mA.

(a) 5   (b) 6   (c) 25   (d) 30

43. Supplementary overcurrent devices shall ____.

(a) not be allowed under any condition
(b) not be required to be readily accessible
(c) be required to be readily accessible and within sight of equipment
(d) be connected only in parallel or series-parallel configurations

44. Metal panelboards must be protected against corrosion ____.

(a) both inside and outside   **(b) outside only**
(c) inside only   **(d) not required**

45. The minimum spacing allowed between bare metal current-carrying parts to ground in a panelboard with voltage not exceeding 250 volts is ____.

(a) 1/2"   (b) 5/8"   (c) 3/4"   (d) 1"

46. If safety switches are rated in horsepower, they must also be marked with a ____.

(a) **current and resistance rating**   (b) **voltage and wattage rating**
(c) **current and voltage rating**   (d) **voltage and resistance rating**

47. The minimum wire bending space required at the top and bottom of a panelboard that has two #3/0 conductors connected to each busbar or terminal in the panelboard is ____.

(a) 8"   (b) 7 1/2"   (c) 7"   (d) 6 1/2"

48. It is permissible to install two wires under the same terminal ____.

(a) **it is not permitted**
(b) **only on branch circuits**
(c) **only on relays mounted on switchboards per the Code**
(d) **when the terminal is identified as allowing more than one conductor**

49. The minimum length required for a junction box in a straight pull is ____.

(a) **six times the trade diameter of the largest raceway**
(b) **eight times the trade diameter of the largest raceway**
(c) **four times the cross sectional area of the largest conductor**
(d) **eight times the cross sectional area of the largest conductor**

50. A 200 ampere panelboard may supply a maximum load of ____ amperes.

(a) **200**   (b) **180**   (c) **160**   (d) **150**

2020

JOURNEYMAN
OPEN
BOOK
EXAM #24

50 QUESTIONS
TIME LIMIT - 2 HOURS

TIME SPENT [   ] **MINUTES**

SCORE [   ] %

JOURNEYMAN OPEN BOOK EXAM #24   **Two Hour Time Limit**

1. In general, switches shall be so wired that all switching is done in the ____ conductor.

(a) grounded   **(b) ungrounded**   **(c) both (a) and (b)**   **(d) neither (a) nor (b)**

2. All branch circuits that supply 125 volt, 15 and 20 ampere outlets installed in dwelling unit ____ shall be protected by an arc-fault circuit interrupter listed to provide protection of the entire branch circuit.

(a) kitchens and laundry areas   **(b) family and dining rooms**
(c) closets and hallways   **(d) all of these**

3. Insulated conductors smaller than ____, intended for use as grounded conductors of circuits, shall have an outer identification of white or gray color.

(a) #4   **(b) #2**   **(c) #1/0**   **(d) #250 kcmil**

4. "Z.P." is an abbreviated marking used for motors to indicate ____.

(a) single-phase   **(b) induction-protected**
(c) thermally protected   **(d) impedance protected**

5. The clearance for 6900v to ground conductors over open land subject to cultivation is ____.

(a) 12'   **(b) 15'**   **(c) 18.5'**   **(d) 22'**

6. Overcurrent protective devices shall be so selected and coordinated as to permit the circuit protective devices used to clear a fault without the occurrence of extensive damage to the electrical components of the circuit. This fault shall be assumed to be ____.

I. between any circuit conductor and the grounding conductor or enclosing metal raceway
II. between two or more of the circuit conductors

(a) I only   **(b) II only**   **(c) both I and II**   **(d) neither I nor II**

7. The ampacity for conductors is derated when the ambient temperature exceeds:

(a) 30 degrees F   **(b) 72 degrees F**   **(c) 86 degrees F**   **(d) 104 degrees F**

8. Transformers isulated with a dielectric fluid installed indoors and rated over ____ shall be installed in a vault.

(a) 112 1/2 kva   (b) 35,000 va   (c) 35 kv   (d) 35 kva

9. Which of the following requires a moisture seal at all points of termination?

(a) underplaster extensions   (b) bare conductor feeders
(c) liquidtight flexible metal conduit   (d) mineral-insulated cable

10. For a feeder supplying household cooking equipment and electric clothes dryers, the maximum unbalanced load on the neutral conductor shall be considered as ____ of the load on the ungrounded conductors.

(a) 40%   (b) 50%   (c) 70%   (d) 80%

11. Formal interpretations of the Code may be found in the ____.

(a) National Electrical Code Handbook
(b) OSHA Standards
(c) NFPA Regulations Governing Committee Projects
(d) Life and Safety Handbook

12. Sign lighting system equipment shall be at least ____ feet above areas accessible to vehicles unless protected from physical damage.

(a) 14   (b) 15   (c) 18   (d) 22

13. Where a transformer or other device is used to obtain a reduced voltage for the motor control circuit and is located in the controller, such transformer or other device shall be connected ____ for the motor control circuit.

I. to the load side of the disconnecting means
II. to the line side of the disconnecting means

(a) I only   (b) II only   (c) either I or II   (d) neither I nor II

14. Post, pedestal, and raised concrete pad types of electrical truck parking space supply equipment shall not be less than ____ aboveground or above the point identified as the prevailing highest water level mark or an equivalent benchmark based on seasonal or storm-driven flooding from the AHJ.

(a) 2'   (b) 2 1/2'   (c) 36"   (d) 42"

15. Type FCC cable shall be clearly and durably marked with ____.

I. material of conductors   II. maximum temperature rating   III. ampacity

(a) I only   (b) II only   (c) III only   (d) I, II and III

16. No swimming pool lighting fixtures shall be installed for operation on supply circuits over ____ volts between conductors.

(a) 24   (b) 50   (c) 120   (d) 150

17. Only wiring methods recognized as ____ are included in the Code.

(a) approved   (b) suitable   (c) listed   (d) identified

18. Service conductors between the street main and the first point of connection to the service entrance run underground is known as the service ____.

(a) drop   (b) loop   (c) lateral   (d) cable

19. EMT installed in a wet location, shall have its coupling and connectors ____.

(a) protected against corrosion   (b) corrosion resistant
(c) raintight type   (d) none of these

20. Dual-voltage motors that have a different locked-rotor kva per horsepower on the two voltages shall be marked with the code letter for the voltage giving the ____ locked-rotor kva per horsepower.

(a) highest   (b) average   (c) lowest   (d) normal

21. The Code requires in a dwelling a minimum of ____.

I.   3 volt-amps per square foot   II.   one 8 kw range
III. two small appliance circuits   IV. one laundry circuit

(a) I and II only   (b) I, II and III only   (c) I, III and IV only   (d) I, II III and IV

22. Outdoor electrical installations over 1000 volts that are open to unqualified persons shall comply with ____.

(a) Chapter 9   (b) Article 225   (c) Chapter 7   (d) Article 110

23. The optional method of calculation is permitted for a multifamily dwelling if ____.

I. each dwelling unit is equipped with either electric space heating or air conditioning or both
II. no dwelling unit is supplied by more than one feeder

(a) I only   (b) II only   (c) both I and II   (d) neither I nor II

24. Messenger supported wiring shall not be used ____.

I. where subject to severe physical damage
II. in hoistways

(a) I only   (b) II only   (c) both I and II   (d) neither I nor II

25. Receptacles installed on ____ ampere branch circuits, shall be of the grounding type.

(a) 15 and 20   (b) 25   (c) 30   (d) 40

26. Class I locations are those that are hazardous because of ____.

(a) the presence of combustible dust
(b) over 8' depth of water
(c) flammable gases or vapors are or may be present in the air
(d) the presence of easily ignitible fibers or flyings

27. Which of the following about the equipment grounding conductor is/are true?

I. does not count as a current-carrying conductor
II. bare, covered or insulated shall be permitted
III. count one for each grounding conductor in conduit fill

(a) I only   (b) II and III only   (c) I and III only   (d) I, II and III

28. Metal faceplates for devices shall be of ferrous metal not less than ____ inches in thickness.

(a) 0.300   (b) 0.003   (c) 0.030   (d) none of these

29. When a controller is **not** within sight from the motor location, the disconnect shall be capable of being ____ in the open position.

(a) down   (b) up   (c) lockable in accordance with 110.25   (d) shut-off

30. A green wire with yellow stripes used in a branch-circuit would be the ____ conductor.

(a) grounded   (b) grounding   (c) neutral   (d) ungrounded

31. Heaters installed within ____ feet of the outlet of an air-moving device, heat pump, A/C, elbows, baffle plates, or other obstructions in duct work may require turning vanes, pressure plates, or other devices on the inlet side of the duct heater to assure an even distribution of air over the face of the heater.

(a) 2 (b) 3 (c) 4 (d) 6

32. In a dwelling, a 20 ampere rated living room branch circuit can be loaded to a maximum of ____ amperes.

(a) 10 (b) 15 (c) 16 (d) 20

33. A cable bundle is a group of cables that are tied together or in contact with one another in a closely packed configuration for at least ____ inches.

(a) 12 (b) 24 (c) 36 (d) 40

34. No receptacle shall be installed within ____ feet of the inside walls of a pool.

(a) 6 (b) 15 (c) 18 (d) 20

35. Electrically heated smoothing irons shall be equipped with an identified ____ means.

(a) disconnecting (b) temperature-limiting (c) cooling (d) shut-off

36. Type TC power and control cable may be used ____.

(a) in outdoor locations when supported by a messenger cable
(b) as open cable on brackets
(c) where exposed to physical damage
(d) none of these

37. Heavy-duty lamps are used on ____ ampere or larger circuits.

(a) 15 (b) 20 (c) 25 (d) 30

38. A switch box installed in a tiled wall may be recessed ____ behind the finished wall.

(a) 1/4" (b) 3/8" (c) 1/2" (d) not at all

39. Raceways on the outside of buildings shall be ____.

(a) arranged to drain (b) weatherproof and covered
(c) rigid conduit (d) none of these

40. A new building will have two service heads, serviced by one service drop. What is the maximum distance apart that the Code permits the service heads to be located?

(a) 36" (b) 48" (c) 6 feet (d) no maximum as long as the conductors will reach

41. What is the area of square inches for a #8 bare conductor in a raceway?

(a) 0.013 (b) 0.017 (c) 0.778 (d) 0.809

42. Receptacles mounted on ____ need not be grounded.

**(a) outdoor circuits   (b) garage walls
(c) portable generators   (d) electric ranges**

43. Splices and taps shall not be located within fixture ____.

(a) splice boxes (b) arms or stems (c) pancake boxes (d) none of these

44. Floor boxes shall be considered to meet the requirements of the spacing of receptacles on walls if they are within ____ to the wall.

(a) 18" (b) 20" (c) 24" (d) 30"

45. ____ may be connected ahead of service switches.

I. Surge arrestors   II. Current-limiting devices

(a) I only (b) II only (c) neither I nor II (d) both I and II

46. Which of the following may **not** be used in damp or wet locations?

(a) AC armored cable (b) EMT (c) open wiring (d) rigid steel conduit

47. Except where computations result in a major fraction of an ampere ____, such fractions may be dropped.

**(a) larger than 0.5   (b) 0.5 or larger
(c) smaller than 0.5   (d) 0.8 or larger**

48. In a dwelling, it shall be permissible to apply a demand factor of ____ percent to the nameplate rating load of four or more appliances fastened in place.

(a) 60 (b) 70 (c) 75 (d) 80

49. The ampacity of a #250 kcmil IGS cable is _____ amperes.

(a) 119   (b) 168   (c) 215   (d) 255

50. Enclosures supported by suspended ceiling systems shall be fastened to the framing member by mechanical means such as _____.

I. clips identified for use   II. screws   III. rivets   IV. bolts

(a) I only   (b) II only   (c) II and IV only   (d) I, II, III and IV

2020

JOURNEYMAN
OPEN
BOOK
EXAM #25

50 QUESTIONS
TIME LIMIT - 2 HOURS

TIME SPENT ⬚ **MINUTES**

SCORE ⬚ %

1. Potential transformers, and other switchboard devices with potential coils shall be supplied by a circuit that is protected by standard overcurrent devices rated ____ amperes or less.

(a) 15   (b) 20   (c) 25   (d) 30

2. Which of the following is a **false** statement?

(a) Where a building is supplied by more than one service, a permanent plaque or directory shall be installed at each service disconnect denoting the location of all other services.
(b) Service conductors supplying a building are permitted to pass through the interior of another building.
(c) Conductors other than service conductors shall not be installed in the same service raceway.
(d) Conductors run above the top level of a window shall be permitted to be less than 3 feet away from a window that is designed to be opened.

3. Type ____ cable consists of three or more flat copper conductors placed edge-to-edge and separated and enclosed within an insulating assembly.

(a) NMC   (b) AC   (c) MI   (d) FCC

4. A cord connector that is supported by a permanently installed cord pendant shall be considered ____.

(a) receptacle outlet   (b) permanent cord   (c) lighting outlet   (d) outlet device

5. Equipment intended to break current at fault levels shall have an interrupting rating at nominal circuit voltage sifficient for the current which is ____ at the line terminals of the equipment.

(a) at maximum   (b) operating   (c) available   (d) required

6. Electrodes of nonferrous metal shall be at least ____ in thickness.

(a) 0.06mm   (b) .186"   (c) 1.52"   (d) 0.06"

7. Examples of resistance heaters are ____.

I. heating blankets   II. heating tape   III. heating barrel

(a) I and II only   (b) II and III only   (c) III only   (d) II only

8. Metal surface raceways having splices and taps shall be permitted as long as the splices and taps and conductors do not fill the raceway more than _____ percent of the area of the raceway at that point.

(a) 40   (b) 50   (c) 70   (d) 75

9. A receptacle installed outdoors in a location protected from the weather or in other damp locations shall have an enclosure for the receptacle that is _____ when the receptacle is covered.

(a) weatherproof   (b) weathertight   (c) rainproof   (d) raintight

10. In determining the dimensions addressing luminaires, the distance to be measured shall be _____ an imaginary cord connected to the luminaire would follow without piercing a floor, wall, ceiling, doorway with hinged or sliding door, window opening, or other effective permanent barrier.

(a) the shortest path   (b) at least 12'   (c) at least 16'   (d) 20'

11. A portable motor which has an attachment plug and receptacle may use this type of attachment as the controller provided the motor does not exceed _____ hp.

(a) 1/8   (b) 1/3   (c) 1   (d) 3

12. The feeder or service neutral load shall be the maximum unbalance of the load calculated. The maximum unbalanced load shall be the maximum net calculated load between the _____ conductor and any one ungrounded conductor.

(a) grounded   (b) grounding   (c) ungrounded   (d) neutral

13. Live parts exposed on the front of a switchboard are present, the working space in front of the switchboard shall not be less than _____ inches.

(a) 24   (b) 30   (c) 36   (d) 42

14. Armored cable installed in thermal insulation shall have conductors rated at _____. The ampacity of cable installed in these applications shall be that of 60 degree C conductors.

(a) 60 degrees C   (b) 194 degrees F   (c) 75 degrees C   (d) 90 degrees F

15. For hallways of _____ feet or more in length at least one receptacle outlet shall be required.

(a) 6   (b) 8   (c) 10   (d) 12

16. In panelboards, where the voltage on busbars is 150 volts and the bars are opposite polarity, held free in air, the minimum spacing between the parts is ____.

(a) 3/4"   (b) 1"   (c) 1 1/2"   (d) 2"

17. Underground service conductors shall have sufficient ampacity to carry the current for the load as calculated and shall have adequate ____ strength.

(a) equivalent   (b) physical   (c) mechanical   (d) conductor

18. A/an ____ switch allows a worker to set a circuit breaker trip unit to "no intentional delay" to reduce the clearing time while the worker is working within the arc-flash boundary.

(a) safety   (b) release action   (c) double break   (d) energy-reducing maintenance

19. The grounding conductor for secondary circuits of instrument transformers and for instrument cases shall not be smaller than #12 ____.

I. metal   II. aluminum   III. copper

(a) I only   (b) II only   (c) III only   (d) I, II or III

20. A current-limiting overcurrent protective device is a device which will ____ the current flowing in the faulted circuit.

(a) reduce   (b) increase   (c) maintain   (d) none of these

21. An office is to be wired with the number of receptacles unknown, the demand for the receptacles is ____ va per square foot.

(a) 1   (b) 3   (c) 3.5   (d) 180

22. In a recreational vehicle park with electrical supply, at least ___ % of the sites shall be equipped with 30 ampere, 125 volt receptacles.

(a) 5   (b) 20   (c) 70   (d) 100

23. No parts of pendants shall be located within a zone measured ____ feet horizontally and 8 feet vertically from the top of the bathtub rim.

(a) 2   (b) 3   (c) 4   (d) 6

24. The lead wires of heating cables are color coded for _____ identification.

(a) lead   (b) voltage   (c) wire   (d) cable

25. Plug fuses must have what specific shape?

(a) octagonal   (b) square   (c) hexagonal   (d) round

26. Luminaires in clothes closets shall be _____.

I.   a surface-mounted or recessed incandescent or LED luminaires with luminaires completely enclosed light sources
II. a surface-mounted or recessed fluorescent luminaire
III. pendant fixture

(a) I only   (b) I and II only   (c) I and III only   (d) I, II and III

27. All heating elements that are replaceable _____ and are a part of an electric heater shall be legibly marked with the rating in volts and watts, or in volts and amperes.

(a) in the shop   (b) by the manufacturer   (c) in the field   (d) none of these

28. Plug fuses and fuseholders can be used in circuits supplied by a system having a grounded neutral and having no conductor at over _____ volts to ground.

(a) 115   (b) 120   (c) 125   (d) 150

29. EMT shall not be used _____.

(a) for exposed work   (b) where subject to severe physical damage
(c) for concealed work   (d) none of these

30. Where a motor is connected to a branch circuit by means of an attachment plug and receptacle and individual overload protection is omitted, the rating of the attachment plug and receptacle shall not exceed _____ or 250 volts.

(a) 15 amperes at 110 volts   (b) 20 amperes at 115 volts
(c) 25 amperes at 120 volts   (d) 15 amperes at 125 volts

31. All type FCC cable connections shall use connectors identified for their use, installed such that _____ against dampness and liquid spillage are provided.

I. electrical continuity   II. insulation   III. sealing

(a) I only   (b) II only   (c) III only   (d) I, II and III

32. The maximum current shall be the stand-alone continuous inverter input current rating when the inverter is producing rated power at the _____.

(a) rms voltage (b) lowest input voltage (c) highest input voltage (d) contact limit voltage

33. Recessed fixtures shall be so constructed that adjacent combustible material will not be subject to temperatures in excess of ____ degrees C.

(a) 60 (b) 75 (c) 90 (d) 110

34. A factory installed duplex receptacle in a baseboard heater, where the heater is to be permanently installed in a commercial building is ___.

(a) prohibited by the code
(b) allowed only when the receptacle is factory connected to the heater circuit
(c) not allowed to be used as the required receptacle outlet for flexible cords with attach-ment plugs, when wired on a separate circuit from the heater circuit
(d) allowed to be used in lieu of the required receptacle outlet for flexible cords with attach-ment plugs, when wired on a separate circuit from the heater circuit

35. Type FCC cable, cable connectors, and insulating ends shall be covered with carpet squares no larger than ____ square.

(a) 24" (b) 914" (c) 36mm (d) 39.37"

36. Vegetation such as trees shall not be used for support of ____ .

(a) lighting fixtures (b) brackets or clamps (c) overhead conductor spans (d) none of these

37. Fixed electric space heating loads shall be computed at ____ percent of the total connected load; however, in no case shall a feeder load current be less than the rating of the largest branch circuit supplied.

(a) 80 (b) 100 (c) 115 (d) 125

38. Circuit conductors supplying power conversion equipment as part of an adjustable-speed drive system shall have an ampacity not less than ____ of the rated input.

(a) 110% (b) 115% (c) 125% (d) 140%

39. Separation of junction box from motor shall be permitted to be separated from the motor not more than ____.

(a) 6 feet (b) 4 feet (c) 1.83 (d) none of these

40. A single 1500w cord and plug connected load on 120v would draw ___ amps, this requires a number ____ wire and ____ circuit breaker for the branch circuit.

(a) 8 - #14 - 15 amp   (b) 10.5 - #14 - 15 amp   (c) 12.5 - #14 - 15 amp   (d) 12.5 - #12 - 20 amp

41. SE cable used to supply ____ shall not be subject to conductor temperatures in excess of the temperature specified for the type of insulation involved.

(a) lighting   (b) appliances   (c) motors   (d) generators

42. Torque motors are rated for operation ____.

(a) at full torque   (b) at F.L.C.   (c) at standstill   (d) with code letter

43. Other equipment with ratings exceeding the low-voltage limit contact limit shall be located at least ____ horizontally from the inside walls of a pool unless separated from the pool by a solid fence, wall or other permanent barrier.

(a) 60"   (b) 4'   (c) 72"   (d) 6'

44. ____ of insulating material that are Listed shall be permitted to be used without boxes in exposed cable wiring.

I. Self-contained switches   II. Self-contained receptacles   III. NM cable interconnector devices

(a) I only   (b) II only   (c) III only   (d) I, II and III

45. The following pool equipment shall be grounded ____.

I.   ground-fault circuit-interrupters
II. transformer enclosures
III. electric equipment located within 5 feet of the inside wall of the pool

(a) III only   (b) II and III only   (c) II only   (d) I, II and III

46. It is the intent of the Code that ____ wiring or the construction of equipment need not be inspected at the time of installation of the equipment, if the equipment has been listed by a qualified electrical testing laboratory.

(a) factory-installed internal   (b) factory-installed
(c) underground   (d) raceway

47. Distances from signs, radio, and TV antennas, tanks or other nonbuilding or nonbridge structures, clearances, vertical, diagonal and horizontal, shall not be less than ____ feet.

(a) 2   (b) 3   (c) 6   (d) 8

48. Any motor application shall be considered as ____ unless the nature of the apparatus it drives is such that the motor will not operate continuously with load under any condition of use.

(a) short-time duty   (b) varying duty
(c) continuous duty   (d) periodic duty

49. An overcurrent trip unit of a circuit shall be connected in series with each ____.

(a) ungrounded conductor   (b) grounded conductor
(c) overcurrent device   (d) transformer

50. The grounded conductor of a mineral-insulated, metal-sheathed cable Type MI shall be identified at the time of installation by ____ marking at its termination.

(a) distinctive   (b) neutral   (c) solid   (d) identified

2020

OPEN
BOOK
FINAL EXAM

80 QUESTIONS
TIME LIMIT - 3 HOURS

TIME SPENT ☐ **MINUTES**

SCORE ☐ %

80 OPEN BOOK QUESTIONS

1. A Universal Serial Bus flush device cover plate that additionally provides a night light and/or ____ output connector(s) shall be listed.

(a) one   (b) two   (c) Class 1   (d) Class 2

2. RV feeders from 208Y/120 volt, 3ø systems shall be permitted to include ____.

I. one equipment grounding conductor II. one grounded conductor III. three ungrounded conductors

(a) I only   (b) II only   (c) I and II only   (d) I, II and III

3. The conductors supplying the supplementary overcurrent protective devices for fixed industrial process heating equipment shall be considered ____ conductors.

(a) supplementary   (b) tap   (c) by-pass   (d) branch circuit

4. In airports where maintenance and supervision conditions ensure that only qualified persons can access, install, or service the cable, airfield lighting cable used in series circuits that are rated up to ____ volts and are powered by constant current regulators shall be permitted to be installed in cable trays.

(a) 1000   (b) 2500   (c) 3000   (d) 5000

5. Low voltage heating power unit shall be an isolating type with a rated output not exceeding ____ volts peak ac.

(a) 30   (b) 42.4   (c) 60   (d) 25

6. GFCI protection shall be provided for lighting outlets not exceeding ____ volts installed in crawl spaces.

(a) 30   (b) 50   (c) 90   (d) 120

7. All audio equipment operating at greater than the low-voltage contact limit and located within ____ from the inside walls of a storable or portable immersion pool shall be grounded and shall be protected by a GFCI.

(a) 6'   (b) 8'   (c) 10'   (d) 12'

8. Locations in which easily ignitible combustible fibers are stored or handled other than in the process of manufacturing are designated as ____.

(a) nonhazardous   **(b) Class III, Division 2**   **(c) Class III, Division 1**   **(d) Class II, Division 2**

9. A disconnecting means is required to disconnect the ____ from the circuit.

(a) motor and controller   **(b) motor**   **(c) motor or controller**   **(d) controller**

10. Circuits and equipment operating at less than 50 volts must use receptacles that are rated at not less than ____ amps.

(a) 15   **(b) 20**   **(c) 25**   **(d) none of these**

11. Most incidents and injuries are initiated by ____.

(a) equipment failures   **(b) people**
(c) incomplete procedures   **(d) inadequate regulation enforcement**

12. Which of the following organizations would maintain records of tested electrical equipment?

(a) Underwriters' Laboratories   **(b) National Fire Protection Association**
(c) National Electrical Contractors Association   **(d) IEEE**

13. Fastening of unbroken lengths of EMT conduit can be increased to a distance of ____ from the termination point where the structural members do not readily permit fastening within 3 feet.

(a) 4'   **(b) 5'**   **(c) 6'**   **(d) 10'**

14. What is the maximum cord-and-plug connected load permitted on a 15 amp receptacle that is supplied by a 20 amp circuit supplying multiple outlets?

(a) 12 amps   **(b) 16 amps**   **(c) 20 amps**   **(d) 24 amps**

15. Enclosures for overcurrent protection devices must be mounted in a/an ____ position unless that is shown to be impracticable.

(a) horizontal   **(b) vertical**   **(c) perspective**   **(d) upright**

16. Heat generated internally in the conductor as the result of load current flow, including fundamental and ____ currents.

(a) dissipation   **(b) alternation**   **(c) harmonic**   **(d) transfer**

17. Equipment grounding conductors must be the same size as the circuit conductors for _____ amp circuits.

(a) 30   (b) 20   (c) 15   (d) all of these

18. When supplying a room air conditioner rated 120 volts, the length of the flexible supply cord must not exceed _____.

(a) 6'   (b) 8'   (c) 10'   (d) 12'

19. A _____ must be located in sight from the motor location and the driven machinery location.

(a) disconnecting means   (b) circuit breaker   (c) fuse   (d) controller

20. Outdoor antennas and lead-in conductors for radio and TV equipment must not cross over open conductors of electric light or power circuits, and must be kept well away from all such circuits to avoid the possibility of accidental contact. Where proximity to open electric light or power service conductors of less than 250 volts between conductors cannot be avoided, the installation must provide a clearance of at least _____.

(a) 12"   (b) 18"   (c) 24"   (d) 30"

21. Effective safe work practices are based on which of the following?

(a) Type of hazard   (b) Manner of exposure   (c) Degree of exposure   (d) All of these

22. When working on live electrical circuits, the type of screwdriver that should be used has a/an _____.

(a) non-conducting handle
(b) double triangle and rated-for-volts handle
(c) ergonomically designed handle for safety
(d) longer blade and square handle

23. Conductors in a non-jacketed multiconductor cable, such as ribbon cable in a permanent amusement attraction shall not be smaller than _____ AWG.

(a) 22   (b) 24   (c) 26   (d) 30

24. For installations consisting of not more than two 2-wire branch circuits, the building disconnecting means must have a rating of not less than _____ amps.

(a) 15   (b) 20   (c) 25   (d) 30

25. Supplementary overcurrent protection _____.

(a) must be readily accessible
(b) must not be used in luminaires
(c) may be used to protect internal circuits of equipment
(d) may be used as a substitute for a branch-circuit overcurrent protection device

26. Electrical services and feeders shall be calculated on the basis of not less than _____ per electrified truck parking space.

(a) 11 kva   (b) 12 kva   (c) 15 kva   (d) 21 kva

27. The largest size grounding electrode conductor to a concrete-encased electrode is not required to be larger than _____ copper.

(a) #10   (b) #8   (c) #6   (d) #4

28. Appliances, _____ provided for public use rated 250v or less and 60 amps or less, 1ø or 3ø, shall be provided with GFCI protection for personnel.

(a) vending machines   (b) tire inflation machines
(c) drinking water coolers   (d) all of these

29. The localization of an overcurrent condition to restrict outages to the circuit or equipment affected, accomplished by the choice of overcurrent-protective devices is called _____.

(a) arc-fault interrupter   (b) overload protection   (c) selective coordination   (d) none of these

30. Torque requirements for motor control circuit device terminals must be a minimum of _____ lbs-inch (unless otherwise identified) for screw-type pressure terminals used for #14 and smaller copper conductors.

(a) 6   (b) 7   (c) 8   (d) 10

31. Where overhead communications wires and cables enter buildings, they must _____.

(a) where practicable, be located below the electric light or power conductors
(b) not be attached to a cross-arm that carries electric light or power conductors
(c) have a vertical clearance of not less than 8' from all points of roofs above which they pass
(d) any of the above

32. A nursing home is an area used for the lodging, boarding, and nursing care, on a 24-hour basis, of _____ or more inpatients.

(a) 4   (b) 20   (c) 50   (d) 100

33. The power in a circuit is 2 W and the voltage is 20 VDC. What is the circuit current?

(a) .10 A   (b) .20 A   (c) .30 A   (d) .40 A

34. The minimum size box that is to contain a flush device must not be less than _____ deep.

(a) 3/4"   (b) 15/16"   (c) 1"   (d) 1 1/2"

35. Receptacle outlets installed for a specific appliance in a dwelling unit, such as a clothes washer, dryer, range, or refrigerator, must be within _____ of the intended location of the appliance.

(a) sight   (b) no specified distance   (c) 6'   (d) 10'

36. Flexible cords approved for and used with a specific listed appliance or portable lamp are considered to be protected when _____.

(a) #18 AWG and larger   (b) #16 AWG and larger
(c) not more than 6' long   (d) applied within the listing requirements

37. In order to _____ NUCC, the conduit must be trimmed away from the conductors or cables using an approved method that will not damage the conductor or cable insulation or jacket.

(a) install in a workmanlike manner   (b) terminate
(c) connect to the fitting properly   (d) all of these

38. The motor branch-circuit short-circuit and ground-fault protective device must be capable of carrying the _____ current of the motor.

(a) starting   (b) inrush   (c) running   (d) overload

39. Central heating equipment, other than fixed electric space-heating equipment, must be supplied by a/(n) _____ branch circuit.

(a) appliance   (b) individual   (c) HARC   (d) controlled

40. The ampacity for the supply conductors for a resistance welder with a duty cycle of 15% and a primary current of 21 amps is _____.

(a) 9.45 amps   (b) 8.19 amps   (c) 11.2 amps   (d) 21 amps

41. Lockout/tagout is an important part of isolating electrical equipment to be worked on. Which of the following should be secured before lockout is executed?

(a) A copy of the OSHA regulations for each person involved.
(b) A supplemental list that shows all involved energy sources and energy isolating devices.
(c) Knowledge that each person involved in the task is in control of all energy sources.
(d) Both (b) and (c)

42. For cord-and-plug connected appliances, an accessible separable connector or ____ plug and receptacle is permitted to serve as the disconnecting means.

(a) a readily accessible   (b) an isolated   (c) an accessible   (d) a guarded

43. The only way to see an electrical hazard is ____.

(a) by wearing a switchman's hood (b) by observing signs and signals indicating its presence
(c) by wearing 3-D glasses   (d) None of these

44. Voltage drop on sensitive electronic equipment systems must not exceed ____ for branch circuits.

(a) 1.5%   (b) 2.5%   (c) 3%   (d) 5%

45. The total number of AC cycles completed in one second is the current's ____.

(a) phase   (b) alternation   (c) frequency   (d) timing

46. Unused openings for breakers in panelboards must be closed using ____ or other approved means.

(a) sheet metal   (b) duct seal   (c) exothermic welding   (d) identified closures

47. Type SE cable is permitted to be formed in a ____ and taped with self-sealing weather-resistant thermoplastic.

(a) doughnut   (b) gooseneck   (c) turtleback   (d) loop

48. The largest size THHN conductor permitted in a 3/8" FMC is ____.

(a) #16   (b) #14   (c) #12   (d) #10

49. At least one 125-volt, single-phase, 15- or 20-ampere-rated receptacle outlet shall be installed within ____ of the electrical service equipment requiring servicing.

(a) 6'   (b) 10'   (c) 25'   (d) 50'

50. When an underground metal water-piping system is used as a grounding electrode, effective bonding must be provided around insulated joints and around any equipment that is likely to be disconnected for repairs or replacement. Bonding conductors must be of _____ to permit removal of such equipment while retaining the integrity of the bond.

(a) cu/al wire   (b) stranded wire   (c) flexible conduit   (d) sufficient length

51. An outdoor disconnecting means for a mobile home must be installed so the bottom of the enclosure is not less than _____ above the finished grade or working platform.

(a) 12"   (b) 18"   (c) 24"   (d) 30"

52. The minimum number of overload unit(s) required for a three-phase motor is _____.

(a) 1   (b) 2   (c) 3   (d) 4

53. Straight runs of 1" RMC using threaded couplings may be secured at intervals not exceeding _____.

(a) 6'   (b) 10'   (c) 12'   (d) 14'

54. All cut ends of flexible metal conduit must be trimmed or otherwise finished to remove rough edges, except where fittings _____.

(a) contain insulated bushings   (b) are listed for grounding
(c) thread into the convolutions   (d) are the compression type

55. A circuit contains two 2,000 ohm resistors connected in parallel. What is the total resistance of the circuit?

(a) 888.8 Ω   (b) 1,000 Ω   (c) 1,200 Ω   (d) 4,000 Ω

56. The building disconnecting means for a one-circuit installation that supplies only limited loads of a single branch circuit must have a rating not less than _____.

(a) 15 amps   (b) 20 amps   (c) 25 amps   (d) 30 amps

57. When determining the number of conductors that are considered as current-carrying, a grounding conductor is _____.

(a) counted as one current-carrying conductor
(b) counted as one conductor for each ground wire in the raceway
(c) considered to be a current-carrying conductor but not counted
(d) considered to be a noncurrent-carrying conductor and is not counted

58. DC microgrid systems used as a source of power for emergency systems shall be of suitable rating and capacity to supply and maintain the total emergency load for not less than ____ hours of full-demand operation.

(a) 2   (b) 3   (c) 3 1/2   (d) 4

59. Receptacles that provide power for water-pump motors or for other loads directly related to the circulation and sanitation system must be located at least ____ from the inside walls of the pool.

(a) 4'   (b) 6'   (c) 10'   (d) 12'

60. Provisions shall be made for sufficient diffusion and ventilation of the gases from the storage battery if present to prevent the accumulation of a/(n) ____ mixture.

(a) explosive   (b) corrosive   (c) toxic   (d) all of these

61. Where motors are provided with terminal housings, the housings must be of ____ and of substantial construction.

(a) metal   (b) plastic   (c) steel   (d) none of these

62. What is the standard abbreviation for power on an electrical diagram?

(a) PAR   (b) PB   (c) PF   (d) PWR

63. The continuous current-carrying capacity of a 1 1/2 square inch copper busbar mounted in an unventilated enclosure is ____ amps.

(a) 500   (b) 650   (c) 750   (d) 1500

64. GFCI protection for personnel is required for all 15 and 20 amp, 125 volt single-phase receptacles installed in a dwelling unit ____.

(a) laundry   (b) garage   (c) shower stalls   (d) all of these

65. Service and feeder conductors may be sized using Table 310.12 for ____.

(a) commercial services only   (b) only multifamily dwelling sevices
(c) any service under 400 amps   (d) only 240/120v, 3-wire services for single dwelling unit

66. Concrete-encased electrodes of ____ are not required to be part of the grounding electrode system where the steel rebars or rods aren't accessible for use without disturbing the concrete.

(a) gas stations   (b) hazardous locations   (c) health care facilities   (d) existing buildings

67. The rating of the attachment plug and receptacle must not exceed _____ @ 250 volts for a cord-and-plug connected air conditioner.

(a) 15 amps   (b) 20 amps   (c) 25 amps   (d) 30 amps

68. Where there is more than one driving machine in an elevator room, the disconnecting means must be numbered to correspond to the identifying number of the _____.

(a) driving machine they control   (b) panelboard it is fed from
(c) the branch circuit feeding it   (d) all of these

69. A feeder must have a protective device with a rating or setting _____ branch-circuit short-circuit and ground-fault protective device for any motor in the group, plus the sum of the full-load currents of the other motors of the group.

(a) 125% of the largest rating   (b) not greater than the largest rating or setting of the
(c) 225% of the largest rating   (d) none of these

70. The symbol for a three-phase delta wound generator consists of a circle with a _____ scribed inside.

(a) cross   (b) triangle   (c) Y   (d) star

71. Cabinets or cutout boxes installed in wet locations must be _____.

(a) weatherproof   (b) waterproof   (c) raintight   (d) watertight

72. Each cable entering a cutout box _____.

(a) can be sleeved through a bushing   (b) shall be secured to the cutout box
(c) can have a maximum 2 cables per connector   (d) all of these

73. The parallel conductors in each phase or grounded conductor must _____.

(a) be terminated in the same manner   (b) have the same cma and insulation type
(c) be the same length and conductor material   (d) all of these

74. For cord-connected equipment such as _____, a separable connector or an attachment plug and receptacle is permitted to serve as the disconnecting means.

(a) drinking water coolers and beverage dispensers   (b) room air conditioners
(c) household refrigerators and freezers   (d) all of these

75. Four devices are connected in one circuit. The current through each of the devices is one-fourth of the circuit current. What kind of circuit connects the devices?

(a) Short circuit   (b) Parallel circuit   (c) Series circuit   (d) Open circuit

76. For systems over 1000 volts, the length of a pull box for a straight pull must be not less than _____ entering the box.

(a) 18 times the diameter of the largest raceway
(b) 36 times the diameter of the largest raceway
(c) 36 times the largest conductor in the raceway
(d) 48 times the outside diameter of the largest shielded conductor or cable

77. The conductor insulation of Type MI cable must be a highly-compressed refractory mineral that will provide proper _____ for all conductors.

(a) resistance   (b) ohmic value   (c) dielectric   (d) spacing

78. Where more than two NM cables containing two or more current-carrying conductors are bundled together and pass through wood framing that is to be fire-stopped using thermal insulation, the ampacity of each conductor is _____.

(a) limited to 30 amps   (b) adjusted by 310.15(B2a)
(c) limited to 20 amps   (d) approved by AHJ only

79. Grounded conductors _____ and larger must be identified by a continuous white or gray outer finish along their entire length, by three continuous white stripes along their length, or by distinctive white or gray marking such as tape, paint, or other effective means at their terminations.

(a) #8   (b) #6   (c) #4   (d) #2

80. In dwelling units, when determining the spacing of general-use receptacles, _____ on exterior walls are not considered wall space.

(a) sliding panels   (b) windows   (c) fixed panels   (d) all of these

ANSWERS

Exam Question Abreviations

1. AHJ   Authority Having Jurisdiction   Article 90

2. AC cable   Armored Cable   Article 320

3. EMT   Electrical Metallic Tubing   Article 358

4. ENT   Electrical Nonmetallic Tubing   Article 362

5. FCC   Flat Conductor Cable   Article 324

6. FMC   Flexible Metal Conduit   Article 348

7. FMT   Flexible Metal Tubing   Article 360

8. HDPE   High Density Polyethylene   Article 353

9. IGS   Integrated Gas Spacer cable   Article 326

10. IMC   Intermediate Metal Conduit   Article 342

11. ITC   Instrumentation Tray Cable   Article 727

12. LFMC   Liquidtight Flexible Metal Conduit   Article 350

13. NUCC   Nonmetallic Underground Conduit Conductors   Article 354

14. RMC   Rigid Metal Conduit   Article 344

15. SE   Service Entrance cable   Article 338

16. SPDs   Surge-Protective Devices   Article 285

17. USE   Underground Service Entrance cable   Article 338

18. UF   Underground Feeder cable   Article 340

19. COPS   Critical Operations Power Systems   Article 708

20. RTRC   Reinforced Thermosetting Resin Conduit   Article 355

ANSWERS   EXAM #1 JOURNEYMAN GENERAL KNOWLEDGE

1. **(b)** #12 AWG
2. **(d)** all of these
3. **(b)** relay
4. **(d)** amber
5. **(c)** an indicating
6. **(c)** increase in current capacity
7. **(c)** effective
8. **(b)** current in each resistor same
9. **(c)** lowers voltage, increases current
10. **(d)** resistance
11. **(b)** current is zero in resistances
12. **(d)** supply battery is weak
13. **(c)** 30Ω
14. **(c)** AC and DC power
15. **(b)** frequency
16. **(d)** develop excess speed
17. **(c)** storing energy
18. **(d)** primary cell
19. **(b)** micrometer
20. **(d)** centrifugal switch
21. **(b)** 50 amps
22. **(c)** reamer
23. **(c)** heating, magnetic and shock
24. **(d)** concealed knob and tube
25. **(d)** outlet with blank cover
26. **(b)** 75 amp
27. **(c)** eddy
28. **(d)** protons
29. **(a)** power
30. **(b)** two coils wound on common core
31. **(a)** corona effect
32. **(d)** pos to pos and neg to neg
33. **(d)** carbon
34. **(d)** growler
35. **(c)** both primary and secondary
36. **(c)** decreased
37. **(c)** induction
38. **(b)** induction
39. **(a)** increase lumen output
40. **(d)** an ohmmeter
41. **(c)** conductor
42. **(a)** series
43. **(a)** always less than the low resistance
44. **(b)** limit current through the lamp
45. **(d)** setting of the overcurrent device
46. **(b)** voltage
47. **(c)** at the far right
48. **(b)** change electrical to mechanical energy
49. **(a)** jumper
50. **(b)** low

To grade yourself on each exam: Divide the number of correct answers by the total number of questions asked.
Example: 38 correct answers ÷ by the total number of questions 50 = 38 ÷ 50 = 76%.

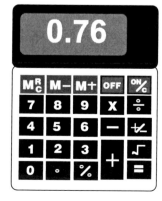

1. **(b)** megger
2. **(d)** tapered thread
3. **(a)** parallel
4. **(b)** consider circuit hot
5. **(c)** air
6. **(b)** toggle bolts
7. **(d)** bathroom
8. **(d)** powdered soapstone
9. **(d)** wattmeter
10. **(c)** main DEF 100
11. **(d)** lower the resistance
12. **(d)** protect end of wire
13. **(a)** LL conduit body
14. **(a)** the use of flux
15. **(a)** reduce shock hazard
16. **(a)** underwriters'
17. **(c)** general purpose DEF 100
18. **(b)** less than any one resistor
19. **(c)** converts into mechanical
20. **(c)** I and III only
21. **(b)** power factor
22. **(c)** 10 ohm resistor
23. **(b)** 1/120
24. **(c)** ampacity DEF 100
25. **(c)** reaming the ends
26. **(b)** 1000
27. **(c)** grounded 404.2(A)
28. **(d)** conductivity
29. **(d)** hacksaw and file
30. **(d)** relay
31. **(d)** clamped perpendicular
32. **(b)** shorted
33. **(a)** volt
34. **(c)** wet location
35. **(a)** may transmit shock to user
36. **(a)** impedance
37. **(a)** rotometer
38. **(d)** all of these
39. **(b)** voltmeter, ohmmeter, ammeter
40. **(c)** iron
41. **(b)** AC or DC
42. **(a)** cartridge fuses
43. **(a)** hanging fixture
44. **(d)** an approved box hanger
45. **(b)** ohm
46. **(c)** supplied by transformers & batteries
47. **(b)** rectifier
48. **(d)** three-way
49. **(d)** non-automatic
50. **(b)** parallel

ANSWERS   EXAM #3 JOURNEYMAN GENERAL KNOWLEDGE

1. **(b)** 3-4wy & 2-3wy
2. **(c)** ease of variation
3. **(b)** copper wire
4. **(d)** electrolyte
5. **(a)** black,red,white
6. **(b)** *Informational Note* 90.5(C)
7. **(a)** reduce shock
8. **(d)** all of these
9. **(a)** currents would circulate
10. **(c)** derating of ampacity
11. **(b)** condenser
12. **(b)** feeder DEF 100
13. **(d)** cond. will not turn off
14. **(d)** an impossibility
15. **(c)** hydrometer
16. **(c)** windings are common
17. **(b)** 20 ampere branch circuits
18. **(a)** tighten the clips
19. **(c)** carbon
20. **(c)** higher volt. & lower current
21. **(b)** copper good conductor
22. **(a)** Kirchoff's law
23. **(c)** pressure
24. **(d)** all of the above 210.21(A)
25. **(c)** protect from damage

26. **(d)** poor contact
27. **(b)** nuts removed frequently
28. **(a)** sum of individual resistances
29. **(c)** shorter life of bulb
30. **(c)** eddy current loss
31. **(b)** green or green with yellow stripes
32. **(b)** do not wear out as quickly
33. **(d)** orange   230.56   110.15
34. **(b)** makes pulling too difficult
35. **(c)** exposed
36. **(d)** electromagnet
37. **(a)** personal injury
38. **(b)** nylon string
39. **(d)** the contact resistance
40. **(c)** relationship between E, I and R
41. **(d)** 3/4" per foot 342.28 344.28
42. **(b)** power factor
43. **(c)** 3 hours DEF 100
44. **(a)** Phase A
45. **(a)** may conceal weak spots
46. **(a)** CO_2
47. **(a)** dry DEF 100
48. **(a)** 1.5
49. **(d)** branch DEF 100
50. **(c)** Insulation of the Conductor

ANSWERS   EXAM #4 JOURNEYMAN GENERAL KNOWLEDGE

1. **(d)** I, II and III
2. **(c)** good PF **not** true
3. **(c)** ohms
4. **(c)** 100a 230.79(C)
5. **(b)** parallel
6. **(b)** green as hot, **not** true
7. **(d)** written consent DEF 100
8. **(c)** 1 megavolt
9. **(c)** both
10. **(c)** **not** true 210.3
11. **(c)** whenever current flows in conductor
12. **(a)** commutator
13. **(c)** 7.5 25 x 60w =1500 x 5 = 7500/1000
14. **(d)** machine
15. **(d)** I, II & III
16. **(c)** neutral carries the unbalance
17. **(b)** counterclockwise
18. **(a)** turn on another circuit
19. **(c)** current lag voltage, **not** true
20. **(d)** 1.0 unity
21. **(b)** variable
22. **(a)** layers of iron sheets
23. **(d)** limit excess voltage
24. **(c)** rate of work performed
25. **(b)** 70.7%

26. **(c)** I & III only
27. **(c)** PVC 24", **not** true   T. 300.5
28. **(a)** equal currents in parallel
29. **(b)** lagging of magnetism
30. **(a)** voltage
31. **(b)** measure of ease of magnetism
32. **(c)** resistance
33. **(c)** either I or II
34. **(b)** reduce to simplest form
35. **(c)** causing AC to be generated
36. **(d)** 410.30(A)
37. **(d)** toggle bolt
38. **(c)** 1/4 as much
39. **(d)** I, II & III
40. **(b)** keep the surface clean
41. **(b)** static electricity
42. **(a)** 1" of concrete
43. **(c)** both
44. **(b)** special tools to make the joint
45. **(d)** I, II & III
46. **(b)** **not** true, 210.9 ex. 1, 2
47. **(a)** 25% 430.24(1)
48. **(d)** Y
49. **(a)** I only wattmeter is series-parallel
50. **(c)** effective difference DEF 100

ANSWERS   EXAM #5 JOURNEYMAN GENERAL KNOWLEDGE

1. **(d)** temperature
2. **(b)** transformer
3. **(d)** I,II or III 410.36(B)
4. **(d)** paper
5. **(b)** AWG or CM 110.6
6. **(c)** tubular
7. **(c)** cool & insulate transformer
8. **(c)** carbon
9. **(b)** cover keep person warm
10. **(a)** stop button
11. **(c)** water & apply vaseline
12. **(d)** squirrel cage
13. **(a)** 15 & 20   406.4(A)
14. **(d)** I, II & III 300.20(A)
15. **(d)** rectifier
16. **(d)** magnetic effect
17. **(d)** conductance
18. **(d)** white and bare wires
19. **(d)** mechanical function DEF 100
20. **(d)** carries the unbalanced 310.15(B5a)
21. **(d)** portable 550.2 DEF
22. **(b)** free of shorts & grounds 110.7
23. **(d)** noncorrosive
24. **(b)** II only DEF 100
25. **(c)** improve finish of threads

26. **(d)** specific gravity
27. **(c)** temperature
28. **(d)** I,II or III 110.13(A)
29. **(a)** commutator bar separators
30. **(c)** insufficient pressure at fuse clips
31. **(d)** elect. & mechanically interlocked
32. **(c)** avoid excessive starting current
33. **(c)** motor starter
34. **(c)** burn more brightly
35. **(d)** broken
36. **(d)** either vacuum or gas
37. **(d)** either I or II 230.70(A)(1)
38. **(d)** all of these
39. **(a)** two 3-way & one 4-way
40. **(a)** artificial respiration
41. **(a)** box end wrench
42. **(b)** ammeter
43. **(d)** csa
44. **(c)** single-pole, double-throw
45. **(c)** resistor
46. **(c)** iron losses
47. **(d)** jerk quickly break any arc
48. **(d)** sustained overload
49. **(d)** NFPA
50. **(b)** LB conduit body

ANSWERS   EXAM #6 JOURNEYMAN GENERAL KNOWLEDGE

1. **(a)** an electromagnet can be switched
2. **(b)** scatters light uniformly in all directions
3. **(c)** in a photovoltaic cell
4. **(a)** armature
5. **(c)** fish tape
6. **(a)** approximately zero
7. **(b)** parallel
8. **(d)** 10 times
9. **(c)** start measuring at the highest range
10. **(a)** a charge
11. **(a)** paper
12. **(b)** knife
13. **(d)** contact resistance at point of contact
14. **(d)** same as
15. **(a)** infinite
16. **(d)** lesser
17. **(a)** above the
18. **(d)** moisture resistant and thermoplastic
19. **(d)** low permeability
20. **(b)** commutator
21. **(b)** will increase
22. **(b)** starting
23. **(c)** cover
24. **(a)** a battery
25. **(b)** oil and soap

26. **(c)** open
27. **(d)** SPDT
28. **(d)** each appliance independent
29. **(d)** voltage
30. **(c)** inductive
31. **(c)** 0.4Ω
32. **(c)** preventing a short between wires
33. **(d)** voltage source and a conductor
34. **(d)** pendant
35. **(a)** highest resistance has the highest voltage
36. **(c)** recording
37. **(b)** eddy current loss is reduced
38. **(c)** dial indicator
39. **(c)** power
40. **(c)** larger plate area smaller distance between
41. **(d)** electrician's knife
42. **(b)** specific gravity
43. **(d)** smaller than the smallest resistance
44. **(c)** generator
45. **(b)** insulator
46. **(d)** high frequency AC in a coil with iron core
47. **(d)** current
48. **(a)** commutator
49. **(c)** length
50. **(a)** its physical size

ANSWERS   EXAM #7 JOURNEYMAN GENERAL KNOWLEDGE

1. **(b)** electrons passing a point
2. **(a)** series
3. **(a)** one coil
4. **(b)** ammeter
5. **(c)** grounded T. 110.26(A1) condition 2
6. **(c)** lighting
7. **(c)** increases the resistance
8. **(d)** effective value
9. **(b)** 1-6 2-5 3-4-7
10. **(c)** 36" edge of basin 210.52(D)
11. **(b)** 2 hot wires use neutral
12. **(b)** 75% 220.53
13. **(c)** I & II PVC or bakelite
14. **(c)** AC and DC tungsten 404.14(B3)
15. **(b)** fuse DEF 100 over 1000v
16. **(b)** service-ent conductors DEF 100
17. **(d)** Article 480
18. **(d)** I, II, & III chain wrench
19. **(c)** hacksaw and ream
20. **(c)** 16"   410.30(A)
21. **(a)** yes 300.3(C1)
22. **(b)** local Code when more stringent
23. **(b)** VD is a percentage
24. **(b)** electrolytic
25. **(d)** zinc finish
26. **(b)** saber saw
27. **(a)** 6-32 x 1"
28. **(c)** be alert at all times
29. **(a)** 90 degrees
30. **(a)** 3Ω will consume the most power
31. **(a)** 35 pounds ceiling fans 314.27(C)
32. **(d)** use a chalk line
33. **(c)** silver improves continuity
34. **(c)** perform their duties properly
35. **(d)** level
36. **(a)** hardened steel surface
37. **(c)** 15 feet over driveways 230.24(B3)
38. **(d)** 60% nipple fill Chapter 9 note 4
39. **(b)** tested to withstand high-voltage
40. **(b)** twisted together tightly
41. **(d)** 12Ω will consume most power in series
42. **(c)** Article 250
43. **(a)** 27 5/16" total sum
44. **(c)** fusestat has different size threads
45. **(c)** symbol for ceiling outlet
46. **(d)** check circuit for a problem
47. **(b)** carborundum
48. **(b)** 0.1875 is the decimal eqivalent of 3/16"
49. **(c)** too much pressure on the drill bit
50. **(b)** L2 fuse is blown

ANSWERS   EXAM #8 JOURNEYMAN GENERAL KNOWLEDGE

1. **(a)** surge arrester DEF 100
2. **(b)** covered DEF 100
3. **(a)** unity
4. **(a)** reduce the current 240.2
5. **(d)** hp is the output
6. **(c)** current develops heat
7. **(a)** inductive exceeds capacitive
8. **(a)** Allen head bolt
9. **(b)** automatic DEF 100
10. **(a)** 120 volts $W = E^2/R$
11. **(a)** may loosen the insulating tape
12. **(d)** steel bushing not used
13. **(c)** ungrounded conductor for switch 404.2(A)
14. **(a)** 0.5625 is the decimal for 9/16"
15. **(b)** the cause of accident
16. **(b)** 420 watts total
17. **(c)** stoppage of breathing
18. **(b)** only the current will change
19. **(d)** solderless connections
20. **(c)** polarized plug
21. **(c)** flush eyes with clean water
22. **(d)** I, II, & III lamps & motors
23. **(c)** III only 3-way switch connection
24. **(b)** 1000v or less 490.2
25. **(a)** 0.125 csa of busbar

26. **(c)** increase VD across the connection
27. **(d)** Δ delta symbol
28. **(b)** hysteresis 300.20 *Info Note*
29. **(b)** I & II only switch
30. **(c)** if one person is hurt
31. **(b)** low resistance in closed position
32. **(b)** 30a receptacle
33. **(d)** I, II, III & IV ground resistance
34. **(d)** cost is less for copper
35. **(c)** six lengths of conduit
36. **(c)** all parts of the circuit not in contact
37. **(d)** hydrometer
38. **(d)** low point
39. **(a)** zinc and copper
40. **(a)** carbon dioxide
41. **(c)** safety switch
42. **(b)** solenoid
43. **(d)** Article 490
44. **(d)** threads over entire length
45. **(a)** stretch the rubber tape
46. **(c)** larger in total diameter
47. **(b)** travel reaches a preset limit
48. **(c)** 10 ohms
49. **(a)** 6" Table 300.5
50. **(b)** a lampholder DEF 100

ANSWERS EXAM #9 JOURNEYMAN GENERAL KNOWLEDGE

1. **(d)** prevent loosening
2. **(c)** saw & ream ends
3. **(b)** voltmeter
4. **(b)** two-gang switch
5. **(d)** LB or T
6. **(d)** cooking DEF 100
7. **(d)** I,II, or III DEF 100
8. **(d)** copper 110.5
9. **(c)** voltage drop
10. **(b)** current
11. **(c)** direct current
12. **(c)** piezoelectricity
13. **(c)** expansion joints
14. **(a)** one-half cycle
15. **(d)** I, II & III
16. **(b)** Chapter 5
17. **(b)** are sure the power is turned off
18. **(a)** real power
19. **(a)** accessible 250.68(A)
20. **(d)** capacitance exceeds inductance
21. **(b)** shall 90.5
22. **(c)** longevity 110.3(A)
23. **(a)** current transformer
24. **(b)** short-circuited
25. **(b)** AC
26. **(c)** 220 $W = E \times I$
27. **(d)** increases as length of wire increases
28. **(c)** safety
29. **(a)** BX
30. **(a)** loose connection
31. **(d)** I, II & III 250.119
32. **(c)** both
33. **(d)** continuously DEF 100
34. **(d)** operation DEF 100
35. **(c)** both DEF 100
36. **(a)** cabinet DEF 100
37. **(c)** 6000 $W = I^2 \times R$
38. **(b)** will not
39. **(d)** larger in total diameter
40. **(b)** 3ø 4-wire
41. **(d)** apply solder to each strand
42. **(d)** make wire pulling easier
43. **(c)** decrease nicking of wire
44. **(c)** oil
45. **(d)** for grounds on 120v circuits
46. **(c)** make a good electrical connection
47. **(a)** filament seldom burns out
48. **(c)** condenser
49. **(d)** ungrounded conductor 240.15(A)
50. **(b)** festoon DEF 100

ANSWERS   EXAM #10 JOURNEYMAN GENERAL KNOWLEDGE

1. **(c)** 6 volt   series-parallel
2. **(d)** locknut outside, bushing inside
3. **(a)** grounded   200.1(2)
4. **(d)** all of these
5. **(b)** becomes stronger
6. **(c)** resistance
7. **(c)** temperature surrounding
8. **(c)** avoid snagging or pulling
9. **(b)** 120v
10. **(a)** remove the fuses
11. **(a)** defective tools cause accidents
12. **(b)** insulation to deteriorate
13. **(b)** even spacing, numerous lights
14. **(b)** accessible
15. **(c)** tungsten
16. **(d)** all of these   DEF 100
17. **(c)** 1/2 the R of one conductor
18. **(b)** same
19. **(c)** limit switch
20. **(a)** common magnetic circuit
21. **(d)** current
22. **(a)** DC motor
23. **(c)** stationary portion
24. **(a)** slow down rust
25. **(c)** oil

26. **(b)** to keep surfaces clean
27. **(a)** rainproof   DEF 100
28. **(b)** direct
29. **(a)** likelihood of arcing
30. **(a)** 30 hertz
31. **(d)** watthour meter
32. **(b)** join wires and insulate the joint
33. **(a)** steel
34. **(d)** test lighting circuit for a ground
35. **(a)** use plenty of solder
36. **(b)** the resistance
37. **(b)** locknuts and bushings
38. **(c)** **not** a safe practice
39. **(b)** heat
40. **(c)** connected in one line only
41. **(b)** circuit breaker
42. **(c)** I and IV
43. **(d)** 50Ω
44. **(b)** corrosive
45. **(b)** fuse clips would become warm
46. **(a)** minimum loads 220.14
47. **(d)** THHN T.310.104(A)
48. **(a)** reamed
49. **(b)** expansion bolts
50. **(d)** fine sandpaper

ANSWERS - TRUE or FALSE

1. False	90.4	assured that equivalent	26. False	230.10
2. True	DEF 100 AHJ *Info Note*		27. False	760.143
3. True	DEF 100		28. True	392.10(D)
4. True	DEF 100		29. False	396.30
5. True	DEF 100		30. True	402.11
6. False	324.10(A)		31. False	404.6(A)
7. True	320.17 & 300.4(A)(1)		32. False	410.16(B)
8. True	314.22		33. False	392.10
9. False	334.12(A2)		34. True	406.9(C)
10. False	501.30(A)		35. True	404.4(C)
11. False	411.4(A)		36. True	410.36(G)
12. True	680.43 ex.1		37. True	210.60(B)
13. False	810.15 & 810.21		38. True	342.42(B)
14. True	352.60 ex.2		39. True	240.10
15. False	353.12(3)		40. True	810.21(D) & 810.15
16. True	362.12(1)		41. False	90.2(B2)
17. False	376.10		42. True	430.87
18. False	376.70		43. True	430.109(B)
19. False	370.10		44. False	430.84
20. True	378.22		45. True	525.32
21. True	348.10		46. False	110.26(E1d)
22. True	384.60		47. True	300.15(G)
23. False	680.43(D4)		48. True	210.11(C3) ex.
24. True	620.37(A)		49. True	250.20(A1)
25. True	702.10		50. False	250.68(A) ex.2

ANSWERS   JOURNEYMAN OPEN BOOK EXAM #1

1. (b) process seal	DEF 100	
2. (a) 72"	691.9	
3. (d) tightening tool	110.14(D)	
4. (a) 60°	425.11	
5. (d) 120v	210.8(E)	
6. (b) arcing	240.87(B) I.N.3	
7. (b) 6' between	328.30	
8. (a) 1/4" x 2"	250.94(B)	
9. (a) 75% of the csa	312.8(B)(2)	
10. (d) I,II,III	210.11(C)(4) ex.	
11. (d) 1,000 sq.ft.	210.71(A)	
12. (d) I,II,III	422.5(B)	
13. (c) 18" under fill	358.10(C)	
14. (c) running boards	330.15	
15. (a) non-threaded	440.9	
16. (a) 50 volts	422.6	
17. (c) trimmed	350.28	
18. (b) 42.4 volts peak ac	424.101(A)	
19. (d) 5,000 volts	392.10(E)	
20. (a) 15kw	445.13(B)	
21. (b) retrofit kits	410.6	
22. (d) GFCI protected	422.5(A)(5)	
23. (a) 50 feet	210.12(A)(3)(b)	
24. (c) 15,000 watts	445.11	
25. (a) #2 AWG	646.9(D)	

26. (a) 48"	551.41(B)(4)
27. (c) flexible cord	240.5(B)(1)
28. (d) fire & burglary	640.1(A)(B)
29. (a) 15 minute	334.10(3)
30. (d) AHJ	DEF 100 "Listed"
31. (c) chemical solvents	300.6(C)(2)
32. (b) 2"	210.12(A)(6)
33. (d) #4 AWG	215.12(C)(2)
34. (a) 6 feet	210.8(A)(9)
35. (d) any of these	406.5(H)(1,2,4)
36. (d) all of these	430.102(B) I.N.
37. (b) personnel	422.5(A)
38. (c) 36"	330.30(D)(3)
39. (a) ⏻	406.3(E)
40. (d) Article 399	399.30(A)
41. (c) automatic	480.10(G)
42. (c) readily accessible	406.4(D)
43. (c) 0.250 inch	314.15
44. (d) all of these	250.194(A)(2,4,6)
45. (a) 1 1/2"	410.10(F)
46. (b) field-cut	300.6(A) I.N.
47. (d) 180 square inch	410.23
48. (a) Wireways	376.100(A)
49. (d) Red brass	344.10(A)(2)
50. (a) 7/8"	310.15(B)(3)(c)

To grade yourself on each exam: Divide the number of correct answers by the total number of questions asked.
Example: 38 correct answers ÷ by the total number of questions 50 = 38 ÷ 50 = 76%.

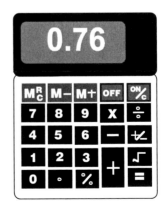

ANSWERS   JOURNEYMAN OPEN BOOK EXAM #2

1. (a) adequate path   320.108
2. (d) 135%   460.8(A)
3. (d) 2,001 volts   328.2
4. (c) 36"   422.16(B1)(2)
5. (b) 10'   312.5(C) ex.
6. (b) two conductors   338.100
7. (c) 7 times   330.24(B)
8. (c) type "O" lamp   410.130(F)(5)
9. (d) wet locations   344.42(A) & 314.15
10. (b) not considered   374.56
11. (c) 30   366.22(A)
12. (c) Table 1   356.22
13. (a) 6'   368.10(C2a)
14. (d) no greater   386.22
15. (a) largest two   220.56
16. (d) four   220.14(I)
17. (b) nonlinear   220.61(C2)
18. (d) b and c   210.18
19. (d) guest suite   DEF 100
20. (a) 10 cubic inches   T. 314.16(A)
21. (d) positive ground   372.18(D)
22. (d) 0.10Ω   Table 9
23. (d) low voltage contact   680.23(A3)
24. (c) 50°C   424.36
25. (a) leveled to   372.18(B)

26. (a) 1/2"   T. 408.56
27. (a) 3"   394.17
28. (b) 0 thru 600 volts   326.2 DEF
29. (a) any hazardous area   332.10(7)
30. (c) flame-retardant   392.100(F)
31. (d) dry location   600.9(B)
32. (b) gasketed   300.22(B)
33. (a) are not blocked   450.9
34. (d) none of these   285.12
35. (d) qualified individuals 225.32 ex.1
36. (d) 12"   470.3
37. (d) 15'   376.30(B)
38. (d) 1,000 volts   410.140(B)
39. (c) nominal   DEF 100
40. (d) 40 amps   440.62(A2)
41. (c) 70 pounds   314.27(C)
42. (d) any of these   399.30(B)
43. (d) all of these   210.12(A)
44. (b) 15 minute   362.10(5)
45. (b) distortion   354.100(B)
46. (d) additional hazards   430.31
47. (d) any of these   250.24(A1)
48. (d) any of these   250.64(C)(1)
49. (c) one additional   250.53(A2) ex.
50. (b) tubes   230.52

**To increase your speed use
the Key Word Index!**

JOURNEYMAN OPEN BOOK EXAM #3

1. **(c)**	#12 copper	230.31(B) ex.	26. **(d)** all of these	210.8(B1-5)
2. **(d)**	60-50	422.11(B)	27. **(b)** 20 ampere	660.9
3. **(d)**	12 times	300.34	28. **(d)** drive through door	210.70(A2)(2)
4. **(c)**	200 amps	Table 392.60(A)	29. **(d)** interrupting rating	DEF 100
5. **(d)**	2001 volts	328.2	30. **(d)** I,II,III & IV	410.24(A)
6. **(a)**	#16 minimum	Table 402.5	31. **(c)** II & III	230.66
7. **(d)**	90%	480.10(C)	32. **(c)** 4" 392.22(B) & T.392.22(A)(5)
8. **(a)**	one is required	210.52(D)	33. **(a)** I only	450.4(A)
9. **(b)**	enamel	250.96(A)	34. **(d)** 10'	378.30(A)
10. **(b)**	3"x 2"x 2 1/4"	Table 314.16(A)	35. **(c)** 12"	450.21(A)
11. **(a)**	167%	450.4(A) ex.	36. **(d)** 50 volts	460.6(A)
12. **(d)**	200va	220.14(G2)	37. **(b)** II only	225.31
13. **(d)**	steel EMT	358.14	38. **(c)** manufactured phase	455.9
14. **(a)**	#4/0 copper	340.104	39. **(b)** 30 amps	230.79(B)
15. **(b)**	200%	Table 430.52 note 3	40. **(d)** I,III & IV	680.2
16. **(a)**	6 feet	680.71	41. **(d)** 800 amps	240.4(C)
17. **(b)**	water pump	230.72(A) ex.	42. **(b)** II only	392.80(A1a)
18. **(a)**	damp location	DEF 100	43. **(d)** tampering	230.93
19. **(b)**	one foot = 12"	470.18(C)	44. **(a)** luminaire	DEF 100
20. **(c)**	accessible	DEF 100	45. **(d)** I,II or III	250.30(A1)
21. **(a)**	AHJ	90.4	46. **(c)** equipment bonding	250.146
22. **(b)**	13 receptacles	605.9(C)	47. **(d)** 24"	402.9(A)
23. **(c)**	3 hours	450.42	48. **(d)** I,II & III	240.60(C)(1,2,3)
24. **(a)**	#18	400.13	49. **(c)** 10'	384.30
25. **(c)**	not more than 6"	110.26(A3)	50. **(b)** 20 amps	430.53(A)

**To increase your speed use
the Key Word Index!**

ANSWERS   **JOURNEYMAN OPEN BOOK EXAM #4**

1.	**(a)**	12"	820.44(B) ex.	26.	**(d)**	60 amperes	250.118(6c)
2.	**(a)**	firestopped	760.3(A) 300.21	27.	**(b)**	800 amperes	240.4(B)(3)
3.	**(d)**	safe installations	90.1(A)	28.	**(c)**	2 1/2' = 30"	250.53(F)
4.	**(d)**	12" separation	450.21(A)	29.	**(d)**	30 volts	522.28
5.	**(c)**	36"	408.18(B) T.110.26(A1)	30.	**(b)**	7'6"	680.43(B1b)
6.	**(d)**	all of the above	440.14	31.	**(d)**	30v	725.41(A)
7.	**(d)**	200 amperes	408.36(A)	32.	**(c)**	22.5'	680.40 T.680.9(A)
8.	**(b)**	protective device	430.62(A)	33.	**(d)**	50'	DEF 100
9.	**(b)**	1/2"	410.116(A)(1)	34.	**(c)**	exposed work	320.10(1)
10.	**(b)**	#14	430.22(G)	35.	**(b)**	#4	312.6(C) 300.4(G)
11.	**(c)**	current of motors	430.24 ex.3	36.	**(b)**	3	T.348.22*note
12.	**(a)**	18"; 36"	422.16(B1)(2)	37.	**(a)**	dry locations	386.10(1)
13.	**(c)**	1 1/2"	410.136(B)	38.	**(c)**	54" = 4 1/2'	334.30
14.	**(b)**	continuous	T.430.22(E) note	39.	**(b)**	1/2"	350.20(A)
15.	**(d)**	same floor	422.34(A)	40.	**(c)**	3;5	344.30(A)(1& 2)
16.	**(b)**	white in color	200.9	41.	**(d)**	bury 2 1/2' = 30"	250.53(G)
17.	**(c)**	30"	110.26(A2)	42.	**(d)**	all of the above	250.118(7a,b)
18.	**(d)**	no limit	225.7(B)	43.	**(c)**	#6 copper	250.53(E)
19.	**(b)**	20 amperes	210.19(A3) ex.1	44.	**(b)**	#10 copper	T.250.122
20.	**(d)**	one and two	210.52(E)(1)	45.	**(d)**	all of the above	250.114(1,2,3)
21.	**(b)**	clock in dining	210.52(B2) ex.1	46.	**(c)**	6 switches	230.71(A)
22.	**(b)**	Class I, Div. 2	500.5(B)(2)(1)	47.	**(a)**	125%	424.3(B) 210.20(A)
23.	**(b)**	Class I, Div. 1	511.4(B)(2)	48.	**(d)**	#1/0	370.20(A)(2)
24.	**(d)**	I, II, III	517.31(A)	49.	**(b)**	1/4"	314.20
25.	**(d)**	as specified in Table	250.24(C)(1)	50.	**(b)**	corrosive conditions	332.12(2)

**To increase your speed use
the Key Word Index!**

ANSWERS   JOURNEYMAN OPEN BOOK EXAM #5

1. **(b)** will not   230.95(C) *Info Note 1*
2. **(a)** is false   300.5(E)
3. **(b)** 8"   424.39
4. **(b)** 6"   300.14
5. **(c)** I & II   220.53
6. **(c)** stranded type   225.24
7. **(b)** 1 1/2"   410.42
8. **(a)** dust   500.5(C)
9. **(b)** 3/4"   342.28   344.28
10. **(b)** shall   Chapter 9 note 3
11. **(b)** 1/4"   352.44
12. **(b)** 200va   220.14(G2)
13. **(b)** #4   314.28(A)
14. **(b)** 6'   250.102(E2)
15. **(a)** direct sunlight   352.100
16. **(d)** all of these   332.104 & 108 & 116
17. **(c)** I or II   550.10(A)
18. **(c)** kva   430.7(B1)
19. **(b)** 4'   422.16(B2)(2)
20. **(a)** sub. increased   300.21
21. **(c)** workmanlike   110.12
22. **(a)** 12 linear feet   210.62
23. **(c)** create a hazard   240.4(A)
24. **(c)** 36 times   314.71(B1)
25. **(d)** 12"   470.3

26. **(b)** first-make, last break   250.124(A)
27. **(a)** lowest   310.60(A1)
28. **(d)** side rail   392.56
29. **(b)** control selected   DEF 100 (over 600v)
30. **(a)** #10   110.14(A)
31. **(c)** 2 1/2"   362.20(B)
32. **(c)** ampacity   Table 402 • 402.5
33. **(d)** all of these   694.1 *Info Note*
34. **(b)** fan circuit   424.63
35. **(a)** 6'   680.22(A1)
36. **(c)** I,II & III   410.52
37. **(a)** 3'   Table 110.26(A)
38. **(c)** 6 pounds   410.30(A)
39. **(a)** as specified in Table   250.24(C1)
40. **(d)** I,II or III   340.10(3)
41. **(b)** FC   322.2
42. **(a)** 2'   220.43(B)
43. **(b)** II only   220.82(B3)(b)
44. **(c)** voltage drop   210.19(A) *Info Note 4*
45. **(c)** 18'   210.6(D1b)
46. **(a)** wet   DEF 100
47. **(b)** #6 copper   280.23
48. **(d)** 1.2v   480.2 DEF *Info Note*
49. **(a)** approved   110.2
50. **(b)** 6'   250.53(A3)

**To increase your speed use
the Key Word Index!**

ANSWERS   **JOURNEYMAN OPEN BOOK EXAM #6**

1.	**(c)**	service drop	DEF 100	26. **(a)**	50 amps	680.26(B)(6b)
2.	**(a)**	1/8 hp	422.31(C)	27. **(a)**	150°C	410.115(B)
3.	**(c)**	I or II	240.30(A1)	28. **(d)**	COPS	708.2 DEF
4.	**(b)**	less per AHJ	430.26	29. **(d)**	150%	430.6(C)
5.	**(b)**	50 volts	445.14	30. **(c)**	cooking unit	422.33(A&B)
6.	**(c)**	III only	450.6	31. **(b)**	protected sprinkler	450.42 ex.
7.	**(c)**	conspicuous	110.27(C)	32. **(c)**	1"	480.10(C)
8.	**(a)**	8'	225.19(A)	33. **(b)**	25%	T.384.22 notes
9.	**(c)**	III only	392.20(D)	34. **(d)**	none of these	300.22(A)
10.	**(b)**	receptacles	210.50(B)	35. **(d)**	75%	388.56
11.	**(d)**	Listing	110.3(B)	36. **(c)**	30 amps	312.11(B)
12.	**(d)**	not required	250.68(A) ex.	37. **(b)**	1"	390.4(B)
13.	**(a)**	#16	680.23(B3)	38. **(d)**	bathrooms	680.72
14.	**(d)**	flexible conduit	300.4(A2) ex.	39. **(d)**	.581 sq.in.	Chapter 9 Table 4
15.	**(b)**	1ø - 3ø	240.85	40. **(d)**	I,II or III	427.37
16.	**(d)**	I,II,III or IV	280.21	41. **(b)**	10'	680.43(A)
17.	**(a)**	I only	314.40(D)	42. **(d)**	thermally	DEF 100 over 600v
18.	**(d)**	I,II or III	410.30(B) • 410.36(A&G)	43. **(d)**	100 pounds	110.31(D)
19.	**(d)**	any of these	625.2 DEF *Info Note*	44. **(c)**	"No Equipment Ground" 406.4(D)(2b)
20.	**(d)**	grd. electrode cond.	250.24(A)	45. **(b)**	2 1/2' = 30"	250.53(H)
21.	**(a)**	24"	110.26(C)	46. **(a)**	outdoor outlets	210.52(B2)
22.	**(d)**	I,II & III	200.10(E)	47. **(d)**	600va	551.73(A)
23.	**(c)**	box listed	314.27(B)	48. **(b)**	12"	600.10(C2)
24.	**(d)**	I,II & III	210.52(G)	49. **(c)**	both I and II	480.10(G)(1& 2)
25.	**(a)**	2 1/4" x 4"	314.17(C) ex.	50. **(b)**	5'	250.68(C)

**To increase your speed use
the Key Word Index!**

**KEY
WORD
INDEX**

ANSWERS   JOURNEYMAN OPEN BOOK EXAM #7

#		Answer	Reference
1.	(c)	25 amps 400.5	T.400.5(A) head.B+
2.	(b)	#18 copper	402.6
3.	(d)	6 pounds	410.30(A)
4.	(b)	concrete	800.47(A)
5.	(a)	Class I Div. 1	516.5(C)(1)
6.	(d)	50 amperes	550.10(C)
7.	(b)	20 ampere	600.5(A)
8.	(a)	14.5'	T.680.9(A)
9.	(d)	2000 amperes	T.392.60(A) note b
10.	(c)	maximum voltage	300.3(C1)
11.	(a)	RHH	T.310.104
12.	(b)	18"	300.5(D1)
13.	(c)	maximum	DEF 100
14.	(d)	6'7"	404.8(A)
15.	(d)	60 sec = 1 minute	460.6(A)
16.	(d)	all of the above	408.19
17.	(c)	6'	440.64
18.	(d)	CO/ALR	404.14(C)
19.	(b)	2 h.p.	430.109(C1)
20.	(d)	all of the above	410.36(C)
21.	(d)	60 amperes	T.430.72(B) Col(C)
22.	(c)	10 penny	398.30(D)
23.	(d)	1 3/16"	314.24(B4)
24.	(c)	MI cable	332.30
25.	(b)	2 1/4" x 4"	314.17(C) ex.
26.	(d)	5 times	334.24
27.	(a)	18" = 1 1/2'	370.30(B)
28.	(d)	2'	T.300.5
29.	(d)	30	376.22(B)
30.	(a)	60°C	340.80
31.	(d)	exposed-concealed	350.10
32.	(b)	4 bends	352.26
33.	(d)	3/4" taper	344.28
34.	(c)	2" concrete	230.6(2)
35.	(a)	run in parallel	250.122(F)
36.	(b)	load	240.50(E)
37.	(b)	#6	250.64(B)(1)
38.	(b)	change locations	250.6(B2)
39.	(a)	directly to wiring	440.60
40.	(b)	#8 solid copper	680.26(B)
41.	(d)	yes, CATVP cable	820.113(B)(2)
42.	(a)	grounding	406.4(A)
43.	(b)	10'	225.18(1)
44.	(b)	grounded neutral	210.10
45.	(c)	100%	220.51
46.	(a)	6'	210.52(A)
47.	(c)	cooking	210.60(A)
48.	(c)	30 amperes	210.21(B1)
49.	(b)	multi-wire	DEF 100
50.	(d)	enamel	300.6(A1)

**To increase your speed use
the Key Word Index!**

ANSWERS   JOURNEYMAN OPEN BOOK EXAM #8

1.	**(d)**	2 1/2" *Note	Table 230.51(C)
2.	**(b)**	II only	430.12(A)
3.	**(a)**	mogul	410.103
4.	**(a)**	1/4"	314.24(B1)
5.	**(b)**	garage	210.8(A2)
6.	**(c)**	I,II & IV	220.12
7.	**(a)**	optional method	220.82
8.	**(c)**	air ducts	250.104(B) *Info Note*
9.	**(a)**	I or III	424.42
10.	**(d)**	temperature rise	368.214
11.	**(d)**	#10	Table 348.22
12.	**(a)**	50%	404.14(B2)
13.	**(a)**	6'	210.52(A1)
14.	**(d)**	Stranded	410.56(E)
15.	**(b)**	10'	Table 680.9(A)
16.	**(c)**	govern. bodies	90.4
17.	**(c)**	70%	220.61(B2)
18.	**(d)**	200a	408.36(A)
19.	**(a)**	83%	310.15(B)(7)(2)
20.	**(b)**	II or III	410.142
21.	**(c)**	I or II	422.16(A)
22.	**(d)**	I,II & III	225.6(B)
23.	**(d)**	all of these	400.14 *Info Note*
24.	**(a)**	raintight	230.54(A) & 314.15
25.	**(d)**	I or III	230.22
26.	**(d)**	all of these	Chapter 9 note 4
27.	**(d)**	front and back	210.52(E1)
28.	**(a)**	6000a	240.60(B) • T.240.6
29.	**(d)**	none of these	386.10(4)
30.	**(c)**	copper	110.5
31.	**(b)**	#18	402.6
32.	**(c)**	2 sq.ft.	250.52(A7)
33.	**(b)**	20a	411.7
34.	**(d)**	I,II & III	250.4(B4)
35.	**(b)**	temporary lighting	590.4(D)(1)
36.	**(b)**	one-half	398.30(D)
37.	**(d)**	I,II or III	324.100(A)
38.	**(a)**	2.5%	647.4(D1)
39.	**(a)**	one conductor	314.16(B1)
40.	**(c)**	18	Tables 4 & 5
41.	**(c)**	2 1/2' = 30"	230.51(A)
42.	**(c)**	bonding jumper	250.98
43.	**(b)**	#8	310.106(C)
44.	**(a)**	two 20a	210.11(C1)
45.	**(d)**	flush	314.20
46.	**(c)**	18"	680.23(A5)
47.	**(a)**	type AC	320.10(4) & 320.12(2)
48.	**(b)**	II only	250.64(B)(2)
49.	**(c)**	75a	240.6
50.	**(c)**	24"	310.15(B)(3)

**To increase your speed use
the Key Word Index!**

ANSWERS   JOURNEYMAN OPEN BOOK EXAM #9

1. **(b)**	.0209	Table 5*	26. **(b)** shall not prohibit	430.14(B) ex.
2. **(d)**	voltage drop	310.15 *Info Note 1*	27. **(c)** 42 devices	408.36 ex. 2
3. **(d)**	I,II & III	410.59(C)	28. **(c)** 1000v	250.24(C)
4. **(b)**	I & II	422.61	29. **(d)** I,II & III	404.14(A1,2,3)
5. **(c)**	panelboard	210.4(A)	30. **(c)** carpet squares	324.1
6. **(d)**	I,II & III	310.10(H2)	31. **(b)** 2 outlets	210.70(A)
7. **(c)**	10 penny	398.30(D)	32. **(b)** beginning of installation	215.5
8. **(c)**	total amp rating	220.18(B)	33. **(c)** 6'	320.23(A)
9. **(a)**	10'	225.4	34. **(c)** number plus one	680.24(D)
10. **(c)**	grounded	200.3	35. **(c)** both I & II	230.7 ex.1 & 2
11. **(b)**	equivalent to	110.14(B)	36. **(a)** 6"	250.94 *Info Note1*
12. **(b)**	50%	210.23(A2)	37. **(c)** either I or II	280.11
13. **(c)**	dry locations	380.10	38. **(d)** shall not exceed 60 days	590.3(B)
14. **(c)**	both a & b	210.4(C) ex.1,2	39. **(d)** 2'	310.15(B3a)
15. **(a)**	watts	430.7(A)	40. **(c)** 15/16"	314.24(B5)
16. **(c)**	insulation	310.15(A3)	41. **(b)** 6'	225.19(E)
17. **(b)**	braces or guys	230.28(A)	42. **(c)** 120/240v Annex D Examples	
18. **(d)**	I,II & III	110.33(B)	43. **(b)** carry the unbalance	310.15(B5a)
19. **(d)**	basin	DEF 100	44. **(d)** 18" - 36"	422.16(B2)
20. **(d)**	I,II or III	225.12	45. **(d)** removed	390.8
21. **(b)**	fished in voids	334.10(A2)	46. **(d)** 40'	225.6(B)
22. **(c)**	25 feet	210.64	47. **(c)** 100%	210.21(B1)
23. **(b)**	bathrooms	240.24(E)	48. **(b)** 30'	366.12(2)
24. **(d)**	I,III & IV	424.19	49. **(c)** shielded	310.10(E)
25. **(b)**	not be less than	230.23(C) • 250.24(B1)	50. **(c)** CM	110.6

**To increase your speed use
the Key Word Index!**

ANSWERS   JOURNEYMAN OPEN BOOK EXAM #10

1.	**(c)**	I & III only	210.6(A1,2)	26. **(d)**	II,III & IV	DEF 100
2.	**(c)**	I & II	110.11	27. **(c)**	MC	330.2 DEF
3.	**(c)**	112 1/2 kva	450.21(B)	28. **(a)**	round	314.2
4.	**(b)**	twice	314.16(C)	29. **(d)**	unswitched	410.12
5.	**(b)**	2' = 24"	324.120	30. **(c)**	good continuity	250.12
6.	**(c)**	grounded	DEF 100	31. **(c)**	12"	Table 300.5
7.	**(b)**	.109	Table 8	32. **(a)**	60° C	334.80
8.	**(d)**	Wooden	110.13(A)	33. **(d)**	removed	374.58
9.	**(a)**	3"	410.116(B)	34. **(a)**	1 1/4"	300.4(A1)
10.	**(c)**	I,II & III	230.50(B1)	35. **(b)**	galvanic action	344.14
11.	**(b)**	#12	225.6(B)	36. **(a)**	5 times	332.24(1)
12.	**(c)**	601a	240.6(A)	37. **(a)**	410a	220.61(B2)
13.	**(c)**	cma	250.122(B)	38. **(b)**	12'	230.24(B2)
14.	**(b)**	300v	324.10(B1)	39. **(b)**	MI	200.6(A5)
15.	**(b)**	II only	110.26(B)	40. **(c)**	48a	422.11(F1)
16.	**(a)**	bonded as required	370.60(1)	41. **(c)**	#14 copper	Table 310.106(A)
17.	**(b)**	continuous	250.64(C)	42. **(d)**	fibers or flyings	500.5(D)
18.	**(c)**	I or II	215.4(A)	43. **(b)**	four	358.26
19.	**(a)**	varying duty	DEF 100	44. **(a)**	75%	386.56
20.	**(d)**	raceway	300.5(C)	45. **(b)**	8000va	220.14(G2)
21.	**(c)**	1/4"	314.17(C)	46. **(b)**	destructive corrosive	330.12(2)
22.	**(d)**	1000a	366.23(A)	47. **(d)**	end seal	332.40(B)
23.	**(a)**	40%	Table 220.83(B)	48. **(a)**	65a	310.15(B3a)(2)
24.	**(b)**	5'	680.26(B7) ex.2	49. **(d)**	0.159	Table 8
25.	**(a)**	energized	300.31	50. **(c)**	.3267	Table 5(A)

**To increase your speed use
the Key Word Index!**

ANSWERS   JOURNEYMAN OPEN BOOK EXAM #11

1. **(d)**	4.40 - 4.49kva	Table 430.7(B)	
2. **(c)**	equip. grd. cond.	215.6	
3. **(d)**	all of above	250.118(6) a,b,d	
4. **(a)**	10' bare #4	250.52(A3)	
5. **(c)**	enclosure	694.2 DEF	
6. **(d)**	all of above	422.16(B2)	
7. **(c)**	115%	430.32(A1)	
8. **(c)**	nonlinear	450.3 *Info Note 2*	
9. **(a)**	at least one	210.52(C)(2)	
10. **(b)**	90°C	410.11	
11. **(d)**	all of these	225.10	
12. **(d)**	6' 7"	404.8	
13. **(a)**	20a or less	427.55(B)	
14. **(d)**	5 1/2' above floor	406.12 ex. 1	
15. **(d)**	24 amps	Table 210.21(B)(2)	
16. **(c)**	9"	392.10(B1a)	
17. **(b)**	two 36" in 20a	250.118(6b,d)	
18. **(b)**	O.C.P.	368.17(B)	
19. **(d)**	no minimum	110.26(D)	
20. **(d)**	5	T. 300.19(A)	
21. **(a)**	rigid nonmetallic	300.4(A2) ex.	
22. **(b)**	6" from storage	410.16(C)(3)	
23. **(b)**	70%	220.61(B)(1)	
24. **(b)**	two	210.52(E)(1)	
25. **(a)**	color braid	400.22(B)	

26. **(c)**	exposed to sunlight	378.12(3)	
27. **(d)**	equip. grd. cond.	386.60	
28. **(d)**	twelve	230.71(A)	
29. **(a)**	service point	DEF 100	
30. **(c)**	must have GFCI	210.8(A7)	
31. **(b)**	4 1/2'	334.30	
32. **(b)**	20 amps	404.14(C)	
33. **(c)**	dump load	694.2 DEF	
34. **(a)**	securely fastened	344.30(A)(1)	
35. **(d)**	sheathed cable	T.396.10(A)	
36. **(d)**	6'	368.56(B2)	
37. **(c)**	8 times	314.28(A)(1)	
38. **(a)**	3"	424.41(D)	
39. **(c)**	50v	460.6(A)	
40. **(d)**	12"	320.30(B)	
41. **(b)**	GFCI equipment	426.28	
42. **(b)**	3'	378.30(A)	
43. **(c)**	45 amp	Table 430.72(B)	
44. **(b)**	50%	450.5(A3) *Info Note*	
45. **(d)**	bond water pipe	250.64(E)	
46. **(d)**	effectively grd.	250.4(A)(5)	
47. **(c)**	6'	210.50(C)	
48. **(c)**	30"	110.26(A)(2)	
49. **(d)**	125%	424.3(B)	
50. **(d)**	40 amps*	422.11(E)(3)	

*5000w/208v = 24a x 150% = 36a
next higher size = 40 amps

**To increase your speed use
the Key Word Index!**

ANSWERS   JOURNEYMAN OPEN BOOK EXAM #12

1. **(b)**	SWD	240.83(D)	
2. **(c)**	II & III	250.62	
3. **(c)**	115%	430.110(A)	
4. **(d)**	1/2"	410.116(A1)	
5. **(b)**	2' = 24"	230.54(C) ex.	
6. **(a)**	1 foot	220.14(H2)	
7. **(a)**	7 pound-inches	430.9(C)	
8. **(d)**	white	200.9	
9. **(c)**	mechanical	230.31	
10. **(d)**	all of the above	770.93(A)	
11. **(b)**	I or III	422.61	
12. **(d)**	1000a	230.95	
13. **(b)**	50' ... 1/3	368.17(B) ex.	
14. **(c)**	III & IV	Chapter 9 note 4	
15. **(c)**	freedom from hazard	90.1(B)	
16. **(c)**	50%	440.62(C)	
17. **(c)**	3 overloads	Table 430.37	
18. **(c)**	#1	310.10(H)	
19. **(a)**	sealed	300.7(A)	
20. **(b)**	I & III	352.28 & 352.48	
21. **(c)**	#12	250.122(A)	
22. **(d)**	3"	408.5	
23. **(b)**	4'	680.24(A2b)	
24. **(c)**	3va	Table 220.12	
25. **(c)**	1/4"	110.12(A)	

26. **(a)**	not required	240.10	
27. **(d)**	150v	250.174(C)	
28. **(c)**	cable tray	392.2 DEF	
29. **(c)**	by hand	362.2 DEF	
30. **(b)**	85%	Table 220.54	
31. **(d)**	1,000 volts	280.1	
32. **(b)**	5'	368.30	
33. **(c)**	omit the smaller	220.60	
34. **(a)**	metal water pipe	250.53(D2)	
35. **(d)**	I & III	110.3(A2,6)	
36. **(d)**	I,II & III	382.10(C)	
37. **(a)**	8'	322.10(3)	
38. **(d)**	3'	410.54(C)	
39. **(d)**	I,II & III	370.10(2)	
40. **(c)**	flame arrester	480.11(A)	
41. **(b)**	-10° C	402.3 *Info Note*	
42. **(d)**	pend., lamps, cables	400.12(A1,2,4)	
43. **(a)**	15a	230.79(A)	
44. **(d)**	16"	410.30(A)	
45. **(b)**	5'	410.151(C8)	
46. **(b)**	30 conductors	376.22(B)	
47. **(a)**	D	310.120(C1)	
48. **(d)**	I,II or III	210.5(C1a)	
49. **(b)**	II and III only	220.12	
50. **(d)**	grounded	410.50	

**To increase your speed use
the Key Word Index!**

ANSWERS   **JOURNEYMAN OPEN BOOK EXAM #13**

1. (c) 20'	342.30(B3)	
2. (a) internal	90.7	
3. (c) parallel	310.10(H3)	
4. (d) grounded	300.13(B)	
5. (a) 60°C	110.14(C1)(a1)	
6. (b) 12"	T. 300.5 Col.4	
7. (c) 20'	250.52(A3)	
8. (c) service head	230.54(B) & 314.15	
9. (d) readily accessible	240.24(A)	
10. (b) yoke	DEF 100	
11. (d) will not	230.95(C) *Info Note*	
12. (b) 3"	300.14	
13. (d) ampere	240.83(A)	
14. (d) metallically	300.10	
15. (b) cord's listing	240.5(B3)	
16. (d) all of these	310.10(H1) ex.1	
17. (d) guest room	DEF 100	
18. (b) tightening torque	110.14(D)	
19. (a) 55 amps	215.2(A2)	
20. (a) white	200.10(B1)	
21. (d) any of these	DEF 100	
22. (a) 9.5'	110.34(E) & T. 110.34(E)	
23. (d) all of these	210.52(G)	
24. (d) all of these	555.9	
25. (a) #6	250.94(4)	

26. (a) power failure	225.38(A)
27. (a) garage	DEF 100
28. (d) permanent ladders	110.33(B)
29. (a) 6'	210.52(A1)
30. (c) bypass isolation	DEF 100
31. (c) 6"	110.26(A3)
32. (b) #8 cu, #6 al	230.23(B)
33. (b) approved	300.5(K)
34. (a) overcurrent	DEF 100
35. (d) different rates	230.2(D)
36. (d) open or closed	230.77
37. (d) all of these	547.1(A)
38. (c) does not apply	300.14
39. (c) inverse-time	DEF 100
40. (a) overcurrent prot.	210.18
41. (d) enclosed	DEF 100
42. (d) circuit	240.4(A)
43. (b) wet	DEF 100
44. (a) branch circuits	210.25(A)
45. (c) purpose is evident	110.22
46. (a) 30"	230.51(A)
47. (d) remote-control	DEF 100
48. (d) not to damage cable	727.10
49. (c) #6	314.27(D) ex.
50. (c) 115%	445.13

**To increase your speed use
the Key Word Index!**

ANSWERS   JOURNEYMAN OPEN BOOK EXAM #14

1. **(c)**	sticks	368.17(C)	26. **(c)** 40%	390.6
2. **(a)**	150mA	410.143(C)	27. **(b)** 2 cu.in.	Table 314.16(B)
3. **(b)**	the L.V. contact limit	680.23(A3)	28. **(b)** #3/0	Table 250.66
4. **(b)**	25 kva	450.11(5)	29. **(d)** 10'	362.120
5. **(b)**	Coordination	DEF 100	30. **(d)** one cond. diameter	370.30(B)
6. **(d)**	grounded neutral	210.10 • 215.7	31. **(b)** Group-operated	460.24(A)
7. **(b)**	T. 220.42	220.42	32. **(d)** 5'	680.22(C)
8. **(b)**	I or II	225.4	33. **(d)** motor-overload device	430.32(E)
9. **(b)**	listed for	250.70	34. **(a)** 1/4"	312.2
10. **(d)**	30a	324.10(B2)	35. **(d)** all of these	590.4(C&H)
11. **(a)**	enclosed in	410.104(A)	36. **(d)** 2"	382.15
12. **(b)**	18"	250.64(A)	37. **(d)** 120 gallons	422.13
13. **(d)**	all of these	210.8(B1,2,3)	38. **(a)** 1/4"	600.41(C)
14. **(b)**	6"	404.5 ex.	39. **(d)** I,II & III	430.82(B)
15. **(c)**	1 1/4"	Tables 4 & 5	40. **(c)** 18"	250.86 ex.3
16. **(c)**	5 3/4"	Chap.9 Table 2	41. **(b)** immediately	590.3(D)
17. **(b)**	55 amps	215.2(A3)	42. **(c)** I & II	328.12 & 328.10(3)
18. **(c)**	5 1/2'	210.52(4)	43. **(c)** cover	314.25
19. **(b)**	#12	680.21(A1)	44. **(b)** bonding	250.90
20. **(c)**	6"	355.20(B)	45. **(d)** grounded	200.7(A)
21. **(d)**	.026	Table 5*	46. **(d)** 25'	250.86 ex.1(2)
22. **(c)**	cable assemblies	250.86 ex.2	47. **(d)** I,II or III	250.53(A2)(1)
23. **(b)**	solder	250.70	48. **(c)** 6440 T.430.248 F.L.C. va = E x I
24. **(c)**	20'	250.52(A3)	49. **(d)** #10	Table 250.122
25. **(b)**	25a	210.18	50. **(d)** 16'	Table 344.30(B2)

**To increase your speed use
the Key Word Index!**

KEY
WORD
INDEX

ANSWERS   JOURNEYMAN OPEN BOOK EXAM #15

1. **(c)** grounded	240.23	26. **(d)** colored stripe	200.6(D)(2)
2. **(b)** 700a	366.23(A)	27. **(c)** 25'	240.21(B2)
3. **(c)** direct burial	340.10(1)	28. **(c)** NEC Tables	430.6(A1) • 430.52(C1)
4. **(b)** joined mech.	110.14(B)	29. **(d)** 1/2" to 4"	358.20(A&B)
5. **(c)** #1/0	372.20	30. **(c)** both I & II	225.25
6. **(a)** 300v	386.12(3)	31. **(c)** both I & II	300.17
7. **(a)** 65a	310.15(B3) ex.3	32. **(d)** 35,000v	328.10
8. **(c)** bushing	300.5(H)	33. **(b)** II or III	240.41(B)
9. **(d)** I & III only	590.3(C)	34. **(c)** 3.5 kva	Annex D example D2b
10. **(c)** 3	T.522.22 Notes	35. **(d)** 8'	250.53(G)
11. **(a)** 300v	410.138	36. **(d)** device-equip.	408.4(B)
12. **(d)** Skin effect heating	426.2	37. **(a)** receptacle	324.42(A)
13. **(d)** open or closed	230.77	38. **(b)** 3/8"	410.62(A)
14. **(c)** 65%	220.82(C3)	39. **(d)** not req. to be access.	250.68(A) ex.
15. **(c)** 5kw	220.54	40. **(a)** dangerous overheating	DEF 100
16. **(d)** 90° C	T.310.104(A)	41. **(c)** 10 cu.in.	Table 314.16(A)
17. **(c)** #18	240.5(B2)(1)	42. **(c)** 36 1/2'	550.10(D)
18. **(d)** accord.	250.102(C)(1)	43. **(c)** both I and II	334.15(B) 334.23
19. **(b)** 50v	110.27(A)	44. **(d)** 18'	230.24(B4)
20. **(a)** #10 copper	250.140(2)	45. **(d)** replacement for existing	240.51(B)
21. **(d)** all of the above	90.1(A& B)	46. **(a)** 12"	210.52(C3)
22. **(c)** both I and II	210.8(A1) & 210.52(D)	47. **(d)** 14' intervals	T.344.30(B2)
23. **(c)** 6530cm	Table 8	48. **(c)** orange	230.56 • 110.15
24. **(a)** 8 breakers	408.36 ex.2	49. **(b)** outside	220.12
25. **(b)** 143a	Table 430.250	50. **(b)** 1/4"	300.6(D)

**To increase your speed use
the Key Word Index!**

ANSWERS   **JOURNEYMAN OPEN BOOK EXAM #16**

1. (d) within 5'	250.68(C1)	26. (c) rated 1000v or less	450.13(A)
2. (b) GFCI	555.19(B1)	27. (b) over 3 gallons	460.2(A)
3. (b) 36"	T. 110.34(A)	28. (d) 150 volts	680.23(A4)
4. (b) service equipment	250.24(A)	29. (d) all of the above	440.62(A)
5. (d) not be necessary	408.3(D)	30. (c) both a & b	430.225(A)
6. (a) 15 amps	230.79(A)	31. (c) plenum	DEF 100
7. (d) service-entrance	T. 250.66	32. (d) abrasives	110.12(B)
8. (b) 12"	230.51(A)	33. (b) not be supplied	210.25(B)
9. (d) storage or work areas	210.8(A5)	34. (c) #6 aluminum	230.31(B)
10. (b) 6"	344.20(B)	35. (d) low as practicable	460.8(B)
11. (c) 6'	210.50(C)	36. (b) two conductors	314.16(B1)
12. (a) dry or moist	334.10(B)(1)	37. (d) all of these	322.10(1)
13. (d) detructive corrosive	332.12(2)	38. (a) equip. grounding	338.10(B2)
14. (b) 15 amps	240.4(D)(3)	39. (c) are permitted	324.10(E)
15. (d) joined at both ends	310.10(H1)	40. (d) manual override	210.70(A1) ex.2
16. (a) immediately	590.3(D)	41. (b) framing members	344.30(B4)
17. (b) not interchangeable	406.4(F)	42. (d) 122°F	353.12(4)
18. (a) 120 volts	210.6(A)	43. (a) assembly	382.40
19. (b) #10	225.6(A)(1)	44. (d) arc-fault	210.12(A)(2)
20. (a) 115/230v	220.5(A)	45. (c) one switch	210.70(A3)
21. (a) 2 sets	215.4(A)	46. (b) 18"	230.24(A) ex.3
22. (d) all locations	210.63	47. (d) supplemented by one	250.53(A)(2)
23. (a) in hoistways	392.12	48. (d) receives its supply	240.21
24. (b) kitchen and bath	210.70(A) ex.1	49. (c) gas pipe	250.52(B)(1)
25. (c) located conveniently	210.60(B)	50. (d) 36"	410.54(C)

**To increase your speed use
the Key Word Index!**

KEY WORD INDEX

ANSWERS   JOURNEYMAN OPEN BOOK EXAM #17

1.	**(b)**	branch-circuit	210.20(A)	26.	**(a)**	6"	Table 300.5
2.	**(a)**	bare copper	338.100	27.	**(b)**	1/8"	314.21
3.	**(c)**	operates	110.4	28.	**(c)**	II & III	394.10
4.	**(c)**	II & III	230.6 (1 & 2)	29.	**(b)**	complete	300.18
5.	**(c)**	135%	460.8(A)	30.	**(a)**	50w	422.43(A)
6.	**(b)**	serious degrad.	310.15(A3) *Info Note*	31.	**(d)**	25 ohm	250.53(A2) ex.
7.	**(d)**	manufacturer's name	314.44	32.	**(b)**	.0353	Table 5
8.	**(d)**	I,II & III	210.25(B)	33.	**(d)**	I,II & III	210.8(A5)
9.	**(d)**	100'	240.5(B2)(2)	34.	**(c)**	I & III	110.21
10.	**(c)**	both I & II	230.71(B)	35.	**(d)**	all of these	250.104(A1)
11.	**(d)**	60° C	340.80	36.	**(c)**	18"	Table 300.5
12.	**(a)**	individual O.C.P.	410.153	37.	**(d)**	need not be polarized	324.40(B)
13.	**(a)**	2.071	Table 4	38.	**(d)**	I & II	320.10(1)
14.	**(b)**	300w	422.48(B)	39.	**(a)**	#1/0	374.20
15.	**(a)**	.0625"	314.40(B)	40.	**(c)**	I or II	250.92(B) (2)(3)
16.	**(c)**	box cover	406.5(C)	41.	**(d)**	I,II,III & IV	310.15(A3) *Info Note*
17.	**(c)**	15a	210.3	42.	**(c)**	gray	200.7(C3) *Info Note*
18.	**(c)**	simult.	404.2(B) ex.1	43.	**(a)**	not be burned	240.41(A)
19.	**(b)**	300va	422.31(A)	44.	**(d)**	36"	408.18(A)
20.	**(b)**	50a	T.310.15(B16) & T.310.104(A)	45.	**(b)**	interrupting	110.9
21.	**(c)**	4 1/2'	348.30(A)	46.	**(c)**	660 ... 750	210.21(A)
22.	**(b)**	4"	110.31(A2)	47.	**(b)**	125%	215.2(A)(1)(a)
23.	**(c)**	right angle	372.18(A)	48.	**(c)**	III only	250.4(B)(5)
24.	**(c)**	both a & b	390.7	49.	**(c)**	NMC	334.116(B)
25.	**(d)**	I,II,III or IV	427.36	50.	**(c)**	clothes closets	240.24(D)

**To increase your speed use
the Key Word Index!**

1.	**(d)**	SO or ST	680.56(B) T.400.4 note 7
2.	**(b)**	.84	T.630.11(A)
3.	**(c)**	grounded	DEF 100
4.	**(d)**	overload	430.6(A2)
5.	**(d)**	both a & b	426.51(B) 427.56(B)
6.	**(d)**	115%	440.12(A1)
7.	**(a)**	33% = one third	460.8(A)
8.	**(d)**	90°C	410.68
9.	**(c)**	75%	366.56(A)
10.	**(d)**	can be accessible	314.29
11.	**(b)**	5'	368.30
12.	**(b)**	10;3'	344.30(A) & (B1)
13.	**(c)**	grounded	200.10(C)
14.	**(c)**	208v to 240v	210.9 ex.1
15.	**(c)**	outside dimensions	220.12
16.	**(b)**	6'	210.50(C)
17.	**(d)**	4 duplex or 8 sing.	517.18(B)
18.	**(b)**	6'	800.53
19.	**(d)**	600v	725.41(B)
20.	**(c)**	18"	680.23(A5)
21.	**(a)**	rigid metal	501.10(A1a)
22.	**(c)**	K,P,B, dinning	210.52(B1)
23.	**(c)**	#10 copper	225.6(A1)
24.	**(c)**	36" = 3'	230.9
25.	**(d)**	all of the above	250.110(2,3,6)
26.	**(d)**	closet or bath	240.24(D,E)
27.	**(b)**	6'	250.53(B)
28.	**(d)**	26"	110.75(A)
29.	**(c)**	14'	600.9(A)
30.	**(c)**	30v	427.27
31.	**(b)**	overload	430.124(A)
32.	**(d)**	190%	430.22(A)(1)
33.	**(d)**	a or b	430.111(B2)
34.	**(a)**	12"	440.65
35.	**(a)**	50 ampere	551.81(1)
36.	**(b)**	reversed	110.57
37.	**(c)**	3'	210.52(D)
38.	**(d)**	125%	215.2(A)(1)(a)
39.	**(c)**	largest	250.122(C)
40.	**(d)**	all of these	210.8(B4)(C)(D)
41.	**(a)**	all	312.7
42.	**(b)**	service cable	334.12(A3)
43.	**(b)**	6" = trade size	344.20(B)
44.	**(c)**	insulating mateial	406.6(A,B,C)
45.	**(d)**	panelboard	408.36(C)
46.	**(b)**	30v	426.32
47.	**(d)**	additional rod	250.53(D2)
48.	**(d)**	30 volts	694.30
49.	**(b)**	12"	T.300.5
50.	**(c)**	single #1/0	392.10(B1a)

**To increase your speed use
the Key Word Index!**

KEY
WORD
INDEX

ANSWERS JOURNEYMAN OPEN BOOK EXAM #19

1.	(c)	panelboard rating	408.36(A) ex.2
2.	(c)	#12	250.122(A)
3.	(c)	by hand	362.2
4.	(d)	150 v	250.174(C)
5.	(d)	3'	410.54(C)
6.	(c)	back fed	408.36(D)
7.	(c)	9'	T.110.34(E)
8.	(c)	100'	T.300.19(A)
9.	(d)	20 pounds	326.112
10.	(b)	enclosed same	215.4(B)
11.	(b)	high temperature	350.12(2)
12.	(c)	ambient temp.	310.15(A)(3)(4)
13.	(b)	12" = 1'	225.14(D)
14.	(b)	600v	250.184(A1)
15.	(d)	conductors, equip.	210.20
16.	(a)	wooden plugs	110.13(A)
17.	(d)	150v	240.50(A2)
18.	(b)	3 circuits 210.11(C1,2) 210.52(B)(1)
19.	(b)	enamel	250.96(A)
20.	(c)	#10	230.31(B) ex.
21.	(d)	100% = equal	210.21(B)
22.	(c)	#4 AWG	430.96 T.250.122
23.	(b)	earth	250.4(B4)
24.	(c)	I and II only	800.48 Info Note 1
25.	(d)	gray	200.6(A)(2)

26.	(c)	green, yellow stripe	250.119(C)
27.	(c)	600v	200.2(A)
28.	(c)	GFI	DEF 100
29.	(c)	#10	310.106(C)
30.	(c)	10 volts	517.64(A1)
31.	(a)	less than 12"	501.15(A4) ex.1
32.	(c)	Largest	314.16(B3,4)
33.	(c)	thermal protector	DEF 100
34.	(a)	0.5958 sq.in.	Table 5
35.	(d)	140%	430.32(C)
36.	(b)	one minute = 60 sec	701.12
37.	(a)	physical damage	378.12(1)
38.	(a)	at least two	517.18(A)
39.	(d)	all of these 550.13(B) ex. & 210.8(D)
40.	(b)	2"	800.133(A2)
41.	(c)	9"	392.10(B1a)
42.	(d)	300%	630.32(B)
43.	(c)	wet locations	340.10(3)
44.	(a)	Class I, Division 1	500.5(B1)
45.	(a)	125%	450.3 T.450.3(A)
46.	(d)	#6	820.100(D)
47.	(a)	incandescent	600.2
48.	(b)	polarized	410.82(A)
49.	(a)	1000va	725.41(A)
50.	(d)	intrinsically safe	504.2 DEF

**To increase your speed use
the Key Word Index!**

ANSWERS   JOURNEYMAN OPEN BOOK EXAM #20

1. **(a)** 70%   T. 310.15(B3a)
2. **(b)** #4   300.4(G)
3. **(c)** back fed   408.36(D)
4. **(c)** listed for raceway   410.64(A)
5. **(d)** 10'   440.64
6. **(a)** 1/8 hp   422.31(C)
7. **(c)** less than   Tables 4 & 5
8. **(c)** pigtail to silver terminal   300.13(B)
9. **(c)** 9'   Table 110.34(E)
10. **(d)** **not** true   210.70(A)(2)(2)
11. **(c)** both I & II   230.23(A)
12. **(d)** I,II & III   250.140(1)(2)(3)
13. **(b)** 15a   Table 210.24
14. **(d)** 8'   230.24(A)
15. **(d)** controlled equip.   DEF 100
16. **(d)** .8 & larger   Chapter 9 Table 1 note 7
17. **(d)** 6' 7"   404.8(A)
18. **(d)** 3 conductors   Table 314.16(A)
19. **(b)** 10'   230.24(B)
20. **(a)** 7'   424.34
21. **(d)** aquarium   250.114(3)b
22. **(c)** 100'   Table 300.19(A)
23. **(d)** 24"   Table 300.5
24. **(d)** #4 copper   Table 250.102(C)(1)
25. **(c)** 1.2426   Table 4 (csa x 60%)

26. **(d)** I,II,III or IV   250.64(B)(2)
27. **(d)** 20 pounds   326.112
28. **(a)** I or II   338.10(B1)
29. **(c)** both I & II   T.400.4 note #2
30. **(b)** enclosed   215.4(B)
31. **(d)** 8 3/4 kw   210.19(A3)
32. **(d)** 20'   680.22(A4)
33. **(c)** 80%   210.23(A1)
34. **(b)** for wet locations   410.10(A)
35. **(c)** nonlinear   220.61(C2)
36. **(d)** metal plugs & plates   110.12(A)
37. **(d)** 5/8"   250.52(A5b)
38. **(b)** high temp.   350.12(2)
39. **(b)** #10   545.4(B)
40. **(d)** 10'   680.51(E)
41. **(d)** I,II & III   410.36(C)
42. **(c)** II,III & IV   422.16(B1)(2,3,4)
43. **(a)** 17 1/2"   Table 360.24(A)
44. **(c)** ambient temp.   310.15(A3)(4)
45. **(c)** either I or II   320.100
46. **(a)** 90° C   Table 310.104
47. **(b)** 12" = 1 ft.   225.14(D)
48. **(b)** 50 pounds   314.27(A2)
49. **(c)** 5000a   240.83(C)
50. **(d)** all of these   DEF 100

**To increase your speed use
the Key Word Index!**

**KEY
WORD
INDEX**

ANSWERS   JOURNEYMAN OPEN BOOK EXAM #21

1. **(a)**	adeq. bond. & grd.	250.116 *Info Note*
2. **(b)**	#1/0	392.10(B1a)
3. **(b)**	II only	200.2
4. **(b)**	support luminaires	352.12(B)
5. **(c)**	#12	410.155(A)
6. **(a)**	5'	T.355.30
7. **(a)**	exposed	370.10(1)
8. **(a)**	isolating switches	404.13(A)
9. **(b)**	header	374.2 DEF
10. **(b)**	hysteresis	300.20(B) *Info Note*
11. **(d)**	90° C	410.11
12. **(b)**	115%	445.13(A)
13. **(c)**	reamed	344.28
14. **(a)**	#8	680.26(B)
15. **(a)**	24" = 2'	320.30(D2)
16. **(a)**	0.053	312.10(B)
17. **(d)**	6' 6" = 6 1/2'	110.26(A3)
18. **(a)**	equal to maximum	300.3(C1)
19. **(d)**	disconnect	230.75
20. **(b)**	6'	210.50(C)
21. **(d)**	small appl. circuit	210.52(B2) ex.1
22. **(a)**	1/16"	300.4(A1)
23. **(a)**	6'	370.18(B)
24. **(b)**	200a	110.26(A)(3) ex.1
25. **(c)**	both I & II	410.62(B)

26. **(c)**	#8	398.30(E)
27. **(b)**	Cover	Table 300.5 Note 1
28. **(c)**	III only	Table 400.4
29. **(a)**	hazardous location	332.10(7)
30. **(c)**	6'	410.117(C)
31. **(b)**	separate box	314.28(D)
32. **(a)**	12"	422.5(A)(5)&(B)(3&4)
33. **(b)**	8'	300.5(D1)
34. **(d)**	2 1/16"	314.24(B3)
35. **(c)**	either I or II	422.16(B3)
36. **(c)**	I,II & III	406.4(F)
37. **(b)**	70%	Table 220.56
38. **(c)**	not true 1 3/4 kw	Table 220.55
39. **(d)**	I,II & III	230.92
40. **(d)**	I,II or III	250.70
41. **(d)**	I,II & III	392.100(A,B,D)
42. **(c)**	45%	T.310.15(B3a)
43. **(d)**	inductive current	300.20(A)
44. **(a)**	#10 cu	225.6(A1)
45. **(b)**	12"	334.30
46. **(c)**	end seal	332.80
47. **(a)**	GFCI	680.32
48. **(a)**	solder	230.81
49. **(a)**	EMT	300.22(B)
50. **(b)**	3'	230.9 ex.

**To increase your speed use
the Key Word Index!**

1.	**(d)**	size 6	353.20(B)	26.	**(b)**	150v	680.23(A4)
2.	**(b)**	induction	427.2	27.	**(b)**	20 amperes	600.5(B2)
3.	**(c)**	30"	110.26(A2)	28.	**(b)**	its temperature	DEF 100
4.	**(a)**	one	250.24(A2)	29.	**(d)**	25 kVA	450.11(A)(5)
5.	**(d)**	all of these	300.50(E)	30.	**(b)**	3 gallons	460.2(A)
6.	**(a)**	temperatures	410.48	31.	**(c)**	accessible; 75%	376.56(A)
7.	**(b)**	manufacturer	406.3(A)	32.	**(d)**	30 amperes	322.10(1)
8.	**(a)**	off position	404.20(B)	33.	**(d)**	buried directly	340.10(1)
9.	**(d)**	all of the above	424.86(1,2,3)	34.	**(b)**	USE	338.2 DEF
10.	**(d)**	600v	760.41(A)	35.	**(d)**	42	408.36 ex.2
11.	**(a)**	3 hours	110.31(A1)	36.	**(b)**	5.5'	210.52(G)(1)
12.	**(a)**	white or gray	322.120(B)	37.	**(c)**	grounded conductor	400.22(F)
13.	**(d)**	removable	314.71(C)	38.	**(d)**	50 pounds	314.27(A)(2)
14.	**(c)**	earth	250.4(A1)	39.	**(c)**	THW or THHN	410.68 T.310.104(A)
15.	**(b)**	series	240.100(2)	40.	**(c)**	112.5 kVA	450.21(B)
16.	**(c)**	identified	250.187(B)	41.	**(c)**	3"	410.116(B)
17.	**(b)**	twelve = 12	336.24	42.	**(d)**	300 watts	422.48(B)
18.	**(d)**	125%	645.5(A)	43.	**(c)**	white marking	200.6(B3)
19.	**(a)**	resistance	427.2 *Info Note*	44.	**(b)**	wooden plugs	110.13(A)
20.	**(a)**	overload protection	430.8	45.	**(c)**	disconnect all	210.4(B)
21.	**(c)**	numbered	620.53	46.	**(d)**	heavy duty	210.21(A)
22.	**(a)**	one	552.41(E)	47.	**(c)**	50 amperes	550.10(A)
23.	**(b)**	Class II	502.115(B)	48.	**(c)**	7 1/2' = 7'6"	680.22(B2)
24.	**(c)**	interlocks	490.45(B)	49.	**(b)**	#14	800.100(A3)
25.	**(d)**	125%	210.20(A)	50.	**(d)**	tightening torque	110.14(D)

**To increase your speed use
the Key Word Index!**

ANSWERS   **JOURNEYMAN OPEN BOOK EXAM #23**

1. (d) shall not   680.26(B)
2. (b) 100 amp   230.79(C)
3. (d) all of these   200.4
4. (c) 42"   T. 110.26(A1) cond. 2
5. (c) 7 pound-inch   430.9(C)
6. (b) Code req.   230.75
7. (b) adjacent   430.75(A)
8. (b) 12"; 6"   410.16(C1,2)
9. (d) GFCI   525.23
10. (d) interrupting   430.82(A)
11. (d) Class 155   450.21(B) ex.1
12. (d) 30 amps   600.5(B1)
13. (a) on premises   517.41(B)
14. (c) static & rotary   455.2 DEF
15. (b) 115%   440.12(A1)
16. (a) 1/3   430.82(C2)
17. (c) enclosures   110.27(B)
18. (d) all of these   424.98(D)
19. (b) attachment   DEF 100
20. (d) at the point   240.21
21. (d) insul. or cov.   547.5(F)
22. (c) 4X or 6P   T. 110.28
23. (a) adjacent to   553.4
24. (a) 175%   T. 430.52
25. (d) 48"   110.26(A) cond. 3

26. (b) 4.5 - 4.99   T. 430.7(B)
27. (c) 2.5', 20'   250.52(A4)   250.53(F)
28. (c) regardless   250.112(D)
29. (c) 7'   110.31
30. (c) 15 amps   240.6(A)
31. (d) not less   110.26(A3)
32. (b) not **natural** gray   200.6(A)
33. (d) not motel bathrooms 240.24(E)
34. (a) 18"   551.30(E)
35. (b) 120 volts to grd.   240.85
36. (d) any of these   445.12(A)
37. (a) 2'   550.32(F)
38. (d) any of these   669.9
39. (a) series shunt winding 450.4(A)
40. (b) not over 300%   630.32(A)
41. (b) 33 1/3%   240.21(B2)
42. (b) 115%   440.12(A1)
43. (b) not required   240.10
44. (a) both inside-outside 312.10(A)
45. (a) 1/2"   T. 408.56
46. (c) current & voltage   404.20(A)
47. (d) 6 1/2"   T. 312.6(B)
48. (d) terminal identified 110.14(A)
49. (b) eight times   314.28(A1)
50. (a) 200 amps   408.30

**To increase your speed use
the Key Word Index!**

ANSWERS   JOURNEYMAN OPEN BOOK EXAM #24

1. **(b)**   ungrounded   404.2(A)
2. **(d)**   all of these   210.12(B)
3. **(a)**   #4   200.6(B)
4. **(d)**   impedance protected   430.7(A) (14)
5. **(c)**   18.5'   T.225.60
6. **(c)**   both I & II   110.10
7. **(c)**   86° F   Table 310.15(B16)
8. **(c)**   35kv   450.24
9. **(d)**   MI cable   332.40(B)
10. **(c)** 70%   220.61(B)
11. **(c)** NFPA   90.6
12. **(a)** 14'   600.9(A)
13. **(a)** I only   430.75(B)
14. **(a)** 2'   626.22(B)
15. **(d)** I,II & III   324.120
16. **(d)** 150v   680.23(A4)
17. **(b)** suitable   110.8
18. **(c)** lateral   DEF 100
19. **(c)** raintight   358.42 & 314.15
20. **(a)** highest   430.7B3
21. **(c)** I,III & IV T.220.12(A) • 210.11(C1&2)
22. **(b)** Article 225   110.31(C1)
23. **(c)** both I & II   220.84(A1,3)
24. **(c)** both I & II   396.12
25. **(a)** 15 & 20   406.4(A)

26. **(c)** gases or vapors   500.5(B)
27. **(d)** 310.15B6 • 250.118 • Chap. 9 note #3
28. **(c)** 0.030   406.6(A)
29. **(c)** lockable   430.102 ex.1
30. **(b)** grounding   250.119
31. **(c)** 4'   424.59 *Info Note*
32. **(d)** 20a   210.23 • T.210.24
33. **(a)** inversely   Table 310.15(B16)
34. **(a)** 6'   680.22(A2)
35. **(b)** temp. limiting   422.46
36. **(a)** supported by messenger   336.10(4)
37. **(c)** 25a   210.21(A)
38. **(a)** 1/4"   314.20
39. **(a)** arranged to drain   225.22 • 230.53
40. **(b)** 48"   230.54(C) ex.
41. **(b)** 0.017   Table 8 • 310.106(C)
42. **(c)** portable generators   406.4(B) ex.1
43. **(b)** arms & stems   410.56(C)
44. **(a)** 18"   210.52(A3)
45. **(d)** both I & II   230.82(1)(4)
46. **(a)** armored cable   320.12(2)
47. **(b)** 0.5 or larger   220.5(B)
48. **(c)** 75%   220.53
49. **(a)** 119a   Table 326.80
50. **(d)** I,II,III & IV   314.23(D1)

**To increase your speed use
the Key Word Index!**

ANSWERS   JOURNEYMAN OPEN BOOK EXAM #25

1.	**(a)**	15	408.52	26.	**(b)**	I & II only	410.16(A1& A2)
2.	**(b)**	is false	230.3	27.	**(c)**	in the field	424.29
3.	**(d)**	FCC	324.2 DEF	28.	**(d)**	150v	240.50(A2)
4.	**(a)**	recpt. outlet	210.50(A)	29.	**(b)**	physical damage	358.12(1)
5.	**(c)**	available	110.9	30.	**(d)**	15a @ 125v	430.42(C)
6.	**(d)**	0.06"	250.52(A7)	31.	**(d)**	I,II & III	324.40(A)
7.	**(a)**	I & II only	427.2 *Info Note*	32.	**(d)**	115%	440.12(A1)
8.	**(d)**	75%	386.56	33.	**(c)**	90° C	410.115(A)
9.	**(a)**	weatherproof	406.9(A)	34.	**(d)**	allowed	210.52
10.	**(c)**	30 amps	600.5(B1)	35.	**(d)**	39.37"	324.41
11.	**(b)**	1/3 h.p.	430.81(B)	36.	**(c)**	overhead spans	225.26
12.	**(d)**	neutral	220.61(A)	37.	**(b)**	100%	220.51
13.	**(c)**	36"	Table 110.26(A1)	38.	**(c)**	125%	430.122(A)
14.	**(b)**	194° F	320.80(A)	39.	**(a)**	6'	430.245(B)
15.	**(c)**	10'	210.52(H)	40.	**(d)**	12.5 - #12 - 20a	210.23(A)
16.	**(a)**	3/4"	Table 408.56	41.	**(b)**	appliances	338.10(B3)
17.	**(c)**	mechanical	230.31(A)	42.	**(c)**	at standstill	430.7(C)
18.	**(d)**	energy-reducing	240.87 *Info Note 1*	43.	**(b)**	as low as practicable	460.8(B)
19.	**(c)**	III only	250.178	44.	**(d)**	I,II & III	334.40(B)
20.	**(a)**	reduce	240.2 DEF	45.	**(d)**	I,II & III	680.6(2)(5)(6)
21.	**(a)**	1 va	220.14(K2)	46.	**(a)**	factory-installed internal	90.7
22.	**(c)**	70%	551.71(B)	47.	**(b)**	3'	225.19B
23.	**(b)**	3'	410.10(D)	48.	**(c)**	continuous duty	T.430.22(E) note
24.	**(b)**	voltage	424.35	49.	**(a)**	ungrounded conductor	240.15(A)
25.	**(c)**	hexagonal	240.50(C)	50.	**(a)**	distinctive	200.6(A5)

**To increase your speed use
the Key Word Index!**

JOURNEYMAN OPEN BOOK FINAL EXAM

1. (d) Class 2	406.6(D)	41. (d) both b & c	NFPA 70E
2. (c) I and II	551.72(B)	42. (c) an accessible	422.33(A)
3. (d) branch circuit	425.22(D)	43. (b) signs & signals	NFPA 70E
4. (d) 5,000 volts	392.10(E)	44. (a) 1.5%	647.4(D)
5. (b) 42.4v peak ac	424.101(A)	45. (c) frequency	General knowledge
6. (d) 120 volts	210.8(E)	46. (d) identified	408.7
7. (d) 5 minutes	690.12(D) I.N.	47. (b) gooseneck	230.54(B) ex.
8. (b) Class III Div.2	500.5(D)(2)	48. (d) #10	T. 348.22
9. (a) motor & con.	430.101	49. (c) 25 feet	210.64
10. (a) 15 amps	720.6	50. (d) sufficient length	250.68(B)
11. (b) people	NFPA 70E	51. (c) 24"	550.32(F)
12. (a) UL	General knowledge	52. (c) 3	T. 430.37
13. (b) 5'	358.30(A) ex.1	53. (c) 12'	344.30(B2) & T. 344.30(B2)
14. (a) 12 amps	210.21(B2) & T. 210.21(B2)	54. (c) thread into	348.28
15. (b) vertical	240.33	55. (b) 1000Ω	2,000 ohm÷2 = 1000Ω
16. (d) transfer	310.2 DEF	56. (a) 15 amps	225.39(A)
17. (d) all of these	T.250.122	57. (d) noncurrent carrying	310.15(B6)
18. (c) 10'	440.64	58. (b) service-entrance	250.102(C)
19. (a) disc. means	430.102(B)(1)	59. (b) 6'	680.22(A2)
20. (c) 24"	810.13	60. (a) explosive	480.10(A)
21. (d) all of these	NFPA 70E	61. (a) metal	430.12(A)
22. (b) double trian.	General knowledge	62. (d) PWR	General knowledge
23. (c) 26	522.21(B)	63. (d) 1500 amps	366.23(A)
24. (d) 30 amps	225.39(B)	64. (d) all of these	210.8(A2)
25. (c) protect	240.10	65. (d) single dwelling	310.15(B7)
26. (a) 11 kva	626.11	66. (d) existing buildings	250.50 ex.
27. (d) #4 cu	250.66(B)	67. (a) 15 amps	440.55(B)
28. (d) all of these	422.5(A) (2,4,5)	68. (a) driving machine	620.51(D)(1)
29. (c) coordination	DEF 100	69. (b) not greater	430.62(A)
30. (b) 7 lbs-inch	430.9(C)	70. (b) triangle	General knowledge
31. (d) any of above	800.44(A1&2) 800.44(B)	71. (a) weatherproof	312.2
32. (a) 4 or more	517.2(DEF)	72. (b) must be secured	312.5(C)
33. (a) .10 amp	I = W ÷ E 2W ÷ 20v =.1 amp	73. (d) all of these	310.10(H2)
34. (b) 15/16"	314.24(B5)	74. (d) all of these	440.13
35. (c) 6'	210.50(C)	75. (b) parallel circuit	General knowledge
36. (d) listing	240.5(B1)	76. (d) 48 times	314.71(A)
37. (b) terminate	354.28	77. (d) spacing	332.112
38. (a) starting	430.52(B)	78. (b) adjusted by	334.80
39. (b) individual	422.12	79. (c) #4	200.6(B)
40. (b) 8.19 amps	T. 630.31(A2)	80. (a) sliding panels	210.52(A2)(2)

THE PREVIEW OF THE ELECTRICAL EXAM

Tom Henry states the electrical exam should contain questions in the field which the electrician is working, need specialized exams. This book contains examples of exam questions and how to prepare for the open and closed book exam questions.

•Book #1 The Preview of the Electrical Exam is **FREE** when purchased with at **least two other books** from The Henry Electrical License Exam Series.

This book contains a 100 Question Exam which you can work and e-mail to Tom Henry and he will personally grade it and return to you the **correct answers** and give you a review on how to improve your score on any weakness you may have.

The Behavior of Electricty
Theory - Ohm's Law - Transformers

OTHER THAN CODE BOOK QUESTIONS -
•NO BOOK QUESTIONS:

General knowledge categories such as the behavior of electricity, theory, Ohm's Law, ac-dc power, voltage drop, power factor, efficiency, cost, tools, safety, plan reading, specifications, etc.

There is no NEC section to locate for **general knowledge** questions, you must select the correct answer by **memory**. These are the questions where **formulas** come into play.

Book #2 contains 6 practice exams and examples with **correct answers**.

OTHER THAN CODE BOOK QUESTIONS -
•NO BOOK QUESTIONS:

General Knowledge - Tools - Safety - Plan Reading - Specifications - Maintenance - Controls - Meters

The **general knowledge** categories test your knowledge of what you have learned from the years spent in the electrical field to **qualify** to take the exam. How much can you remember from your training?

The NEC is updated each 3 years, **general knowledge** categories remain the same over the years in most cases.

Book #3 contains 8 one hour practice exams with **correct answers**.

The National Electrical Code   Chapter One

ARTICLE 90 thru 110

Introduction, Definitions, Requirements for Electrical Installations.

Preparing for the exam, common sense will tell you to **study an hour a night** for a week is better than an all day cram.

The difficulty occurs when you say **National Electrical Code book**. Most applicants taking an exam are **not** familiar enough with the Code book and it's easy to understand why only 30 out of 100 pass an electrical exam. Many are *unsuccessful* because they failed to *read* the question correctly.

Your score on the open book exam depends on how familiar you are with the **National Electrical Code book**. Most exam applicants run out of time and are not able to find all the answers to the questions within the limited time.

You must understand Article 100 Definitions. If you don't understand the definition, you will have trouble with answering the questions correctly.

In writing these books on OPEN BOOK questions for **locating the section** of the NEC, I'm using a different format. *I want you to write down what section of the NEC that states the fact.* This will help you in using your memory cells and eliminate guessing. **I'll give you the correct answer**.

EXAMPLE: Each meeting room of not more than _____ sq. ft. in other than dwelling units shall have outlets for nonlocking-type, 125 volt, 15 or 20 ampere receptacles.

(a) 250   (b) 500   (c) 750   (d) 1000

Section ____210.71(A)____ .

Book #4 contains 6 one hour practice exams with **correct answers** and **section** where found.

The National Electrical Code   Chapter Two

ARTICLE 200 thru 285

Wiring and Protection. Calculations of Demand Factors, Services, Overcurrent Protection, Grounding, etc.

Chapter Two is a big one! Article 220 is Load **Calculations.**

Article 220 - Branch-Circuit, Feeder, and Service Load Calculations.

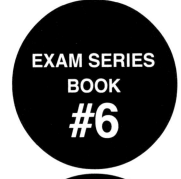

EXAM SERIES BOOK #6

EXAM SERIES BOOK #7

EXAM SERIES BOOK #8

EXAM SERIES BOOK #9

EXAM SERIES BOOK #10

The National Electrical Code   Chapter Three

ARTICLE 300 thru 399

Chapter Three Wiring Methods and Materials is big! It contains 8 exams on boxes, NM cable, conduits, PVC, cable trays, open wiring, etc.

The National Electrical Code   Chapter Four

ARTICLE 400 thru 490

Chapter Four Equipment for General use contains 8 exams on cords, fixture wires, switches, appliances, space heating, luminaires, motors, transformers, batteries, equipment over 1000 volts, etc.

The National Electrical Code   Chapter Five

ARTICLE 500 thru 590

Chapter Five Special Occupancies contains 8 exams on hazardous locations, commercial garages, air craft hangers, bulk storage plants, health care facilities, assembly occupancies, carnivals, TV studios, mobile homes, marinas, etc.

The National Electrical Code   Chapter Six

ARTICLE 600 thru 690

Chapter Six Special Equipment contains 8 exams on signs, elevators, welders, X-ray, swimming pools, solar, fuel cell system, wind electric, etc.

The National Electrical Code Chapters 7-8-9 Calculations

ARTICLE 700 thru Chapter 9

Book #10 contains 5 exams on special/conditions, communication systems. And examples on Tables most used, cooking equipment demand factors, box fill calculations, motor calculations, etc.

Pricing as of November 2019 •Subject to change in 2020.

•Book #1 The Preview of the Electrical Exam is **FREE** when purchased with at **least two other books** from The Henry Electrical License Exam Series.

Example: Purchase books #2 and #3 and receive Book #1 Free!

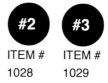

#2 ITEM # 1028   #3 ITEM # 1029

Each book is $19 and you are receiving 3 books for $38 + Shipping or $12.66 a book!

The BEST BUY is all 10 books The Henry Electrical License Exam Series
ITEM # 1037 $171 + Shipping   ($17.10 per book)

#2 ITEM # 1028   #3 ITEM # 1029   #4 ITEM # 1030   #5 ITEM # 1031   #6 ITEM # 1032   #7 ITEM # 1033   #8 ITEM # 1034   #9 ITEM # 1035   #10 ITEM # 1036

Tom Henry's
**Code Electrical Classes Inc.
and Bookstore**
7449 Citrus Avenue
Winter Park, Florida 32792

**THE ELECTRICIANS BOOKSTORE
1-800-642-2633**

SAME DAY SHIPPING...
 Call 1-800-642-2633
OR FAX
(407) 671-6497

7 DAYS MAX

 OPEN

EASTERN TIME
MONDAY - FRIDAY 8am - 5pm
ANSWERING MACHINE, FAX, or
www.code-electrical.com
24 HOURS - 7 DAYS A WEEK

 Call 1-800-642-2633 today!

•Note: Call Monday thru Friday 8 am to 5 pm Eastern time and a person will answer the phone and eliminate pressing all the buttons only to get a recording. *It's called the personal touch.* Without the customer we don't exist!

READ THE BOOKS THE ELECTRICIAN'S READ

WORLDWIDE LEADER IN ELECTRICAL EDUCATION

1-800-642-2633
E-mail tomhenry@code-electrical.com
ONLINE SHOPPING AT
http://www.code-electrical.com

Tom Henry's Code Electrical Classes Inc.

Since 1979 we have taught electrical exam preparation classes in 21 states, 84 cities and St. Croix in the Virgin Islands.

Schedule a class in your city by calling 1-800-642-2633.

Alabama
Birmingham, Huntsville, Mobile, Montgomery

Arkansas
Little Rock

Connecticut
Hartford

Florida
Fort Myers, Fort Lauderdale, Lakeland, Tampa, St. Petersburg, Bradenton, Sarasota, Winter Haven, Jacksonville, Ocala, Leesburg, Daytona Beach, Orlando, Kissimmee, Winter Park, Haines City, Cocoa Beach, Ft. Pierce. Naples

Georgia
Atlanta, Macon, Gainesville

Hawaii
Honolulu

Indiana
Fort Wayne, Indianapolis, South Bend, Evansville, Muncie, Kokomo, Michigan City, Elkhart

Iowa
Des Moines, Cedar Rapids

Kansas
Wichita, Manhattan, Topeka, Salina, Dodge City

Kentucky
Louisville, Owensboro, Lexington

Louisiana
New Orleans, Shreveport, Baton Rouge, Covington

Michigan
Detroit, Grand Rapids

Mississippi
Jackson

Missouri
St. Louis, Kansas City, Springfield, Joplin, St. Joseph

North Carolina
Raleigh

Ohio
Columbus, Cincinnati, Akron

Oklahoma
Oklahoma City

Pennsylvania
Allentown

South Carolina
Columbia, Greenville, Spartanburg

Tennessee
Chattanooga, Memphis, Knoxville, Johnson City, Nashville, Jackson

Texas
Dallas, Lubbock, Amarillo, Wichita Falls, Waco, Odessa, Corpus Christi, Abilene, Longview, Plainview, San Angelo, Houston, San Antonio, College Station

http://www.code-electrical.com